P9-BBQ-131

A GUIDE TO ROMAN BRITAIN

By the same Author

ALL MEN ARE NEIGHBOURS

THE LOST PHARAOHS

MADAME TUSSAUD

THE BULL OF MINOS

LIFE UNDER THE PHARAOHS

ONE MAN'S JOURNEY

THE MOUNTAINS OF PHARAOH

A PROJECT OF DIMENSION BOOKS

A GUIDE TO Roman Britain

by

LEONARD COTTRELL

CHILTON BOOKS — A DIVISION OF CHILTON COMPANY
Publishers PHILADELPHIA AND NEW YORK

First American Edition by Dimension Books, 1966

Published by Dimension Books, Wilkes-Barre, Pennsylvania in association with Chilton Books and simultaneously in Toronto, Canada by Ambassador Books, Ltd.

Library of Congress Catalog Card Number: 66-22873

ACKNOWLEDGMENTS

FOR permission to reproduce copyright material in this book the author and publishers are indebted to Brian Blake, M.A., and the Editor of the *Manchester Guardian* for the extract from " The Solway Defences "; M. R. Hull, M.A., F.S.A., for the quotation from " Roman Colchester "; Mrs. George Bambridge and Messrs. Macmillan & Co. Ltd. for the extract from " Puck of Pook's Hill " and the verse from " A Song of Mithras," by Rudyard Kipling; Penguin Books Ltd. for the extracts from " Roman Britain," by Professor L. A. Richmond; the University Court of Glasgow University and Miss Anne S. Robertson for the quotation from the " Handbook to the Cultural Collections in the Hunterian Museum" ; The Society of Authors and Messrs. Jonathan Cape Ltd. for the verses by A. E. Housman; and to T. F. Wright, Esq., and the *Birmingham Post* for the extract from " The Roman Midlands."

CONTENTS

To

JOHN AND SUSAN

FOREWORD TO FIRST AMERICAN EDITION

It is ten years since this book was first published in England, and although reprinted several times with minor amendments there, it has remained substantially an account of a journey of some 3,500 miles through Roman Britain in 1955.

During the past ten years so many new discoveries have been made that the first publication of this new edition in America provides a welcome opportunity to bring the work up-to-date. This has been done (a) by correcting any information published in the first edition which has since had to be revised in view of new discoveries, and (b) by adding to each chapter a brief Appendix summarizing discoveries made, and new theories propounded, since my first account was written.

I must, however, warn all non-archaeologists (archaeologists need no warning) that the pace of research and investigation during the past decade has been so accelerated that a book, by its very nature, can never be completely up-to-date. A glance through the press-reports and learned journals for one year alone reveals that almost every week, somewhere in our island, new excavations, re-excavations and re-interpretations, are enlarging and deepening our view of Roman Britain.

I used the word 'accelerated' advisedly. Progress in understanding the Roman invasion and occupation of Britain has continued since the seventeenth century, but since the end of the Second World War our horizons have expanded at a bewildering rate, due mainly to two causes. The first is the improvement and advance in archaeological techniques, and the use of new methods which were not available to our predecessors, e.g. aerial photography. The second is adventitious; the inevitable changes which are overtaking Britain in the mid-twentieth century, road building, housing expansion, and the rebuilding of old towns and the construction of new ones. These have produced a crop of archaeological discoveries, some of them accidental.

This in turn has brought into being a new kind of archaeological operation, 'rescue-digging'. Hardly a day passes without some harassed, overworked professional archaeologist being faced with an urgent work of rescue. Willing volunteers must be recruited and a 'blitz' operation mounted to record all available information before the site is buried under a housing estate. In London, bulldozers operating near Cannon Street Station revealed Roman remains of a huge outdoor swimming-bath. Near Chichester, workmen digging a water-main stumbled on the pavements of a Roman palace of unprecedented magnificence. At Faversham, in Kent, building contractors working on a new development site near the Grammar School discovered other Roman remains which turn out to be those of a Roman villa. At a farm near Lavenham in Suffolk, a ploughman turns up a gladiator's helmet; while almost at the same time, a blacksmith at Hinton St. Mary in Dorset, building a shed on his land, finds a superb mosaic pavement bearing the portrait of a young man with the Christian monogram CHI-RHO, which is now generally accepted to be a portrait of Christ, and has been purchased by the British Museum.

A Roman marching-camp turns up on a Hertfordshire hill-top; a fine collection of Roman 'Samian' pottery is discovered at Alcester in Warwickshire; the redevelopment of Chester reveals the barracks of the 20th Legion which Agricola commanded; schoolboys at the tiny hamlet of Llanymynech in Montgomeryshire find 33 coins left in a cave by Roman miners searching for copper; and other camps, invisible from the ground, reveal their outlines in aerial photographs. These, though unlikely to be found by the most assiduous motorist, cyclist or walker, are worth studying in the photographs. To the writer there is something almost magical in the fact that the military operations conducted by the Romans against their enemies in Wales, Northern England and Scotland, though mentioned only briefly by their own historians, are now showing unmistakable traces through the lens of an aerial camera.

The written records of these fierce campaigns, which brought Emperors to Britain, and wore out more than one Roman Governor, are sparse. Yet, year after year, the dim outline of Roman marching camps, with their firm rectilinear outlines, appear like "spirit-photographs" under a landscape which, from the ground, seems to contain no feature earlier than the eighteenth century A.D. Probably most of them will never be seen from ground level, since many were temporary earth-works thrown up to protect the tents of an army on the march; yet there they are, at Ancaster in Lincolnshire, at Irechester in Northhamptonshire, near Stretton in Staffordshire, and most numerous in Northern England and Scotland.

Tacitus can thrill us with his stories of his father-in-law, Agricola, Governor of Britain, whose seven year campaign subdued the North and brought about the almost complete subjugation of Caledonia. Yet the photographic prints of the aerial photographer can show us the actual camps which Agricola made, and which Tacitus never saw. Nor is the earthbound traveller likely to see them either, because they are truly ghosts of the remote past, made tangible only in the developing tanks of 20th century photographers. Not all of them are associated with Agricola of course; their hard symmetrical outlines gleaming faintly through the blanket of ploughland and meadow, mark the track of armies whose movements are only vaguely recorded, if at all. This fact is both frustrating and fascinating. For instance, there have been revealed, in recent years, certain forts near the line of the Fosse Way, the Roman road which ran from the Bristol Channel to the Wash. Did these mark the line of the first frontier which Rome drew after their initial advance, but long before she was forced to conquer the North?

Then there is a marching-camp discovered in 1965 on a hill-top overlooking the Colne Valley, at Aldenham, near Watford. It has long been conjectured that this was the route which Caesar took; was this one of his camps? Again at Ancaster, in Lincolnshire, near the Roman town of Causennae, a Roman fort has been found occupying an important strategic point where an east-west road crossed the Ermine Street. A turf rampart had been deliberately dismantled; this was done, as has been suggested, during the systematic destruction of military sites in the early 70's A.D. when the 9th Hispana Legion moved from its old base at Lincoln to its new base at York.

Again, at Godmanchester in Huntingdonshire, a Roman fort of the late 2nd century has recently been found, with substantial ramparts, trench, and remains of a palisade; yet so far it has yielded no sign of human habitation. Mr. Michael Green, who directed the excavation, has stated that he believes that the fort may be associated with the troubled period when the British Governor, Claudius Albinus, tried to make himself Emperor. Historians say that Claudius took garrison troops away from Hadrian's Wall, and other places, and marched southward, where he was met and defeated by the true Emperor, Septimus Severus. Was this a Severan marching-camp, built and occupied briefly during that urgent campaign?

Puzzles such as these are absorbing to those for whom archaeology is a search for facts, and not merely a treasure-hunt. Others may well ask, "Why tantalize us with visions of camps and forts and roads which are now mere crop-marks visible only from the air, if at all?" The answer is surely that if there is one quality which we need to bring to the study of Roman Britain it is disciplined imagination. There are, of course, many Roman monuments which need little or no interpretation; the great swimming-pool at Bath, the mighty walls at Colchester, Silchester and Caerwent; the splendid mosaics found at Fishbourne, the Ackling Dyke in Wiltshire, and above all, Hadrian's imperial frontier, snaking across the naked fells of Northumberland from the North Sea to the Atlantic.

Yet, in the majority of cases, the seeker for Roman Britain must look for subtler signs; the line of a long vanished road, once trodden by the Legions, now a slightly raised embankment running across a field; or a few worn stones marking the site of a fort, a settlement or a villa. The search for these relics of the people who governed Britain for four centuries will have little appeal for those to whom only the Colosseum or the Pont du Gard can testify to the might of Rome. For the rest, especially those who long for escape from the overcrowded highways, whether by car, bicycle, or on foot, I can heartily recommend that they follow the Imperial Eagles.

LEONARD COTTRELL

July 1966

INTRODUCTION

THERE have been many books on Roman Britain, and one needs some justification for adding yet another. May I therefore outline the plan underlying this work, explain what it is and, almost as important, what it is not?

It is primarily a personal account of travels in search of Roman Britain, covering more than 3,500 miles and embracing a considerable part, though not all, of the Home Counties, Southern and Western England, East Anglia, the Midlands and South Wales, Northern England and Scotland. Wherever practicable, these journeys have been made along the line of the Roman roads, where they are still passable, and readers who wish to follow the same routes should be able, with the aid of a set of Ordnance Survey Maps, to do so. Incidentally, although most of my journeys were by car, I have been a motorcyclist, a cyclist and a walker, and their requirements have been kept in mind when preparing this book.

My journeys have taken me to Roman towns, villas, forts, settlements, and to scores of local museums, and I have described every place visited. My original ambition was to visit *every* Roman site in the British Isles, but experience soon forced me to modify this plan. There are so many Roman remains to be seen in these islands that a work which included them all would be too bulky to be practicable, unless each item was drastically condensed, reducing the book to little more than a catalogue.

Instead, I have aimed at a workable compromise. Each section deals with a particular tour, and includes fairly full descriptions of the route and the sites visited. However, where an area includes Roman antiquities which I have not yet been able to visit personally, or which are of limited interest to the general reader, there are brief summarising accounts based on the latest available information.

The book, therefore, is not a comprehensive descriptive survey of every Roman site in the country, though it can be used as a practical guide to the sites visited. Equally it is not an historical exegesis, beginning with an account of the invasion and occupation, and going on to describe, under appropriate headings, the Roman military system, Romano-British towns, country life, law and administration, and so on. Excellent books of this type already exist, such as the late Sir Ian Richmond's "Roman Britain", Collingwood's "Roman Britain and the English Settlements", Winbolt's "Britain Under the Romans" and others, and I wish to acknowledge here the abundant help I have derived from them.

I would like especially to thank Dr. John Morris, Lecturer in Ancient History, University College, London, for help and advice, for reading the manuscript and suggesting improvements.

There may be readers who do not wish to go deeply into the subject, and for them I have tried to work into my narrative references to such aspects of life in Roman Britain as will make their visits to sites more interesting and enjoyable. Also, since no understanding of an historical epoch is possible without a framework of dates, there is a chronological table of the main events in the history of Britain under the Romans, and a list of Roman place names and the English equivalents.

By these means I have tried to avoid cluttering up the narrative with too many dates and dynasties, while providing the basic historical framework as a reference. At the same time, I strongly recommend that serious students, as distinct from casual travellers, should regard this volume as a companion to the authoritative but highly readable accounts of Roman Britain mentioned above. The more the reader knows about the four centuries during which Britain was a province of the Roman Empire the more pleasure and profit he or she is likely to get from this book.

Undoubtedly the most fascinating way of exploring Roman Britain is to follow in the track of the Legions, by using the original roads as far as possible. These ancient highways are in themselves the most impressive relics of the Roman occupation, and the more one travels along them the greater becomes one's respect for the men who planned and built them. Often their line is followed by modern trunk roads; how many of the motorists driving along A1 from Stamford to Lincoln, for instance, realise that they are using a road which Emperors trod more than seventeen centuries ago?

Others have become what are known as 'good class secondary roads', often far superior, in directness and freedom from traffic, to the overcrowded main highways which have replaced them. Motorists who take the trouble to trace the course of these ancient roads on an Ordnance Survey Map (where they are clearly marked) will often find that they reach their destinations more quickly and much more pleasurably than by following the main roads.

There is a third category of Roman road which will appeal especially to the walker and the more adventurous cyclist. It is not widely known that even where a highway has completely passed out of use as a road, or even a lane, its course can often be traced as a raised mound, known as an *agger*, running across fields, through woods, over open downland, ignoring the meandering Anglo-Saxon lanes which have succeeded it.

For the walker and cyclist, there is no more fascinating way of seeing England than by trying to follow these forgotten highways with the help of an Ordnance Survey Map. Two magnificent examples spring to my mind. There is the Ackling Dyke, one of the finest surviving stretches of a Roman road in the West of England, where it branches off the main Blandford road and runs for miles over open downland, a high embankment, 6 feet high and more than 20 feet broad. Cars cannot use it, but walkers can. Then there is the last stretch of the Ermine Way as it approaches Lincoln, the Roman *Lindum Colonia*.

Though I did manage to negotiate it, with difficulty, in a sports car, walkers are unlikely to be troubled by motor traffic, and will have the satisfaction of approaching Lincoln as the Ninth Legion did, on foot, and along the same ancient way.

There is another, more subtle reason why it is more satisfying to approach Roman towns and settlements along the roads which their builders themselves used. Apart from Hadrian's Wall and such places as Caerleon, Caerwent, Richborough and Porchester, there are very few Roman sites in Great Britain in a state of preservation comparable with those on the Continent, in Africa and the Middle East. There one may see amphitheatres, theatres, even whole towns, standing almost at the height to which they were built. In Britain, alas, one finds all too often that the place one has journeyed far to see is little more than a few mounds in a field or a broken pavement in the basement of a Departmental Store.

There are several reasons for this. One is that our northern climate is unkind to ancient buildings. Another is that Roman towns such as Timgad and Leptis Magna in Africa have been deserted and unoccupied for centuries, whereas *Lindum Colonia* lies buried under medieval and modern Lincoln, *Eboracum* under York, *Glevum* under Gloucester, *Corinium* under Cirencester, and so on. Only occasionally, as in the case of Silchester (*Calleva Atrebatum*) is a Romano-British town covered only by a blanket of earth.

However, I found that by using, whenever possible, the network of roads which the Romans built, and familiarising myself with the original Roman names of towns and settlements, these sites, however scanty their remains, gained enormously in significance. The signpost says " to Colchester ", but *you* are on your way to Camulodunum, Cymbeline's city. The lorries grind and thunder their way northward through St. Albans, shaking the windows of Boots Cash Chemists, but you are at the gates of Verulamium which Boudicca put to fire and sword when the Iceni rose in their anger. And when, leaving

Cirencester, you take that long, lonely road which soars and swoops over the Cotswolds and the Berkshire downs, and come at last to Silchester, *you* see more than a group of sodden fields, ringed by a tall thickset hedge. That hedge, dark against the sunset, marks the outer wall of *Calleva Atrebatum*, capital of the Atrebates, and under those fields lie the streets, the baths, the forum, the houses of a once gracious city.

By " you " of course I really mean " I ", for this is essentially a personal and subjective approach to Roman Britain; and while I hope that readers will share at least some of my preferences and dislikes, there are bound to be points on which we shall differ. Therefore I would like to state frankly at the outset that my approach is human rather than technical. I am less interested in the construction of Roman buildings than in the lives of the people who lived in them. I am more interested in ferreting out what can be known about the daily life of a Legionary soldier than in the high strategy of generals or the political manœuvres of Emperors. Also, while respecting the Romans as soldiers, engineers and administrators, I must admit that there are some features of their civilisation which I find dull, and others—such as their fondness for gladiatorial sports—repellent. And the dreary standardised patterns of their domestic objects and interior decoration recall the least attractive aspects of our own age.

Again, this book records journeys through a country richly endowed with monuments of many periods, and only the most rabid enthusiast would hurry from one Roman site to another while ignoring everything non-Roman *en route*. To visit the Roman remains at Lincoln and ignore the Cathedral, to go to Old Sarum and by-pass Salisbury, to explore the Roman lead mines in the Mendip Hills without looking at the wonderful group of Iron Age barrows not far away, would be absurd. Therefore, occasionally I have strayed out of Roman Britain into earlier or later periods of British history.

This was also in the nature of a sentimental journey.

Twenty years ago I visited, on foot or by bicycle, many of the sites mentioned in this book, especially those in the Midlands and the North. But it so happens that I have seen relatively little of the British Isles since 1945. My duties as a B.B.C. correspondent have usually taken me abroad each year to places as far apart as Mexico and Siam, Newfoundland and Australia. In Europe and the Middle East I have had the good fortune to see some of the most splendid monuments of Roman genius—Palmyra in Syria, Baalbeck in the Lebanon, Leptis Magna in Libya, the Pont du Gard, the Amphitheatre at Arles, and the Imperial City itself. But until this year I had not had the opportunity of spending an entire summer and autumn exploring the Roman monuments of my own homeland, so that when the opportunity came I embraced it with a fresh mind and a lively enthusiasm.

Summarised accounts of this journey were broadcast by the B.B.C. in my programmes " A Tour of Roman Britain " and " Roman Roads ". I would like to thank the British Broadcasting Corporation for the facilities they gave me, and for allowing me to re-use some of the material I gathered on this journey.

Even if the reader's interest in Roman remains is of the slightest, still they will provide him with an objective which will take him far off the beaten track, away from the stench of the main roads, to discover how much of our lovely land still remains unspoiled, despite airfields, factories, satellite towns and suburban development. If readers experience only half the pleasure which has come my way while preparing this book, they will be richly rewarded.

CHAPTER ONE

THE WATLING STREET

In planning my itinerary I tried, as far as possible, to follow in the path of the Roman Army, and trace the successive stages of the invasion, conquest and occupation of Britain, district by district. Kent, therefore, came first on the list, for it was here that the Legions first set foot on British soil.

Let us start, therefore, from London, along the line of the old Watling Street, which runs from the capital through Rochester and Canterbury to the coast. And since the first part of the journey is not particularly interesting, we might pass the time by discussing why the Romans came to Britain in the first place, and what kind of people were the Britons whom they conquered.

There was no " British " nation in the modern sense; only a number of independent tribes who had migrated to Britain from Gaul (modern France), some of them not many centuries before the Romans came. The Belgæ, for instance, began to arrive about 200 B.C. They were at least as civilised as the Homeric Greeks. Like them, they were often governed by a tribal aristocracy, and ruled by hereditary chiefs. Like them they were fine craftsmen and produced superb works of art; examine some of the Celtic shields, weapons, golden ornaments and other objects in museums and compare their vigorous, lively spirit with the tame, derivative Græco-Roman art which the invaders introduced.

Little is known of their literature, but doubtless some Celtic Homer sang their tribal lays; anyone who has enjoyed the stories of King Arthur, has listened to the faint echo of Celtic poems which were recited more than a thousand years before Mallory's armour-plated chevaliers. King Arthur, in fact, was probably a Celtic chieftain who resisted the Saxon invaders after the Romans left Britain.

They were brave and skilful warriors, as Cæsar reported, using the horse, the chariot and the spear with deadly effect. Their religion was animistic. "The whole Gaulish nation," wrote Cæsar, "is to a great degree devoted to superstitious rites; and on this account those who are afflicted with severe diseases, or who are engaged in battles and dangers, either sacrifice human beings for victims, or vow that they will immolate themselves."

Why did Cæsar invade Britain? Not, one may be sure, because of his abhorrence of these superstitious practices, but more probably because the Britons had been aiding their kinsmen, the Gauls. That, at any rate, was his excuse.

Professor Richmond in his "Roman Britain" writes:

"Roman public opinion felt distant Britain as almost legendary, the source of mineral wealth, its very size and definition as an island in doubt, a new world of awesome isolation and uncharted risk. This explains the excitement with which Rome received the news of an invasion of Britain by Cæsar and judged it an exploit of unexampled enterprise and daring, adding new laurels to him who had conceived it and new prestige to the name of Rome."

* * * * *

With this in our mind let us take the Watling Street out of London, along the line of invasion which Cæsar probably followed (he is believed to have crossed the Thames somewhere near Westminster). Watling Street, though built by the Romans, probably followed the line of an earlier British trackway and must be one of the most ancient highways in the British Isles. First, crossing London Bridge, near which probably stood a Roman bridge, we take the Old Kent Road to New Cross, where we bear left towards Dartford, Gillingham and Rochester. Shooter's Hill, a pleasant green oasis in the surrounding drabness, was a sighting point which the Roman surveyors used when planning the road.

Further eastward the road, now a 25-foot highway, passes through pleasant undulating country which, alas, is rapidly disappearing under the encroaching tide of new villas.

Away to the north lie the factories and powerhouse chimneys of Dartford, where the silhouettes of great cranes mark the course of the Thames, which the old road follows.

Two miles south of Bexley Heath the road crosses a broad common usually crowded at weekends with parked cars, then enters suburbia again, where the Watlington Street continues straight on for Dartford, but we take the right turn along A2 towards Rochester.

The road breasts a steep chalk hill in a dead straight line, crowded with coastward streaming traffic, then Rochester appears on its hill above the Medway, with Gundulph's great Keep and the Romanesque cathedral, grey in the sunlight. The Watling Street climbs again out of the town, where flat-fronted Georgian houses preserve a fragment of Augustan elegance, and almost immediately carries one into Chatham, switchbacking over chalk hills covered with houses. Rochester, incidentally, covers the ancient Roman settlement of Durobrivæ.

Notice that, contrary to popular belief, the Roman road does *not* follow a continuously straight line. The roads were planned to link the principal centres of population; some of these, such as Silchester (Calleva Atrebatum), Colchester (Camulodunum) and St. Albans (Verulamium) were old British tribal capitals. Others, like Caerleon, in Monmouthshire, were legionary fortresses; and there were intermediate military stations and settlements *en route*. The main difference between the Roman and the Saxon roads were that the former were carefully surveyed in advance and planned to link the towns by the quickest possible route. The Romans drove their military highways through virgin territory, taking the shortest practicable route. The road-builders of the Middle Ages had to consider property-owners.

The method which the Roman surveyors seem to have used in planning their roads was probably as follows.

Having determined the direction of their projected road, they sighted from hill-top to hill-top, or at least from high points. Between these sighting points the road ran as straight as possible, while making allowances for natural obstacles; for instance, a road might be diverted slightly to one side in order to cross a river or stream at the most convenient point. Where a valley was steep sided, the road might be carried diagonally down the hillside on terraces and then resume its original alignment when it had climbed the further bank. The typical Roman road, therefore, has few if any curves, but proceeds in a series of straight lengths, with slight changes of alignment on high ground, and if you trace their course on an Ordnance Survey Map you will often see where these changes occur.

Generally I used the ¼-inch maps, which are detailed enough for most requirements, while covering reasonably large areas (twelve maps cover the whole of England, Wales and Scotland). For detailed surveying of smaller areas, however, I used the 1-inch maps, which are particularly useful to walkers and cyclists, since they show footpaths and small lanes in close detail. But for the motorist the ¼-inch maps are quite adequate.

Do not make the mistake, however, of imagining that because a road follows a Roman alignment that it necessarily rides on top of its Roman forbear. It may well do so, but sometimes, when the original road has been worn out by constant use, our lazy Saxon ancestors would improvise a rough track alongside it, rather than repair the old highway. When this has happened you can sometimes see the older road running beside the modern one as a slightly raised bank. We shall meet many examples of this on our travels.

Again, one often finds instances in which the modern road, while following the Roman original for many miles, suddenly curves away from it. If you consult the map you may find that a lane continues the alignment of the Roman road and may lead you through interesting and little-known country to the place where the modern road takes up the alignment again. But make sure first that there is a through route, especially if you are a motorist. Walkers will probably find that there is at least a field track which preserves, or should preserve, the ancient right of way.

However, the route we are following now, along the Watling Street, provides no such pleasant diversions. It has borne traffic for nearly 2,000 years and its original appearance has been completely lost. Yet still it is the old road which the Legions trod, and as we finally clear Rainham, and see, above a forest of TV aerials, the chalk downs beckoning to the east, we glimpse for the first time, a bit of England which probably looked very much the same to the Romans. After Sittingbourne a few miles brings us to the pleasant little village of Bapchild, with its inviting-looking inns. And then the real country begins—Kent, the " Garden of England " begins to justify its title. Red oast-houses, their conical roofs at a slight slant, become more frequent, and on either side of the Watling Street stretch the hopfields, with their peculiar but not unpleasant vegetable smell.

Beyond Teynham the old road strides on magnificently, bearing an enormous load of heavy traffic. When I last travelled it the tall hawthorn hedges were beginning to blush with autumn berries. Around the warmly-weathered brick of Ospringe the hop-fields spread greenly on all sides. Beyond Boughton the giant steel radar towers reminded me that to-day our fortress walls are literally castles in the air, and of air; vapour-trails high in the blue were another reminder of an invasion threatened but frustrated.

For this is the invader's historic road through the gateway of Britain. Cæsar's Legions, Hitler's Luftwaffe, both came this way. An Englishman would sadly lack imagination who could travel that road and not feel its powerful spell; especially the stretch from Boughton eastward, then every rise in the switchback reveals it cutting through the Kentish orchards, as swift and straight as a Legionary's spear, pointing directly to the gates of Durovernum, which the Saxons called Canterbury.

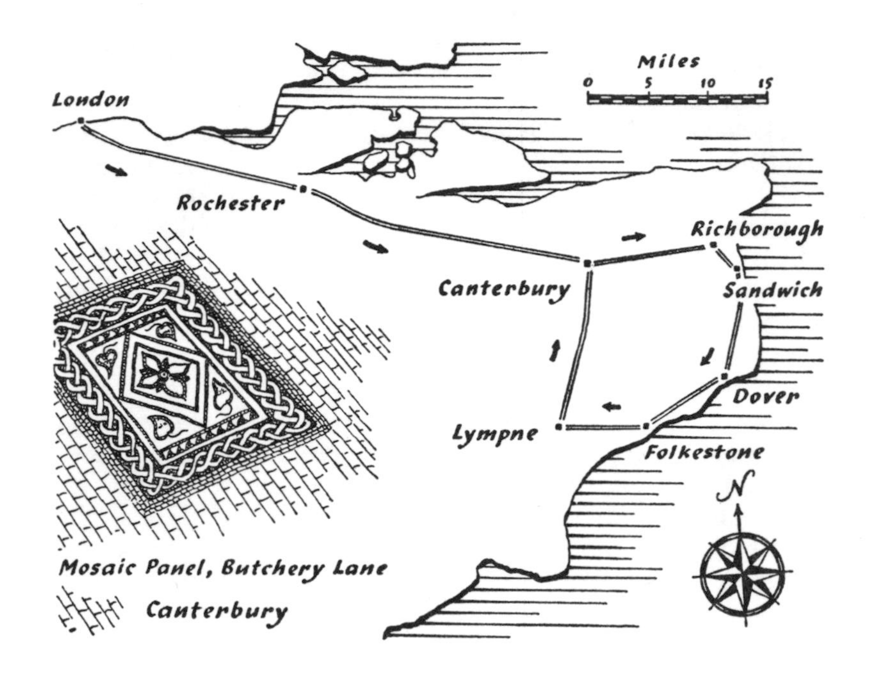

CHAPTER TWO

ROMAN CANTERBURY

I suggest that the visitor spends at least a day and a night at Canterbury; there are several excellent hotels. Evening and night-time, when traffic is thinner, enable one to get much closer to the spirit of the place, and at such times even the faint, far-off voice of Rome can occasionally be heard. At least another day is needed to complete the tour of Richborough, Walmer, Dover, Folkestone and Lympne, described in the next chapter, a tour which ends where it began—Canterbury. Not that this short tour exhausts the possibilities of Kent by any means. There is the impressive fort at Reculver, to the north; there is the recently discovered, magnificent villa at Lullingstone; there are remains of a Roman settlement at Springhead, between London and Rochester and other Roman or Celtic sites of which so little remains that they will have little appeal except to the most imaginative.

On the first day the newcomer to Canterbury will almost certainly wish to see the medieval city. Starting with the Cathedral, the splendour of which needs no comment from me, he should then visit the King's School in its venerable, tree-shaded grounds, and then wander as his fancy takes him along the narrow streets, helped by the excellent little " Pilgrim's Guide ", published by the City Council.

There are enough churches to satisfy the most ardent medievalist—St. Martin's, Holy Cross, St. Peter's, St. Augustine's Abbey and, above all, Grey Friars. This must not be missed, if only for its walks beside the Stour. The view from its tiny lancet windows across the gardens, walks and streams is memorable. So are the Dane John Gardens, with their lovely avenue of limes, where you can see a relic of the Roman period, though not of stone. The grassy mound in the centre is one of a group of Roman mound burials of the first or second century, which became known later as the " Dongeon Hills ".

From the Dane John Gardens you get a superb view of the south-eastern stretch of the ancient City Wall, with its projecting turrets, thirteen of which remain, although until 1691 all the twenty-one turrets and six main gates were intact. The existing wall stretches in a great arc from the Castle on the south-west to a little beyond the King's School on the north-east, although there are fragments adjoining St. Radigund's Street on the north, and Pound Lane on the north-west, where it joined the West Gate. Though the upper part of the present wall is medieval, some sections have been proved to stand on Roman foundations, and it is probable that most of the Romano-British city, Durovernum

Cantiorum, stood within the line of the present walls. Most Romano-British towns were small by modern standards; when they received their walls or ramparts later in the third century A.D. they usually covered about 100 acres, rarely more. Roman Canterbury was larger than this, on account of its suburb built beyond the line of the fortifications.

The best way to get an idea of what Durovernum looked like is to begin by climbing the Cathedral Tower, taking with you the excellent little map contained in the Official Guide. From the roof of the Tower on a clear day you get a splendid view of Canterbury lying cupped within its circle of hills. In this way you can resist for a while the prevailing medieval spirit of the city.

Let your eye follow the line of the existing walls, and then continue them in imagination from the Castle northward to the western branch of the Stour, along the river, and past the West Gate to where Pound Lane and St. Radigund's Street carry the line back to the King's School.

Within that area lay Durovernum, built, we now know, on the site of an earlier Belgic settlement of timber and mud huts. Remains of these huts have been found in most of the areas explored by the archæologists. It is clear that the city was not of Roman foundation, but a continuation of an earlier Belgic settlement. Nor was this the earliest occupation. On a site near Castle Street, the excavators discovered the remains of a palisade and ditch of an early Iron Age settlement of about 200 B.C. From the Cathedral Tower it is easy to see why such a site would be chosen for habitation and defence, partly protected by the river.

But where were the streets of Durovernum? Romano-British towns, we know, were usually symmetrically planned, with streets arranged in a grid pattern. This seems to have been the case with Roman Canterbury. Two main lines of Roman street have been discovered, one running roughly in line with Burgate, a little to the south side of the Cathedral, and the other at right angles to this and running from a point near the Roman Catholic Church (which you can pick out quite easily just south of Burgate) in a south-easterly direction under the main street. Of course, there must be many other Roman streets buried deep beneath the modern city.

Other excavations have brought to light remains of Roman buildings, the most remarkable of which are the foundations of a great theatre, with walls at least 12 feet thick and a diameter estimated at 250 feet. It stood where Watling Street joins St. Margaret's Street a little to the south of the Roman city centre. St. Albans, in Hertfordshire, can no longer claim to possess the only remaining Roman theatre in Great Britain. The Canterbury theatre seems to have been the larger of the two (250 feet against 190 feet), though this is unlikely to worry the people of St. Albans, as only a fragment of the newly-discovered theatre is visible, whereas the St. Albans theatre lies completely exposed in idyllic surroundings. Coins found on the site of the Canterbury theatre indicate that it was built in the reign of Trajan or more probably Hadrian, that is, sometime between A.D. 98 and 138.

What would you have seen if you could have stood at this same elevated spot in 55 B.C., the year in which Cæsar landed? Nothing, probably, but clusters of timber and wattle-and-daub huts, the river flowing between them and crops growing and cattle grazing in small, unhedged fields. If then, like a film director, you could " dissolve " to the same scene 200 years later, in the middle of the second century A.D., you would see a complete transformation. The huts would have gone. In their place would be symmetrically planned streets of well-built houses of stone and timber, with red-tiled roofs, enclosed by a high wall of grey stone, with turrets at intervals, and impressive towered gateways where the main roads entered the city.

You would see the open forum or market-place, surrounded by large public buildings; you would see pillared temples, basilicæ, and the great open-air theatre with its tiers of seats. You would see citizens in Roman dress entering and leaving the public baths, and others, of the richer sort, being set down from their litters at the porches of their handsome villas; while in the poorer quarters of the town, where the streets were narrower and the dwellings smaller, the artisans plied their trades; the saddlers, cobblers, weavers, tanners, carpenters and smiths.

But among the thousands crowding the streets and piazzas, it is doubtful if one in ten was a Roman of Italian origin. Most of them would be descendants of the same tribesmen who lived in the mud and timber huts a couple of centuries earlier. That was the measure of the revolution which the Romans achieved in the brief 100 years after the Claudian conquest of A.D. 43. They introduced into Britain the Mediterranean conception of a town, as they had done in Gaul earlier.

" An occupation," writes Richmond,[1] " in conferring peace and order, brought about the conditions in which population and productivity might be substantially increased. The tribute yield of the Three Gauls was doubled in fifty years. . . . The instrument of civilisation used by Rome in achieving such results was the town and the many-sided attainments of amenity and social grace which successful civic organisation involves."

He then goes on to describe how such towns were founded. The normal method in Celtic lands was through the aristocratic families, who were encouraged to adopt Roman ways and give their sons a Roman education.

Abroad they would see Roman towns and on their return would wish to imitate them. Tribal revenues, family pride and the desire to show superiority over rivals would do the rest. Once the desire to build an urban tribal centre for festivals and markets had manifested itself the Roman Government stepped in and offered to help. Along would come the surveyors and architects to lend a hand and see that the land was properly parcelled

[1] " Roman Britain," by I. A. Richmond (Penguin Books).

out and the streets laid out in the correct Roman manner. This is the way in which such towns as Londinium, Ratae Coritanorum (Leicester), Eboracum (York), Regnum (Chichester) and others came into being. But it was a gradual process and did not immediately follow the occupation. First the aristocratic families had to be indoctrinated with Roman culture. When the time arrived a nucleus for the new town existed in the old Celtic tribal centre with its wooden shacks for traders and artisans.

In their prime such Romano-British towns were probably rather like the smaller English country towns in the eighteenth century, in which the local gentry had their town houses, while retaining their rural estates, and where civic business could be conducted and markets held. In the peaceful conditions ensured by the Roman occupation, and linked by straight, well-surfaced roads, they were probably very pleasant places to live in, certainly far superior to the insanitary medieval huddles which succeeded them.

I am afraid I have kept the reader on the Cathedral Tower for rather a long time, so let us descend now and see what still remains of Roman Canterbury. There is not much, compared with other Roman cities which we shall visit later, but what exists is worth seeing. Whether or not the newly-discovered remains can still be seen when this book appears will depend on local conditions. Rebuilding is going on fast, and some remains will certainly be re-buried, if they have not been already, but it is worth making a few discreet inquiries concerning the walls of the great theatre, which are near the junction of Watling Street and St. Margaret's Street, also the bath-building under the Royal Fountain Hotel car park, and the remains of the Roman gateway near the Riding Gate.

Some of the objects found during the recent excavations are shown in the Royal Museum in the High Street, which also contains Roman and pre-Roman antiquities from other parts of Kent, and should not be missed. Look especially for the massive silver ingot found at

Richborough Castle, which we shall visit to-morrow; an impressive token of the mineral wealth, which was one of the reasons for the Roman invasion of Britain. There is also a small but fine collection of Roman and Anglo-Saxon glass of lovely shape and fine texture; also, of course, the inevitable collection of Roman pottery, including the glazed red " samian ware ", which some may find more attractive than I do.

On the whole, however, I found the post-Roman objects in the Canterbury museum more interesting than the Roman, especially the two famous Jutish " rune-stones ", the oldest inscribed burial memorials ever found in Britain not belonging to a Celtic or Romano-British population. For Canterbury—Cant-wara-byrig—is primarily an English shrine, the cradle of our race; and no city motto is more fitly chosen: " Ave Mater Angliæ! "—" Hail, Mother of England! "

Yet there are still moments when an imaginative ear can catch the echo of that older city which flourished here before the blond sea-rovers arrived in their long-ships. After dinner, take a stroll along Palace Street, then bear right along the Borough, keeping the walls of King's School on the right; then, having crossed the City Ditch, turn right along the rampart path beside the most perfect stretch of the City Walls. At night, particularly by moonlight, you might imagine yourself beside the walls of Roman Durovernum, which must have looked much the same. Indeed, at one point, called Queningate, you will find a fragment of a Roman entrance, embedded in the medieval masonry. From this gate the Roman road left for the great port of Rutupiæ, modern Richborough. Further along, where a bridge crosses the site of the old Riding Gate you are near the spot where Frere and his fellow archæologists recently discovered the foundations of another Roman gate-tower. In fact, it is now certain that the whole of the medieval *enceinte* is of Roman origin. The base of the Roman wall was 7 feet thick, built of large coursed flints, in front of an earth bank.

When you have followed the wall as far westward as you wish, turn back and retrace your steps to the Queningate. Through that gate more than ten generations of Roman citizens passed to and from their great port of Rutupiæ; Emperors, generals, ambitious young officers arriving in the Province for the first time; the same men promoted and campaign-hardened, returning to Rome; messengers bearing news from far off provinces of the Empire—from Germany, Egypt, Syria; young British blades returning from the Imperial City to shock their fathers with court scandal and a foppish foreign accent; and innumerable humbler men, women and children.

As you make your way back through the narrow, silent streets you may imagine that you hear not a platoon of the Buffs returning to barracks, but a troop of legionaries grounding spears under the great archway while the officer sings out the Latin password as he did eighteen centuries ago.

CHAPTER THREE

CÆSAR CAME THIS WAY

FIVE Roman roads left Canterbury: Watling Street, which came in from London on the west, and left on the south *en route* for Dover (Dubris); another road which left Canterbury via the Queningate for Richborough (Rutupiæ); a northern road which connected with the fort of Reculver (Regulbium) on the north coast of Kent; and a southern highway, now called the Stone Street, which linked the city with Lympne (Portus Lemanis), a seaport which now lies landlocked in the desolate Romney marsh.

Four of these five roads can still be followed, in whole or in part, to-day. The tour which follows starts with the road to Walmer (near which Julius Cæsar landed) and from thence to the Roman port of Dover, Folkestone with its Roman villa, and on to Portus Lemanis, returning to Canterbury via the ancient Stone Street, one of the best-preserved stretches of Roman road still in use in the South of England.

Take the Sandwich road (A257) from Lower Bridge Street, which follows the City Wall which we explored last night. The first part—a short stretch of about 100 yards—runs straight to the gateway of St. Augustine's Abbey, where you must turn right and make a detour, but the original Roman road ran straight through what are now the Abbey grounds. About half a mile further on you pick up the original line of the old road, and just beyond Her Majesty's prison you will see an unobtrusive little lane on the left with a signpost " to St. Martin's Church ". Avoid, if you can, the temptation to press on to Richborough, and turn up this side lane, which leads to one of the most ancient and historic churches in the British Isles.

The little church of St. Martin is nothing much to look at from the outside; just a pleasant towered church of Kentish flint on a slope overlooking a singularly dull road of twentieth-century villas. Yet this is is the only church in Britain which has known continuous Christian worship for at least thirteen centuries without apparent interruption.

When St. Augustine came to England in the sixth century—only 200 years or so after the end of the Roman occupation—he undoubtedly used this church, which had been restored before his time for Queen Bertha; and it was within this tiny building that her husband, King Ethelbert, King of Kent, was baptised. Its history may go back even earlier than that; some authorities suggest that it may be associated with the Roman Christians and St. Martin of Tours, but that is little more than conjecture. Of its association with King Ethelbert and his Queen, however, there is no doubt whatever.

Inside, near the tower, you will see an ancient font; traditionally the one in which King Ethelbert was baptised. It is made up of twenty-two separate pieces of Caen stone, but originally they formed part of a single block. Perhaps it was shattered by the invading Danes when they sacked the city. If this was so, it may well be that the pieces were piously preserved and later re-united when Christianity was restored, and the exterior re-ornamented in a later style in order to cover up the damage.

When St. Augustine climbed the slope to the church to baptise King Ethelbert, the great Roman walls of Canterbury must still have been standing. The Roman road, though decayed, would still be visible, and perhaps the Latin language had not entirely died out among the common people. It is an odd experience to stand in the drab little street which now fronts the ancient church, a street with roofs bristling with TV aerials, and hear the bell ring for Matins from a building which boasts the longest continuous tradition of Christian worship in the British Isles.

Now return to the Sandwich road and continue along it for about ten miles. It is a pleasant journey through typical Kentish countryside; there are villages of time-weathered brick such as Littlebourne and Ash, and at Wingham there is a handsome old inn, the " Red Lion ", which was Wingham College until the dissolution of the monasteries; then it became the home of the Palmer family and is at present a public house.

About a mile beyond Ash, where the main road (A257) takes a sharp turn to the right, look out for a narrow lane on the left signposted " Richborough Castle, Ancient Monument ". When I travelled it in the late autumn a mist hung over the flat, low-lying fields, and there was a damp sea-breeze heavy with the smell of cabbage.

Under an overcast sky, lit by intermittent sunshine stood the venerable walls of Richborough, standing on a flat knoll about 80 feet above the flat meadowland which stretches without interruption to the sea-coast about six miles away. From the clipped turf surrounded by neat Office of Works fencing rose the three surviving flint walls standing to a height of about 10 feet, impressive even in ruin. They enclose what was, for nearly four centuries, the principal southern port of Roman Britain—Rutupiæ. Try not to think of it as an " Ancient Monument ". There was no wire fencing here when Claudius made it his supply depot, and the poet Juvenal commended its oysters. For generations of Romans, their wives and children, Rutupiæ was their first sight of Britain—and their last. Claudius and Vespasian came this way. The warships and transports anchored against the walls which the sea washed, where now there are only reedy meadows where the cattle graze, and small boys scamper over the great ditch which once protected the fortress.

Once a great marble monument rose above the grey walls, probably commemorating the conquest of Britain; a landmark to the ships out in the Channel and for miles inland. But that was in the heyday of the occupation, when Agricola's forts barred the way to the Caledonians 400 miles to the north, when the fierce Silures of South Wales had been subdued; when great roads such as the Ermine Street, the Fosse Way, Watling Street, straddled the land, when such proud cities as Durovernum, Londinium, Uriconium and Eboracum were rising to astonish and impress the British tribesmen.

But there was another phase of history which left its mark on Richborough, a phase which began towards the end of the third century after Christ. Two centuries had passed since Claudius landed in our island, as long a period as separates us from George I; a time when the Celtic inhabitants of Britain had long grown accustomed to Latin culture, when their princes and men of rank had grown used to life in well-ordered cities; when they had learned to relax in the *calidaria* and *tepidaria* of their baths; when they travelled on well-surfaced, well-policed roads, by chariot or on horseback, travelling from London to Scotland in just over a week.

A new menace came to them from across the sea which had brought the conquerors—no longer regarded as conquerors—three centuries ago. Fierce warriors from Germany came in their long-ships, sailing up the Thames Estuary, attacking the south-east coast, ravaging, slaying and looting. The derelict port of Rutupiæ became one of a chain of fortresses by which the Romanised Britons attempted to defend themselves against the barbaric Teutons, the men in the winged helmets.

Around the shores of Britain, south and west along the coasts of Dorset, Hampshire, Sussex, Kent and northwards along the coasts of East Anglia and Yorkshire, they built forts from which their fleets could operate against the pirates, intercepting as they approached or as they retreated. These coastal defences were known as the *Litus Saxonicus*—the Saxon Shore—and were commanded by an officer who bore the title of *Comes Litoris Saxonici*—Count of the Saxon Shore; and of these forts Rutupiæ was one of the greatest. It is from this period that we can date the mighty walls which still dominate the knoll. These lonely, forsaken walls, grimly outlined against the sky, have seen dramatic events. Two usurping Emperors may have known them. The first was Carausius (A.D. 286–293), the bold and daring admiral who commanded the *classis Britannica*, which might be called the first British Navy. Probably in his time they surrounded the monument with ditches, converting it to a look-out, from which the defenders could watch for the approach of pirates.

The other usurper was Magnus Maximus, called by his detractors " the Rutupian Robber ", who seized power in A.D. 383, towards the end of the Roman occupation. A fascinating fact is that the story of his usurpation, and even his name—disguised as Maxen Wledig, is preserved in a Welsh legend. In a final bid for power he took troops from Britain to the Continent, but he was defeated and killed.

When the clouds hang low over the Kentish flats and the straight horizon is a hard pencil-line drawn across the leaden sky an atmosphere of ancient melancholy hangs over Rutupiæ. The silence is never quite complete. Occasionally it is broken by the bellow of jets from a nearby fighter airfield, and when these sounds cease there is still the cawing of rooks and the mewing of gulls. No modern buildings clutter up the ancient walls, save the discreet timber hut of the Curator, and other wooden buildings which house a fine collection of Roman objects found on the site—samian ware, a rich collection of amphoræ (wine-jars) and more intimate articles—women's ornaments, cosmetic jars, etc., which speak of the time when the green enclosure was covered with streets of houses in which lived the officials and their wives.

After Sandwich take the Dover road, which meanders past low-lying meadows, cabbage fields, and occasional clumps of trees sheltering comfortable Georgian houses from the winter gales. Skirting the unattractive purlieus of Deal and following the signpost to Walmer Castle, you come suddenly on to a magnificent stretch of pebble beach. It slopes down fairly steeply to the sea, and here, with the waves lapping your feet, you are on or near the very ground where Cæsar's warships grounded almost exactly 2,000 years ago, and where the Standard Bearer of the Tenth Legion leaped into the sea and waded ashore, holding aloft the Imperial Eagle.

At your back, enclosed by ancient trees, stands Walmer Castle, the official home of the Lord Warden of the Cinque Ports. To your right lie the chalk cliffs on which Cæsar's men saw the British defenders crowding along the crest. Cæsar describes vividly how the British on the cliff-tops followed the Roman ships as they cruised along the coast seeking a suitable landing-place. And on the ground behind the beach must have been fought the battle in which the British charioteers exhibited their desperate skill, as described by the Roman general.

To-day there is probably no more peaceful scene in all England. With your back to the tarmac road and its parked cars you can look out across the unchanging sea, lulled by the regular, rhythmic breaking of the waves, forever flinging forward and dragging back the rounded pebbles, blue and brown and white. The keen salt air blows in from the Channel. The gulls cry above the long-drawn sucking hiss of the undertow. It is a place for reverie.

This is where it all began; everything you will see on your tour, everything which Rome has left in these islands, pleasant villas in sheltered Cotswold valleys; stately Bath; the Amphitheatre at Caerleon; Hadrian's Wall snaking across the Northumberland fells; towns, forts, marching-camps, settlements, and the straight, purposeful roads which link them—all these began here.

It is doubtful if Julius Cæsar intended his invasion to be anything more than a reconnaissance in force. His first expedition was a failure.

His second and more successful attempt in the following year may have helped to restore his slightly damaged prestige. For in his youth Julius Cæsar was far from being the conventional hero-dictator of the school history books. He was, in fact, what the eighteenth century would have called a " blade " and we a playboy. He was an athlete, a fine swordsman, an accomplished horseman. He was also a fop and a dandy, and his amours—which apparently embraced members of both sexes—were notorious. But when he became a military commander his success was dazzling. In Gaul he subdued 300 tribes, took 800 hill-forts, and brought the whole vast territory of what is now France under Roman dominion. Yet, when he attempted the invasion of Britain, his earlier reputation followed him. The Roman wits suggested that he wished to invade the island in order to procure for his mistresses choice specimens of the pearls for which it was famous. His initial failure must therefore have irked him considerably.

Next year he made no mistake. Detachments from five legions, with 2,000 cavalry and strong contingents of archers and slingers, followed him across the Channel. On July 7th, A.D. 54, the army landed between Sandown Castle and Sandwich, and dug themselves in. Hearing that the main British force was at Bigbury near Canterbury, Cæsar pressed on to engage them, and launched the Seventh Legion against the British fortress, the earthwork of which can still be seen west of the city. This disposed of, he was ready to march on Wheathampstead, the headquarters of Cassivellaunus, the British King, but was recalled by the news that a high wind had wrecked forty of his transports. For ten days the army delayed and then, after hauling up the ships out of reach of the tide, began the march inland.

Cæsar's march was probably roughly along the line of the road which we followed from London to Canterbury. He crossed the Medway above Rochester, and the Thames somewhere near Westminster, where the legionaries forded the river at low tide, their shields held above their heads. At this period London did not exist; the capital was at Wheathampstead, to which Cæsar now marched. It quickly fell, though Cassivellaunus had slipped out and organized an attack on the Romans' supply base, probably near Worth in Kent. But the attempt failed and the leader, the Celtic prince, Lugotorix, was taken prisoner.

This time Cæsar was satisfied. He marched back to Worth, wrote a triumphant letter to Marcus Cicero announcing his success, and, after receiving the submission of Cassivellaunus and other British Kings, re-embarked for Gaul. Britain did not see another Roman army for nearly 100 years.

* * * * *

From Walmer it is only a five-mile drive to Dover, where the mighty thirteenth-century *enceinte* of Dover Castle frowns from its hillside above the harbour. Dover also was a Roman port—Dubris—but its remains are buried under modern buildings. One relic of the Roman occupation, however, does remain; the *Pharos* or lighthouse which now serves as the east tower of the medieval chapel within the castle walls. One wonders how many of the thousands of visitors who in summer wander across the green courts realise that this weather-beaten tower stood there for at least a thousand years before the castle was built?

Dover Castle is, I suppose, the most magnificent of its kind in the United Kingdom, but we must make an effort to forget the medieval fortress and try to imagine the green hill as it was in Roman times, when the lighthouse dominated the scene—a solitary grey tower by day, but at night a bonfire blazed from its roof, guiding the Roman galleys on their way across the Channel. From the ground to a height of about 40 feet the structure is recognisably Roman, built of stone and flint, with the usual horizontal bonding courses of red tiles. The upper part is medieval.

The view from the Pharos is one of the finest in Great Britain, a rich panorama starting with the Keep of Dover Castle on the north-east, and then, as the eye sweeps eastward and northward, taking in the chalk downs and the smoking chimneys of Dover far below, with the Channel steamers moving in through the outstretched arms of the harbour entrance and the smoke of other ships far out across the grey water. This, truly, is historic ground. Inevitably one recalls the Norman Constables of Dover, who held the keys to England, but it would be a mistake to think of Roman Dubris in that way. When the keepers of the Roman Pharos looked out across the Channel to the hazy line of the Gaulish coast, they were not, as we are, looking at a foreign country, but at another province of the same great Empire of which Britain was a part. The people over there, in Gaul, spoke the same Latin language, lived in the same kind of towns, worshipped the same gods, shared the same culture, though with regional differences. Similar currencies were used, from Scotland to Syria, from Vienna to Barcelona, and linking these far-flung provinces was a network of fine, straight well-surfaced roads, along which one could travel from the Tyne to the Euphrates safely and with little inconvenience.

Nor was it a superficial unity imposed by force from above. True, it was founded on military conquest, but once achieved it became a confederation of peoples who could attain common Roman citizenship. The Emperor Hadrian was a Spaniard. Julius Classicianus, Legate of Britain, came from the Rhineland. Among the Roman tombstones scattered throughout the museums of Britain you will find the names of Greeks, Batavians, and even people from far-off Palmyra in Syria. A few years ago I visited this romantic ruined city, lost in the desert wastes east of Damascus. This year I came across the memorial stone of a Palmyrenian archer who served on Hadrian's Wall, in Northumberland. He had settled in the North of England and married a British wife. Both would have spoken Latin, the common tongue of the Empire.

Similarly, one finds tombstones of British officers who served in the Roman Army in Germany, North Africa and other places. All were Romans.

When the fire on top of the Roman Pharos at Dover went out for the last time, much more was extinguished than the light. With it died European unity, and Man's first attempt, however imperfect, to establish a world state. Eighteen hundred years afterwards we are as far from either ideal as ever. We have, however, television and the hydrogen bomb.

Further along the coast lies Folkestone, where, on a stretch of cliffs known as "the Warren" stand the foundations of what used to be one of the best-preserved Roman villas in the South of England. Unfortunately, some of it has slipped down over the cliff-edge, and what remains is so shamefully neglected as to make one very cynical concerning the depth of the alleged public interest in archæology.

From Folkestone to Lympne the best way is via the toll-road, which takes one along the coast, with views of the Channel away to the left, and so on through Sandgate, another ancient seaport which the sea has forsaken. Hythe, equally fascinating, comes next, after which you should turn off the main Ashford road to the left along B2067. Continue along narrow, winding lanes to Lympne, famous among other things for its airport. The village itself, although pleasant, is not in any way outstanding, but turn left along the narrow lane near the County Members Inn, and you will come suddenly upon one of those vistas in which all that we nostalgically associate with the name England is embodied. So much of our lovely country has been and is being despoiled, and every year more of it disappears under the tide of standardised villas, petrol stations, factories, multiple stores, etc. Yet, every now and then, and usually without being sought, the old England suddenly reveals itself.

Such a moment came to me at Lympne, when, in the fading light of a mellow October day, I was looking for the ruins of the third great Roman port on the Kentish coast, Portus Lemanis. After 100 yards the narrow lane I have described turns in a loop opposite the venerable grey stone manor house, Lympne Place. Here I parked the car and entered the churchyard beside the great house. To the right rose the grey bulk of the twelfth-century church, with its squat square tower, like a Norman keep. To the right the crenellations of the Manor House parapet continued the line of the church roof. It was etched against the sky of cirrus clouds, like the scales of a goldfish; the kind of view the early nineteenth-century landscape artists loved to paint.

Rooks cawed in the great trees of the park, and cattle lowed in a nearby shippen. I retraced my steps, passing the Manor House, until I reached a little shop called the Lympne Castle Stores, where a narrow track to the left led steeply downhill. A footpath branched off to the right through a coppice. I made my way along this, through the trees, and suddenly found myself on the edge of a steeply descending slope, almost a cliff which overlooked a vast stretch of the Romney Marsh. The flat line of the horizon divided the picture, and beyond gleamed the sea.

Here nothing had changed. Perhaps the most recent innovation was the Military Canal, made in the time of Napoleon. Otherwise there remained only the flat, dun-coloured fields, crossed by canals; a few isolated farms, occasional clumps of dark trees, and in the foreground a tumbled expanse of uncultivated land. My glance followed the line of the slope down, down, until suddenly checked by a few ruined walls of grey stone, tilted at odd angles and lying forlornly among the coarse, hummocky grass. And that was what I had come to see—Portus Lemanis, the name of which still survives in Lympne.

Portus Lemanis was another of the Forts of the Saxon Shore, of which Rutupiæ was the most important. It was garrisoned by a regiment of Tungrians from Belgic Gaul. To the west lay Anderida, now called Pevensey, in Sussex, the remains of which are still impressive, and after Pevensey came Portus Adurni, now called Porchester Castle, near Portsmouth.

Here were epitomised twenty centuries of British history. There were the ruins of the Roman port from which the sea had long receded. There rose the bulk of the Norman church built by another race of conquerors. Beyond it was the medieval Manor House, built perhaps on the site of a Saxon demesne, but speaking more distinctly of the Plantagenets. The park, with its carefully sited clumps of trees, was of the seventeenth and eighteenth century, civilised and well-ordered, but ending abruptly where the marsh began—the ancient sea-bed over which the Roman warships sailed on their way to intercept the Teutonic raiders.

Below me the Military Canal caught the last gleam of daylight, recalling Wellington, the Martello Towers and *le petit Caporal* with his spyglass on the cliffs above Boulogne. Above, a solitary fighter streaked back to its base, the flat roar of its jets flung back by the hillside; a reminder of yet another attempted invasion.

And then it was quite dark, and only the regular pulsing light of the Dungeness lightship marked the line of the unseen coast.

* * * * *

From Lympne, almost opposite the County Members Inn, take B2068, signposted Canterbury and London, and after a mile you cross the road between Hythe and Maidstone (A261); continue straight on, avoiding the right-hand fork on to A20, and take the road which continues almost due north (still B2068). This, scheduled as a secondary road, is none other than the historic Roman Stone Street, which, starting at Portus Lemanis, strides straight across the Weald to Canterbury, Roman Durovernum. The traveller will discover with amusement that if he faithfully follows the Legions on his journeys he will find himself almost automatically using the old Latin names.

The section of Stone Street which stretches for fourteen miles between Lympne and Canterbury is one of the best examples in Britain of a Roman military highway still in use. Part of its attraction lies in the fact that, on the one hand, its identity has not been blotted out under the tarmac of a great trunk road, nor, on the other has it degenerated into a mere cart-track. It is still a well-used highway, preserving its original width in most places, and, apart from a slight deviation near Horton Park and Canterbury itself, it runs in an almost perfectly straight line.

Driving along Stone Street on a fine night can be impressive, because of the darkness, which by shutting out the surrounding landscape, concentrates the mind on the road itself. If the headlights suddenly picked up the gleam of a legionary's helmet, or one were to hear the clatter of a cohort of Tungrian cavalry on their way to Portus Lemanis, it would only realise what one's imagination had already painted.

To complete the illusion, when at last you enter Canterbury from this direction you pass straight through one of the great gateways piercing the curtain wall. Almost you expect to hear the challenge of the sentry as you pass under the arch, at the end of your first tour of Roman Kent.

For a sketch of recent and even current discoveries in Roman Kent, see *New Discoveries*, beginning on page 285.

CHAPTER FOUR

CLAUDIUS AND COLCHESTER

To Tiberius Claudius Cæsar Augustus Germanicus, the son of Drucus; Pontifex Maximus; in the eleventh year of his Tribunician power; his fifth consulate and the twenty-first occasion of his being saluted Imperator; Father of the State and the People of Rome—because, without any mishap he received in unconditional surrender eleven conquered British kings, and for the first time reduced transoceanic barbarians under the power of the Roman people.

THAT inscription in honour of the Emperor Claudius was found some years ago on a large marble slab in Rome. It is now in the Palazzo Barberini, and commemorates, in suitably grandiose terms, the conquest of Britain by Claudius, though in fact the bulk of the work was done by his general, Aulus Plautius, while the Emperor himself stayed only sixteen days in the island. From the Claudian invasion, as historians call it, we date the beginning of the real conquest and occupation of Britain.

We know considerably more about this expedition than about that of Cæsar. We know, for instance, that the troops selected for the occupation were four legions, the Second Augusta, previously stationed on the Rhine at Strasbourg, the Twentieth Valeria Victrix from the Lower Rhine, the Fourteenth Gemina from the Middle Rhine, and the Ninth Hispana from Pannonia. With them came many auxiliary troops, cavalry, archers, slingers, etc., from Gaul, from Thrace, and other provinces. The fact that these veteran troops at first refused to embark speaks volumes for Britain's dire reputation. To the Romans Britain was beyond the edge of the known world. The outer ocean, they believed, spilled over the edge of the flat earth like a waterfall, and the soldiers and sailors called upon to make the crossing were extremely reluctant to operate in such dangerous waters. In fact at first they refused to move from their bases on the Rhine. The fact that they did eventually move was due to one of those fascinating historical accidents which occur from time to time. Dio Cassius, the historian, tells us what happened. The Emperor Claudius sent as his emissary a certain Narcissus, who was a freed slave. When he got up to speak the troops jeered at him. Then some wag shouted "*Io Saturnalia!*"—referring to the Christmas celebrations when slaves dressed up as their masters. The legionaries roared with laughter, the tension broke, they listened to Narcissus, and crossed.

A future Emperor was among the commanders; Vespasian commanded the Second Augusta. The expedition was commanded by Aulus Plautius, at the head of some 50,000 men.

The basis of the Roman Army was the Legion. Each Legion was known by a number, and as far as can be ascertained, comprised about 5,000 heavy infantry, and 120 "dispatch riders"—light horsemen for scouting and message-carrying. It was commanded by a Senator (which sounds odd to modern ears, but I will explain later the system of military appointments), six military tribunes—young men of rank for whom the army was the first stage in their political career—sixty centurions, equivalents of sergeants, corporals, and lance-corporals.

The weapons of the legionary were two; the *pilum*, a slender javelin with a long iron point, and beautifully balanced for throwing, and the *gladius* or short sword which could cut and thrust. He wore a helmet with cheek-pieces, the upper part of his body was protected by segmented plates of iron or bronze—the *lorica segmentata*, and he carried a long shield of semi-cylindrical shape. Under his armour he wore a leather tunic reaching to the knee, and on his feet leather boots called *caligæ*. For this reason the Roman infantry soldiers were nicknamed *caligatæ*—those who wore the *caligæ*—"foot-sloggers" in fact. This, incidentally, is how the Emperor Caligula got his name. When the child was born his father held him up in front of the troops with words to this effect: " Here he is—one of you! He will be a *caligula!* " (little foot). The delighted troops yelled " Caligula! Caligula! " and the name stuck to the Emperor for the rest of his life, though he failed to achieve the military prowess for which his father had hoped.

The legionary's method of fighting was first to hurl the *pilum*, and then, drawing his short sword, close with the enemy in hand to hand combat. These were the men who conquered most of the known world: " the iron legionary," as Sir Charles Oman wrote, " who, with shield fitted close to his left shoulder and sword-hilt sunk low, cut his way through the thickest hedge of pikes, turned back the onset of the mailed horsemen of the East, and stood unmoved before the wildest rush of Celt or German."

I shall have more to say about the legionary's life in a later chapter, when we visit Caerleon, but in the meantime we must consider his companion-in-arms, the Auxiliary. Whereas the legionaries were Roman citizens, the Auxiliaries were not. They were recruited among the subject peoples of the Empire, divided into infantry cohorts of some 500 to 1,000 men, and cavalry troops known as *alae*. It is well to remember the latter word, as shall find it often on Roman tombstones throughout the country.

The word, which means " wing ", was used because that was how the auxiliary cavalryman operated, on the wings of the army, protecting the heavily-armed legionaries who bore the main weight of the attack.

The Romans also had quite formidable artillery, the use of which they inherited, like many other things, from the Greeks. There were *catapultæ* and *ballistæ* for hurling stones or javelins for considerable lengths. Some of the stone missiles from the *ballistæ* have been found near the Roman forts in Scotland.

They also understood what we call " combined operations " in which the land and naval arms co-operated. Tacitus has a lively account in his " Agricola " of how the soldiers and sailors who took part in the invasion of Scotland camped together, and of the rival boasting which went on between them..

> " The war was pushed forward simultaneously by land and sea; and infantry, cavalry and marines, often meeting in the same camp, would mess and make merry together. They would boast, as soldiers will, of their several exploits and adventures, and match the perilous depths of woods and mountains against the hazards of storms and tides, the victories on land against the conquest of the ocean."

Such passages—and would there were more of them in the works of Roman historians—bring us very near to the men who conquered Britain.

Unfortunately, with a few exceptions like the one just quoted, most accounts of the Roman Army are dry official chronicles of battles and campaigns written by historians of whom most had probably never seen action. The life of the soldier off-duty, the stories which he swapped with his comrades while relaxing in the hot baths, at dice in his barracks, or round the camp-fire at night while the sentries peered into the darkness, wary against a Belgic raid, will never be known. Yet one can imagine them. What an army it must have been in which to serve! Think of its composition; in its ranks there would be men from the mountains of Macedonia, Orientals from Syria, effervescent, laughter-loving Greeks from the Ægean islands, swarthy Berbers from North Africa, blond warriors from the forests of Germany. What songs were sung, what dances danced, in those grim Northumbrian forts, when, their weapons laid aside, the men relaxed and recalled the stories and the music of their far-off homeland? One thinks of the gambling, the spilled wine and the drunken quarrels over women, the lusty, vigorous life of which now nothing remains but a dice-box in some provincial museum, and a few ruined walls above which the curlews cry.

These, then, were the men who followed their commander, Aulus Plautius, across the grey waters of the Channel in A.D. 43. Like the Allies in 1944, they aimed to land at several points in order to conceal from the enemy the direction of the main attack. Of these three beach-heads, one was probably Rutupiæ (Richborough) where the Romans built up a big maritime supply base.

The British forces opposed to the invaders were commanded by two chieftains, sons of Cunobelinus—Shakespeare's Cymbeline, whose headquarters were at Camulodunum (modern Colchester). One was Togodumnus, the other Caratacus, the legendary Celtic leader who was to be a thorn in the invaders' side for years, and whose name survives in the Welsh hero Caradoc.

What happened after the Roman forces had landed and deployed is vividly described by Professor Richmond in his " Roman Britain ", and I cannot do better than quote direct from his account:

> " The British forces . . . depended too much upon natural obstacles and too little upon their powers of manœuvre, thoroughly underrating the ingenuity and resource of Roman troops in the face of river crossings. At the first pitched battle, on the Medway, the Roman auxiliary troops crossed and caught the charioteers off their guard, and in the two day battle which followed, Vespasian, commander of the Second Legion, achieved a successful surprise attack, while Hosidius Geta won a resounding victory by firmly sustained pressure and bold personal risk. The next river was the Thames itself across which the Britons retreated without arranging for an effective rearguard action and allowed their retreat beyond the river to be cut off by Roman troops who had crossed uncontested, even using a bridge. The lack of counsel here displayed was no doubt due to the previous death of Togodumnus; and it is the more readily explicable when it is realised that on the death of Cunobelinus, Togodumnus had taken the old kingdom, in Essex and Hertfordshire, while Caratacus had taken the westward kingdom of the Middle Thames, Hampshire and Surrey. Thus, on defeat on the Medway, the Britons must in fact have split into two groups, one retreating westward under Caratacus, the other, leaderless, making headlong for home north of the river."

Thus the way to Camulodunum, in Essex, lay wide open, but on the Thames Aulus Plautius paused, to allow time for the arrival of the Emperor Claudius who led the final march on the British capital. After a campaign lasting only sixteen days, Claudius entered the city in triumph to receive its submission and later that of other unnamed British tribes.

* * * * *

The next stage of our journey takes us from London to Colchester along the Roman road which was laid down not long after the conquest, and which passes through the country which Claudius traversed on his triumphal march on Camulodunum. The first fifteen miles of the road pass through London's urban sprawl, and when at last the road emerges beyond Romford it is a broad modern highway (A12), partly double-tracked, passing through Brentwood and the still delightful villages of Mountnessing and Ingatestone. On it goes, through pleasant rolling country of hedgerows and ploughland, dignified by ancient trees, which, when I last took this road, glowed with the colours of autumn. It is almost impossible to see in this crowded tarmac strip, choc-a-bloc with lorries and nervously-driven saloons, the route which Claudius's legions took on their way to Camulodunum. It bears on its flanks the inevitable appendages of a main coast route—cafés advertising " dainty teas ", large petrol stations, and huge signs advertising the delights of Clacton and Southend. Yet this is the ancient road, and the original metalling still lies beneath the modern highway, which for most of its length closely follows the Roman alignment.

Generally it keeps to the high ground, occasionally changing direction on hilltops, and it has, in spite of its modern appearance, that indefinable atmosphere of a road which has been in constant use for many centuries. The many coaching inns in the villages through which it passes remind us of earlier generations of travellers, and many of the trees which border it must have been seen by ten generations of travellers.

Of all counties Essex is perhaps the most difficult to associate with Rome. It is obstinately Saxon. The names on the signposts—names like Halstead, Braintree, Malding—the fair-haired, fair-skinned, kindly Saxon faces; the clayey soil of the fat fields; all these speak more clearly of these stubborn, slow-thinking, slow-moving German ancestors of ours than of the volatile Latin peoples whom they finally overwhelmed.

The modern road swings round Chelmsford to the south and then for a long stretch continues on high ground, passing through Hatfield Peverel and Witham. Marks Tey, an undistinguished sprawl of modern villas, garages, and a few ancient houses, is the point where the " Great Road " which we have been following was joined by another Roman road from the north-west. From here traffic from both roads joins for the last four miles to Colchester.

After passing through the little unspoiled village of Lexden (famous for its tumulus excavated thirty years ago) we enter modern Colchester through an avenue of limes, after observing the proud notice—" Colchester, Britain's oldest recorded town ".

In this active, bustling and attractive city, thronged with cars, lorries and military transports, it is very difficult to find relics of ancient Camulodunum. But they exist and are worth the effort of discovery. The ancient city crops up in unlikely places, where one least expects to find it. Nor are the modern inhabitants indifferent to their city's history. It was refreshing to find, in the " snug " of the Gate Head Inn, a portrait of Cæsar in bright colours above a painting of the Roman Balkerne Gate, evidently the work of a local amateur. The military element in Colchester is still strong, and the legionaries would certainly have appreciated the accompanying mural in the same pub, which depicts two Tommies in battledress reclining in some Elysian meadow accompanied by a buxom, diaphanously-gowned nymph who holds in one hand a guitar and in the other a glass of Daniel's Pale Ale.

We could do worse than follow her example, and while relaxing after our journey, consider what ancient Camulodunum was like, and what can still be seen of it.

CHAPTER FIVE

THE STRONG PLACE OF CAMULOS

It is important to remember, when we speak of the "British" resistance to the invasions of Cæsar and Claudius, that we do not mean a united people. The country was divided up into tribal areas, each under its local ruler; for instance, there were the Coritani, whose capital was where Leicester now stands; there were the Dobunni, occupying part of the Cotswolds and Gloucestershire, and ruled from what is now Cirencester; there were the Brigantes of Yorkshire, the Iceni of East Anglia, and Silures of South Wales, and many others. None of these remoter tribes took part in the resistance to Claudius, though later, when their own territories were attacked, some of them fought bravely. But in the initial stages of the invasion the brunt of the Roman attack was borne by the southern tribes. Among these were the Trinovantes, who occupied roughly the area which we now call Essex; their ancestral capital was Camulodunum, which means "the strong place of Camulos"—Camulos being a Celtic war-god.

Cassivellaunus, who fought Julius Cæsar, had invaded the territory of the Trinovantes, and Mandubracius, the son of the defeated Trinovantian king, had sought the protection of Rome. One of the conditions imposed on Cassivellaunus by Cæsar was that he should cease harrying the Trinovantes. But in 10 B.C., forty-five years after Cæsar had withdrawn, it seems that the Trinovantes had been conquered by Tasciovanus, the successor to Cassivellaunus, for coins of this date bear the name Camulodunum. Afterwards the invaders seem to have been expelled, but not for long, for at the beginning of the first century the Trinovantes came under the domination of Dubnovellaunus, King of Kent. Not long afterwards,

Dubnovellaunus in turn was driven out and appeared, like several of his predecessors, as a suppliant in Rome.

The names alone of these gentlemen, all seemingly ending in " aunus " or " umnus ", are enough to fog the brain of anyone seeking to unravel the tangle of Romano-British relations at this period, and I shall not weary the reader with more of them. No more, that is, except the greatest of them all, Cunobelinus. This King, after annexing the territory of the Catevellauni, in Middlesex and Hertfordshire, and later that of Kent also, made himself ruler of South-Eastern Britain, so that he became known to the Romans as *Rex Britonnorum*, King of the Britons. When Shakespeare wrote his play about this monarch, he called him Cymbeline, not Cunobelinus.

The site of Cymbeline's city lay under Sheepen Farm, just west of modern Colchester. Elements of its defences can still be seen. These great earth-works, built in three successive lines of ditches and banks are impressive. You can see them on the west side of Colchester near Lexden, where they are known as Gryme's Dyke, the Triple Dyke and the Lexden Ramparts. The ditches are 30 feet deep, large enough to stop modern tanks, let alone chariots. The best way to locate them is with a large-scale Ordnance Survey Map, where they are clearly marked.

It was partly due to family quarrels between Cymbeline and his sons that Claudius invaded Britain. One of them, Adminius, had been sent packing in A.D. 40, and almost succeeded in persuading Caligula (the " little boot ") to invade the island. Other disgruntled exiles approached Claudius at the time of Cymbeline's death, and there may well have been among the party which triumphantly entered Camulodunum in A.D. 43.

Some readers may wonder why the Roman Emperor directed his main attack on this little Essex town and not on Londinium, which was destined to become the most important city in Roman Britain. But at this time Londinium did not exist, and it was therefore quite natural that Claudius should make for the tribal capital of the *Rex Britonnorum*. Colchester's history goes much further back than that of London, and its citizens have every right to boast that theirs is " the oldest inhabited town in England ".

Although there may well have been a Roman military camp at Camulodunum in the early years of the occupation, none has yet been found.

A word of explanation concerning *Coloniæ*, of which Colchester is an example. As I explained in the chapter on Canterbury, most of the so-called Roman towns of Britain were in fact British settlements re-planned in the Roman manner and occupied mainly by the Romanised Britons. But there were exceptions. Some of the towns were deliberately planned as colonies for time-expired legionaries who were given land on which to settle. Camulodunum was such a *Colonia*; Lincoln was another.

The fact that the land was thus forcibly annexed for the benefit of foreign troops is important, because it helps to explain why the Trinovantes rose in support of the Iceni tribe when they revolted some years later under Boudicca (Boadicea). The only relic of this first Colonia is the platform of the great Temple of Claudius (which we shall see when we visit the Castle), because the colony was burned to the ground when Boudicca and her followers sacked it less than twenty years later. What we see of Roman Camulodunum to-day is the rebuilt town which succeeded it.

It is as well to start with the Balkerne Gate, the largest Roman gateway in Britain. To get to it from the Gate Head Inn, go down Crouch Street, take the first turning on the right—Balkerne Lane—and after about 200 yards you will come upon a public-house the " King's Head ", known locally as " The Hole-in-the-Wall ", which stands on a high bank to the right of the lane. Here stands a substantial part of the great West Gate of the Roman city, 107 feet wide, with two archways originally capable of accommodating two lines of wheeled traffic, and on each side of these are two narrower archways for pedestrians. That on the right still survives. These in turn were flanked by quadrant-shaped bastions, of which all the right-hand bastion and part of the left still remain. These bastions or towers contained guard-rooms.

Although some antiquaries deplore the fact that the " King's Head " now sits on top of the gate, I, for one, cannot regret it. The Gateway might have suffered a much worse fate, and what more appropriate site could be found for a convivial meeting-place than the great gateway where the citizens of Camulodunum lounged and gossiped nearly 2,000 years ago?

I was also glad to notice that the municipality of Colchester has placed a memorial plaque on the brick wall in front of the Roman one, showing the original appearance of the Balkerne Gate; a commendable piece of civic spirit worthy of " the oldest recorded city in Great Britain ".

Colchester can boast one of the best-preserved Roman city walls in Great Britain, and it is well worth the effort of making the entire circuit, preferably on foot. They have a circumference of some one and three-quarter miles, and enclose an oblong area of approximately 100 acres.

Starting from the Balkerne Gate, go down Balkerne Hill, where the remains of the wall are of the finest, standing almost to their original height of 12 feet, to which should be added the 3 additional feet of the parapet. The walls are 8 feet thick, built of rubble and mortar, originally faced on both sides with squared masonry, alternating with tile courses. In places these can still be seen. On the top one must imagine the rampart walk for the sentries, protected by the parapet, now missing. At the bottom of the hill turn right with the wall and follow it almost as far as North Hill. The North Gate stood here, part of which was revealed under the pavement in 1944.

Nothing of the wall can be seen from this point to the Rye Gate, through part of it being buried under the pavement, but from the Rye Gate onward one picks it up again along the Park Folly; there is a particularly good example of the inner face in Castle Park and a little further eastward, in Holly Tree Meadow, even the rampart is preserved. Near the eastern end of this stretch of the North Wall there are well-preserved remains of a Roman gateway, within which one can still see a section of the great drain or *cloaca*. Archæologists tend to get very excited over well-preserved drains. For those who share their enthusiasm, this one is 1½ feet wide, lined with tiles, and runs from the remains of the Mithraic Temple alongside the Roman street—now buried—to this gate, and thence to the north-west. The River Colne, which you can see in the valley away to the north, must have received the sewage from the Roman town.

Near the north-east corner of the Roman city part of the defensive ditch can still be seen. This is perhaps the most picturesque part of the Roman wall, crowned by trees, growing in the Friends' Burial Ground on the other side. But the western section of the Wall, where it still survives, is mostly hidden behind houses and in gardens and is inaccessible. The East Gate was demolished in the seventeenth century. If the traveller persists patiently until he comes to Priory Street he will find other well-preserved sections of the wall, with internal towers and bastions, running along behind the houses of Priory Street and sometimes visible from yards and back-alleys. In one such yard I saw a bizarre sight—a group of television aerials waiting erection, and leaning against the worn stones of the 1,800-year-old wall. That was typical of a large part of Roman remains still visible in Britain. They are rarely isolated and remote; the throb of modern life is still around them.

Along the south side of the town, through Vineyard Street, and St. John's Street, portions of the wall have recently been revealed, and more will probably be cleared as rebuilding takes place. Unlike some towns, Colchester is proud of its Roman remains and is anxious to show them to the best advantage whenever this is possible. Finally, we come back to the Headgate, and from here, if our stamina allows, we can return along Balkerne Lane and so through the Balkerne Gate, past the hideous red-brick Water Tower, and so through a narrow alley to North Hill.

At this point we are on the original line of the Roman road which entered through the Balkerne or West Gate. Ahead of you lies the modern High Street, which continues the line of the ancient road. From here, the " top of the Town " as the people of Colchester call it, you look left down the steep slope of North Hill to the valley of the Colne. If you could have stood here, say, in the third century, you would have seen a large number of handsome villas on the hill slopes to your left hand and, straight ahead of you, a broad straight street leading to the south side of the great Forum, or market-place, dominated by the huge Temple of Claudius, the high roof of which would be visible from here.

Go past the Town Hall, West and East Stockwell until you come to the Castle Grounds on the left. Here, where the great Norman Keep rises foursquare from its dry-moat, stood the Temple of Claudius, surrounded by a wide piazza, the Forum, which was the focal point of Roman Camulodunum. It measured about 600 feet in length and 400 feet in width, and was surrounded by magnificent buildings, the foundations of which are mainly buried.

For a full description of these buildings, and indeed for the rest of Roman Colchester, I strongly recommend the reader to consult Mr. Hull's " Roman Colchester ", which can be bought for 2*s*. at the Museum. It is one of the most readable and authoritative accounts of a Roman city I have encountered on my travels, extremely well written by an archæologist who not only knows his subject, but loves it and knows how to capture the imagination of the lay reader. I wish that all such handbooks were as interesting.

Of the Claudian Temple he writes:

" In the centre " (of the Forum) " stood the great temple of Claudius, build about A.D. 50, on such an elaborate scale that the Romans themselves ridiculed the ambition of the founder. It was of a well-known classical style, with a deep portico eight columns wide and four deep. Colonnades ran along each side, but only half-engaged columns across the back. This plan is almost the same as that of the Temple of Mars Ultor in the Forum at Rome. A complete reconstruction can be seen in the Museum."

Of this magnificent building nothing now remains but the great platform of masonry upon which it stood. This was the podium upon which Roman temples were raised high above the prevailing ground level. In order to save stone and mortar, which was difficult to obtain here, the interior of this platform was built in the form of four vaults, the shorter cross wall serving as a support for the front walls of the cells (the one large hall) which makes the plan cruciform. These vaults were purely constructional and were not intended to be used; consequently there was no entrance to them, nor any means of inter-communication.

Not long after the Norman Conquest the conquerors built their great Keep at Colchester, and chose as their site the Roman forum which at this time (*circa* 1076) provided a copious supply of building material. They cleared the Temple ruins, thus exposing the platform, and around this built the walls of their great tower. The flat top of the podium or platform provided the ground floor, and on it they built massive dividing walls. But evidently they were quite ignorant of the fact that the foundations were not solid, but hollow vaults, with the result that in time the western vault cracked, and the wall must have moved considerably at the top also. This is why the west wall has completely disappeared. The vaults were accidentally discovered by a Mr. John Wheeley in 1683, when he was attempting to demolish the Castle, and to-day it is possible to visit them. These vaults alone constitute the largest Roman building still surviving in Britain. What the Temple above them was like can only be imagined.

Camulodunum must have abounded in temples. There was one a little to the north of the Claudian temple.

There was another in Cheshunt Field on Gosbecks Farm, and there was also a Temple of Mithras, part of which can still be seen. It lies in the Holly Trees Meadow, north-east of the Castle, and was explored between 1927 and 1929.

" A squarish room with red concrete floor had an entrance lobby at its north-east corner which led to a stair-well leading down to an underground chamber. This chamber was carefully walled with tiles laid in pink mortar and had a floor of thick concrete in which heavy timber baulks had been embedded in a curious plan. . . . The plan of the timbers in this underground room coincides with that of the internal arrangements of a Mithraic Temple, as also does the general plan." (M. R. Hull).

You will find the remains of this underground room of the Mithraic Temple at the south end of Holly Trees Meadow, in the Castle Park, and from it a street ran to one of the Roman postern gates, which can also be seen.

Although the recent discovery of the London Mithræum has attracted much deserved publicity, it should be remembered that there are several Temples of Mithras in Britain, such as this one, and several on the Roman Wall in Northumberland, but they are rare on civilian sites such as Colchester and London. Mithras, a Persian god, was very popular with the Roman Army. The cult seems to have taken the form of a society, with Lodges, and its proceedings were strictly secret. However, we do know that one of the rites of initiation consisted in making the novice lie for a long period in a narrow underground chamber above which a fire was lit, in order to test his powers of endurance.

The remains I have described comprise practically all that can be seen of Roman Colchester still *in situ*. It is as well to see them before you enter the Castle itself, which must on no account be missed, because it contains one of the finest collections of Romano-British objects in Great Britain.

The heavy eleventh-century walls of the Keep are built from the ruins of Camulodunum; you will immediately notice the Roman tiles in herringbone formation; and the

Norman arches of the narrow windows are also built of Roman tiles. Before you mount to the first floor, notice the well-preserved mosiac pavement which once adorned the town house of some wealthy citizen of Roman Colchester.

When I first visited the Castle Museum I must admit to being disappointed. There seemed too many dusty glass cases overcrowded with not very interesting pottery, and hundreds of bronze and other instruments fixed on display cards as if in an ironmonger's shop. But this was an unfair judgment. The fact is that Colchester has yielded such a number and variety of objects from its four centuries of Roman occupation that one would need a larger building even than the Castle adequately to display them all. And as Colchester is equally rich in objects from earlier and later periods, all of which have to be represented, it is not surprising that the Museum authorities have little space in which to spread themselves.

But persevere; climb the wooden stairs to the gallery on the first floor of the Keep, and in particular do not miss the display of Romano-British antiquities in the annexe near the top of the stairs, especially the fascinating models which will give you a far more vivid picture of what Camulodunum looked like than any words of mine.

Before I attempt to describe the contents of the Colchester Museum, I think I should state frankly at the outset the method I propose to adopt in dealing with this and similar collections. No attempt will be made to draw up a careful catalogue of the objects. Such catalogues already exist in most museums, and it would obviously be impossible to include everything which is likely to interest the reader. Instead I have picked out those things which have appealed to me personally, without suggesting that they are necessarily the most important or significant. The objects which attracted me in the main are those which throw light on the daily life of these remote ancestors of ours; the ornaments with which the women adorned themselves, the games they played, the dishes they ate off; such trifles as a child's money-box, a pair of eye-brow pluckers, the tools which a blacksmith used in his smithy.

Among the bewildering mass of material in the Castle Museum notice particularly the tombstone of a Centurion of the XXth Legion, who is shown standing in a carved niche, carrying a swagger stick. He wears greaves (*Ocreæ*) which were one of the marks which distinguished the Centurion from the private soldier. This tombstone was found nearly 100 years ago outside the City Wall. Near it was a lead cyst containing charred bones, probably those of the officer himself, together with a small glass vessel and a cup. The Centurion is depicted with one hand resting on his staff of office, and his dagger at his right hip. A translation of the accompanying inscription reads as follows:

"*Marcus Fevorius Facilis, son of Marcus of the Pollian Tribe, Centurion of the XXth Legion, Verecundus and Novicius, his freedman, placed it. This is the spot.*"

A centurion commanded 80 men.

There is also the almost inevitable tombstone, the like of which you will see in most museums of Roman antiquities, depicting an auxiliary cavalryman riding over a prostrate foe (in this case depicted with long hair). This particular officer was a *Duplicarius* of the First Ala of Thracians. His name was Longinus and his father bore the extraordinary name of Szapezmatchus. There is also a specimen of a military diploma given to one Saturnus, a Briton. Such diplomas, which were awarded to soldiers granting them citizenship at the end of twenty-five years' service are often found on Roman sites in Britain and elsewhere.

Among the curiosities of the Colchester Museum are a set of moulds used by forgers to cast counterfeit coins, a theatre-pass made of pottery, with the initials "R.B." inscribed on it, and a curious jug with a slot, obviously used as a money-box. There is a set of surgical instruments, including forceps and tweezers, a hanging inkstand, and among the smiths' work a very modern-looking pair of pliers, such as one uses for removing iron nails from packing-cases. An exact duplicate could be bought in any ironmonger's shop to-day.

The artistic standard of most Roman ornaments found in Britain is extremely low. There is something tawdry and mass-produced about the numberless little votive statuettes of Mercury, Hercules and Minerva, and of the Emperors with their frequently unpleasant faces. Occasionally, however, one comes across something which pleases the eye; the glassware, for instance, is often graceful and attractive both in shape and texture, and the red-glazed " Samian " bowls, dishes and cups, though the ornament is often mechanical and repetitive, are usually of handsome shape.

In the gallery near the top of the stairs is a Roman lead coffin containing the remains of a woman, the outline of whose skeleton has been clearly impressed upon the lid owing to earth pressure. In it were found the remains of a casket containing glass ointment phials and bone hairpins. Roman antiquities *en masse* can become dull, and one Roman lead coffin tends to look very like another. But sometimes one's flagging interest is suddenly roused by the sight of a tiny pair of gold earrings fixed to a board next to a group of human teeth and skull fragments. One looks closer and finds that they belonged to a girl of sixteen. Who was she? A soldier's daughter perhaps, by a British mother? She too knew Colchester, she too passed perhaps under the same gateway though which you walked this afternoon, and saw the view from the top of North Hill; bathed, perhaps, in the same River Colne which flows through the valley.

Before you return to the ground floor be sure to see the fine collection in the annexe which is approached by an archway in the Norman wall near the lady in her lead coffin. Here you can see a fine model of the Balkerne Gate with its twin entrances flanked by smaller passage ways for pedestrians. Children especially will be fascinated by this and other models in the room. Tiny figures are amusingly grouped outside the main archway of the Gate—a waggoner with a cartload of timber, a group of citizens watching a cock-fight, an ox-cart loaded with wine jars, and a couple of builders, one mixing mortar while his companion lounges on a pile of red tiles. A legionary's shield rests against the gateway—a nice touch—and on the roof two sentries stand on guard.

Before leaving the Castle, ask the Curator to show you the massive Roman vaults beneath the Keep. These once supported the platform of the Temple of Claudius, which is also visible. This makes a fitting end to one's first visit to this busy, thriving, fascinating city. For although Colchester is proud of its antiquities, there is nothing dead or even moribund about it. There is a feeling of continuous life, even at night, when the pubs are crowded with troops from the nearby barracks, and the Roman walls shake under the vibration of military lorries. That, apart from the lorries, is probably how the legionaires knew it, and that, I hope, is how it will remain, the oldest inhabited town in Britain, and still very much alive.

For current developments, see section on *New Discoveries*, p. 285.

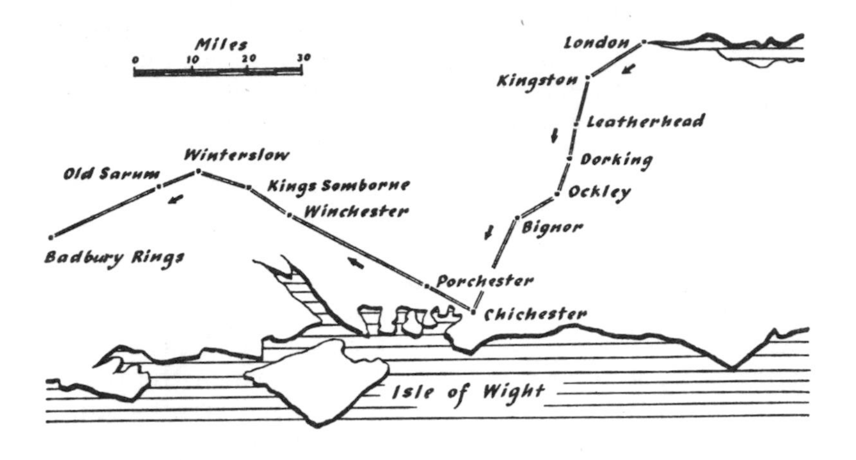

CHAPTER SIX

THRUST TO THE WEST

ACCURATE contemporary records of the early years following the Claudian invasion are not numerous. We do know, however, that Vespasian, in command of the Second Legion, advanced south-westward along a line which is roughly followed by the main road—London, Silchester, Winchester, Southampton; Winchester, Dorchester, Exeter. The Fourteenth and Twentieth, with their auxiliaries, moved north-westward, probably as far as Wroxeter, near modern Shrewsbury. The famous Ninth Legion marched northward and eventually occupied Lincoln. These were not lightning campaigns, because, although some of the British tribes made rapid submission, e.g. the Kingdom of Sussex, others gave the invaders a lot of trouble. The biographer of Vespasian writes of the vigorous resistance of two native tribes, and the storming of over twenty native fortresses. These two tribes were probably the Belgæ of Wiltshire and the Durotriges of Dorset. We can be fairly certain of this, in spite of the paucity of written records, because when two great Dorset hill fortresses, Maiden Castle and Hod Hill, were excavated, the diggings revealed that both camps had been attacked and taken by the Romans. The storming of Maiden Castle, brilliantly told by Sir Mortimer Wheeler in the Office of Works guide which you can buy on the spot, is one of the most dramatic stories ever revealed by the spade alone. Other British camps in this area will probably tell the same stories when they are excavated.

I have tried to make our tour of Roman Britain follow, as far as possible, the successive stages of conquest and occupation. One can only do this in a rough sort of way, because at times several campaigns were taking place simultaneously in different parts of the country, and also because my main concern must always be the convenience of the traveller. For instance, it is a natural step, after visiting Somerset, to take the ferry across the Bristol Channel and see the the Roman sites of South Wales. As it happens, however, the final conquest of the Silures of Monmouthshire and Glamorgan did not take place until several years after South-West England had been subdued. Also it is clear that many of the Roman sites which we shall visit on our journeys will not have any connection with the initial period of conquest, and the visible remains of most will date from a period of two or three centuries after it. Nevertheless, the pattern of invasion and occupation does provide us with a rough guide and when we tour the West Country, as we shall do in this and the following chapters, it will help us if we imagine that we are following in the track of Vespasian.

Before we pick up his main line of advance from Winchester, however, we must first make the trip from London to *Noviomagus* (Chichester), via the Stane Street, because it passes through some of the loveliest Sussex countryside, and takes in some particularly interesting Roman sites. Unless you are a purist, I advise skipping the first part of the original road, which ran from London Bridge south-west by way of Tooting. Far better take the main trunk road through Kingston, Leatherhead and Dorking, where you will come to the line of the original Roman road.

It passes through Dorking and then for a time follows the main A24 road. If you look at the map ($\frac{1}{4}$-inch Ordnance Survey, Sheet 12) you will notice that south of Dorking the modern road wanders away east of the Roman line, then returns to it about two miles beyond Holmwood Station. From this point for a distance of some four miles the modern road rides along the original *agger*, through the charming village of Ockley, and so on to Oakwood Farm, where it suddenly deviates to the south. From here to a little beyond Rowhook the original Stone Street can be traced for most of the way, sometimes as a grass-grown track, sometimes as a line of hedgerows, but continuing along its original alignment until it strikes the modern road again about a mile and a half north of Slinfold. This stretch is well worth exploration by walkers, but motorists will have to stick to A24.

At a point on the map marked " Roman Wood " the Stone Street turns away left (A29) towards Pulborough. It continues in a dead straight line, precisely following the alignment of the original Roman road for a distance of over twelve miles—a glorious stretch for the fast driver if he is lucky enough to have it to himself. Beyond Pulborough the original road was laid out some way to the west of the modern highway, but it can still be traced by walkers and cyclists as a narrow lane. On the Ordnance Survey map it can be seen tracking south-west past the Iron Age fort near Hardham, and then travelling roughly parallel with A29, parting from it a mile beyond Coldwaltham to pass near Bignor and over the Downs to Chichester. The modern road makes a wide detour to the east, and does not rejoin the Stane Street until within a few miles of the town, but if we are wise we shall leave A29 when we see the sign-post to Bignor, for here is one of the best-known Roman villas in Southern England, a fascinating site in a lovely setting.

Motorists should continue along A29 as far as Bury, and then take the first turning on the right just before reaching the inn. You will be rewarded by an enchanting drive through a maze of by-lanes which will lead you gently beside the downs, through West Burton and Bignor itself, with a fine manor house near the roadside; and so to Bignor Hill where you will have to leave the car and take the footpath to the villa.

Walkers, however, may prefer to take a more direct route to Bignor along a lane which branches off the main road about a mile south of Coldwaltham.

The ruins were discovered accidentally by a farmer in 1811. Fortunately, he had the intelligence and good taste to have them properly excavated and planned, and sufficient business acumen to see that the fine mosaic pavements were adequately protected from the weather and then thrown open to the general public, as they have been ever since. In the first room there is a stone cistern let into the floor, where a fountain once played, surrounded by mosaic figures of dancing nymphs. Move to the next great room and you will see a particularly well-preserved pavement with figures of Cupids fighting as gladiators. Juno is there also, with her peacocks. A passage leads off to a bath, also quite well preserved, and you see again, as on most villa sites, remains of the hypocaust or heating system which we saw at Canterbury. Remember, when you see these remains, that they are only a few fragments which are exposed, and the fact that each is covered by a separate shed makes it very difficult for the layman to visualise the villa as a whole. Bignor villa was one of the largest and most luxurious of its kind, originally covering an area of 650 by 350 feet. The rest of the foundations lie buried under the fields.

As this is the first Roman villa we have encountered on our tour, perhaps this is the place to consider Romano-British villas in general. Many people—myself included—have imagined that all these buildings were the country residences of Roman officials, and, in trying to picture them as they were, have thought of them as the

Roman equivalent of our country houses. Although some may have been occupied by the invaders, most were undoubtedly occupied by Romanised Britons who had learned to live in the Roman manner. Just as they aped the Romans in the planning of their towns, so they copied, or tried to copy, the type of country house which some of them had seen on the Continent. But, like the Roman villas in the country near Rome itself and like our own country houses, the Romano-British villas were not simply pleasure palaces. Their owners farmed the land. Some were run by bailiffs on behalf of absentee landlords.

" While country houses erected for pleasure existed in the Roman world," Richmond writes, " they were almost exclusively the privilege of the very wealthy. The normal Villa was not a liability of this kind, but a profit-making farm, and the very richest villas in Roman Britain show no departure from this economic basis. Comfortable on the average, luxurious at best, and squalid at worst, the Roman-British villas ranged in size from cottage to mansion, and the associated acreage varied accordingly."

Bignor was particularly large and luxurious, with over fifty rooms grouped around a large rectangular courtyard, and a huge walled enclosure to the south-east. Many of these rooms would have been occupied by the estate servants; some would be farm labourers, others might have been fullers, dyers, weavers, for these great establishments would be largely self-contained and self-supporting. The same estate would raise sheep, shear them, weave the cloth and market it. There would also be the carpenters who made the fences and gates, and fashioned the furniture for the great house; there would be smiths who made the ploughshares, spades, hoes and other tools, examples of which can frequently be seen in museums. And there would be many women employed in spinning and weaving.

These were the producers of wealth. What of the men and women who spent it? As far as the British aristocrats were concerned, I fancy that they were not unlike the English kings and nobles of the seventeenth century, eagerly imitating the manners of the French court. Just as Charles II and his courtiers aped French dress and manners, French architecture, French culture, so I imagine that these British noblemen and *bourgeoisie*, living on the very fringes of the great Empire of which they formed a part, would copy Roman fashions.

Take as a single example the well-known mosaic pavements with their classical themes. I am not an admirer of Roman mosaic work. Even at its best, in Italy and France, there is something laboured and mechanical about it; the work of native craftsmen working in an unfamiliar and probably uncongenial medium, laboriously copying from pattern books. But to the British landlord of Bignor and his family these huge, elaborately designed pavements with their Græco-Roman deities, their cupid gladiators, their allegories of the four seasons, would be the visible manifestation of their owners' taste and culture; and as they reclined on their couches in the Roman manner, speaking Latin with a strong British accent, warmed by the gentle heat of the hypocaust under the floor, they may have felt as newly-rich millowners of the nineteenth century felt as they displayed to their friends their imitation Tudor mansions.

Of course there are exceptions to this general rule—for example, in the recently-discovered villa at Lullingstone in Kent, there is lively and pleasing design depicting Europa and the Bull, forming the centrepiece, with a verse-couplet which, it has been suggested, "has the amateurish ring of an impromptu production of the dining table". At Otford, also in Kent, the wall-plaster was painted with pleasing Vergilian scenes, with quotations from the poet, and at Aldborough were found nine standing figures of the Muses, with a Greek inscription. In the latter villa, by the way, there is a semi-circular unornamented section of the pavement on which originally stood the three couches for the diners, who of course are reclining in the Roman manner. Such fine examples which are usually of later date—

third or fourth century—strongly suggest that they belonged to the home of a man of taste as well as wealth, a home in which good conversation and literary entertainment mingled with choice food and wine, as in Rome itself.

Most of these villas went through several stages of development; when you visit one, therefore, do not think of it as a house built at one time and occupied for a limited period. Imagine it rather as an ancestral home, growing like a tree from century to century; a place in which families were born, grew up and died, which saw weddings and homecomings, periods of prosperity and sometimes of dearth. Above all, let your mind picture more than the group of elegantly dressed diners reclining in the *Triclinium*, or relaxing in the baths. To scores of humbler men and women these great buildings were also the centre of their lives; the field labourers driving the plough over the same meadows which the Sussex worker ploughs to-day; the reapers in high summer; the shepherds with their flocks, the smith at his forge; and their wives and daughters gossiping as they sat teasing the wool under the sun-shadowed colonnade. Around them were the country sights and sounds with which we are familiar; cattle lowing in the sheds, fowls clucking and scratching, dogs barking and pigeons cooing in the eaves.

* * * * *

From Bignor the motorist must return by the way he came, as far as A29 and continue along it, skirting Rewell Wood, which abuts on to historic Arundel Park, with its mighty trees and noble gates. All this country will repay a leisurely explorer with time on his hands. There are Celtic fields on the Downs near Amberley, an encampment on the north of Arundel Park, and a lovely stretch of unspoiled parkland between Burpham and Slindon, which can only be explored satisfactorily on foot. The walker who is sufficiently painstaking may be able to locate the Flint Mines on the Downs north of Clapham; all these are indicated on the 1-inch Ordnance Survey map.

He can also, if he wishes, trace the line of Stone Street from Bignor over the South Downs until it is joined by the modern road near historic Halnaker House, from which point A285 follows the ancient alignment as far as West Hampnett. Here signposts point to another historic spot—Tangmere Airfield—famous in the Battle of Britain.

Almost immediately after leaving the road junction near West Hampnett the outskirts of Chichester appear, with their gasworks and rows of red-brick villas, as depressing as the approaches to most British towns. Once one has threaded the narrow streets and entered the heart of the city there is much to please the eye; sedate Georgian houses of flint, with graceful porticoes, the elegant front of the Queen Anne County Hall, the superb fifteenth-century Market Cross, and the long, shadowy bulk of the Cathedral, flanking South Street. Here the big green and yellow omnibuses wait to carry home the inhabitants of Selsey, Sidlesham, East and West Wittering and other villages whose delightful names appear on the destination boards. One of these villages, Bosham, has a special interest for those interested in Roman Britain. It was a major port. The chancel arch of the church stands on massive Roman pillars, and the town possessed a life-size statue of the Emperor Trojan (now in the British Museum).

Modern Chichester has little to show of its Romano-British ancestry save the line of the main streets which cross in the centre, and the venerable city walls which, though of medieval construction, stand on Roman foundations. Many objects of Roman and pre-Roman date have been found here, for this was Noviomagus, tribal capital of a district called Regnum, occupied by the Regnenses, and Roman coins of pre-Claudian date suggest that the Regnenses were in contact with Rome at an early date, and when Claudius launched his invasion,

Cogidumnus, the native ruler, became a " client king " under the Romans.

Richmond, indeed, goes so far as to suggest that the territory of the Regnenses was used by Vespasian as a springboard for his attack on the west, and this may well be so. Cogidumnus certainly owed much to the Romans, for they appointed him *rex et legatus Augusti in Britannia.* This title, together with the name *Tiberius Claudius Cogidumnus*, appears on a remarkable inscribed stone found in Chichester. It is a dedication of a temple to Neptune and Minerva by a guild of iron-workers.

One hopes that the Chichester Council will continue to encourage the development of a fine museum in "Little London," which houses an interesting and growing collection, excellently presented.

After staying the night at the Dolphin Hotel—which has one of the most elegant eighteenth-century dining-rooms in England—I drove along A27, which closely follows the line of the Roman road which connected Chichester with Porchester (Portus Adurni) and the Isle of Wight. At the signpost " to Old Bosham " I turned off the main road to this delightful flint and red-brick village. It overlooks a broad, tidal inlet dotted with coloured sailing dinghies which at low tide lie slantwise on the brown mud. Here the gulls gather, looking for scraps, and the salt air is laced with the strong tang of seaweed. There is a distinct and pleasing air of amateur yachtsmanship about the place; a smell of tar, rope and wet paint. The little houses are scattered around the inlet under the huge windy sky, and the only focal point is the squat-towered church where King Canute's daughter is buried.

After exploring the winding lanes of Hayling Island, I returned to the main road and followed it to Bedhampton. Beyond this village the modern road goes south-west of the Roman road, traces of which can be seen in a wood near Parbrook, and as a well-defined *agger* further west. Except for a short section, it is not negotiable by cars, but excellent for walkers, who would find it profitable to explore this stretch. After lunch at the "Red Lion" at Fareham, I returned along A27 to Porchester, a straggling nondescript village with much modern development along the main road, but on turning right along a lane signposted "Porchester Castle" I came to the remains of the older village.

Near the end of this lane one comes quite suddenly on one of the most impressive Roman monuments in the British Isles. It is a fortress standing to a height of 30 feet and more, in one corner of which stand the much later Norman Keep. From the top of this one gets a splendid view not only of the Roman fort, but of the approach to Portsmouth harbour beyond. Here you can marvel at the toughness of the Roman walls which have withstood the ravages of more than fifteen centuries. Portus Adurni, as Porchester was called in Roman times, was another of the strong points designed to protect Britain against the Saxon raiders in the third and fourth centuries. These mighty walls, with their projecting semi-circular towers of flint masonry, seem at first to be medieval. They might well be taken for fourteenth-century work of the time of Edward III, like Conway Castle, but in fact they were already 1,000 years old when that King came to the throne.

The layout is as usual quadrilateral, with gates symmetrically placed in the middle of each of the four walls. The West or Sea Gate opens straight on to Portsmouth Harbour, and as you approach it across the green turf you can see the giant cranes of the Naval Dockyards on the far side of the harbour. The sea channel comes right up to the walls of the fort, as it did in Roman times; therefore Portus Adurni preserves its original appearance far more than does, say, Richborough or Portus Lemanis.

Sailing dinghies with the brightly painted hulls lie at anchor where the Roman ships were moored. The grey battleships, looming hugely across the grey water, remind us that Porchester too was a naval base. But to-day, on Sundays, the hoary old fortress is a playground for the youth of Porchester, and small boys may be seen illegally scrambling along the rampart walls from which the fourth century garrison guarded the coast against Saxon raiders.

For current developments, see section on *New Discoveries*, p. 285.

CHAPTER SEVEN

HAMPSHIRE, WILTSHIRE AND DORSET

We have followed the Stone Street from London to Chichester, and then eastward along another Roman road which linked that city with Portus Adurni (Porchester). From here a third Roman highway used to run north-westward to Winchester, the tribal capital of the Belgæ; the Romans called it Venta Belgarum. The southern section of this road has been lost, or exists only in fragments, so that for most of the way one must use the modern highway. From Fareham take A32 as far as Wickham, then along A333 through Bishops Waltham. Between this village and the fork at Fisher's Pond you cross the original line of the Roman road, which ran in a more direct line to Winchester. Those who have the time and inclination can, if they wish, turn off to the right along a narrow lane just beyond Fisher's Pond and come on to a short two-mile fragment of the old road just north of the hamlet of Owlesbury. It provides a delightful and unfrequented approach to Winchester, ideal for walkers and cyclists and, of course, for motorists who are not in a hurry. Whether you make this detour or follow A333 you will eventually arrive at the ancient capital of the Belgæ, standing proudly on its hill above the Itchen.

There is hardly anything to be seen of Roman Winchester, apart from remains of the amphitheatre, now called the Devil's Punch Bowl, just outside the East Gate, some Roman masonry in the walls of Wolvesey Castle, and as at Canterbury medieval walls follow the line of their Roman predecessors. But if the visitor is short of time he would be foolish to allow these fragments to keep him from exploring the Cathedral and other medieval monuments, in which the city is so rich. He should, however, try to see the Museum, where there are some quite interesting Roman antiquities from Winchester and other Hampshire sites.

Five Roman roads radiated from the city, besides the one to Porchester. One north-east to Silchester (between Reading and Basingstoke); another by the north to join the main western route which ran between London, through Silchester, to Bath and Bristol; a third went due south to the port of Clausentum, near the modern Bitterne; the fourth was aligned almost due west, pointing to Old Sarum near Salisbury. This is the one which we shall follow.

Leave Winchester by A31 (Romsey, Salisbury, Bournemouth), but go slowly, keeping careful watch for a narrow lane leading off to the right about a mile from the city centre. It is best to consult the Ordnance Survey map to make sure of this turning, but once you have located it you are on one of the most delightful stretches of Roman road in the West Country, narrow, unfrequented and passing through some of the loveliest countryside in Hampshire. At first you will see the *agger* or raised bank running through the front gardens of suburban villas. Then it passes alongside hedges, through coppices and farmyards, until at last it becomes a tree-covered lane. There is a particularly interesting portion with side-ditches, just beyond a little rise about one mile from the commencement of the lane, at a point where another narrow road (signposted Sparsholt and Hursley) crosses it. About 5 yards northward along the Hursley road you will see where the modern road has cut through the Roman embankment opposite a gate near the signpost.

Beyond these cross-roads, the modern road mounts the *agger* and travels along it for some distance, the ditch being clearly visible on each side. Approximately half a mile beyond the cross-roads the lane suddenly swings to the left (S.W.), and at this point there is a particularly good example of the *agger* which is followed on its left (southern) side by a cart track. Here several test pits had been sunk when I was there, and the original

Roman metalling, mainly flint, lay on the surface. From this place, on a hilltop, the eye can easily follow the line of the road, which climbs the next ridge to the right of a coppice. Although I managed to scramble through this section with some difficulty in a sports car, I do not recommend it for motorists; but walkers and cyclists would be well advised to explore it further.

Beyond Kings Somborne take the main Southampton road for one and a half miles, then turn right along the road to Broughton. It is a pretty winding road, which crosses the Test River in a series of hump-backed bridges where one can loiter happily, watching the fish rise.

Here the Roman road bears left, re-crossing the Wallop Brook at Bossington House. Watch carefully for a narrow lane leading off to the left, through a wood. This is the original Roman highway which climbs the ridge above the valley of the Wallop. There is a Round Barrow (Iron Age burial mound) near the right of the road, just before it enters the next patch of woodland. Marked Beech Barrow on the map, it is crowned with small trees, with a good view to the north across the valley. These burial mounds were usually erected on prominent sites. One is reminded of the passage in the " Iliad " in which Achilles buried the ashes of his friend Patroclus and piled above them a great mound which would be visible from afar. Such burials were only given to men of note, chieftains and their families.

Beyond Buckholt Farm (Ordnance Survey Map 167) the lane crosses another at right-angles immediately opposite the original Roman road, which here degenerates into a cart track, descends a slope and for one mile passes through Node's Copse. This track, though narrow and rough in parts, can be negotiated by cars with a reasonably high ground clearance. The *agger* can be clearly seen all the way, until the road enters a lane leading from West Titherly to Winterslow.

Just beyond the point where the road enters the lane leading from West Titherly to Winterslow there is a pleasant inn, the " Red Lion ", which provides welcome refreshment for those who may have become tired of following the legions.

From this point onwards follow the lane through Middle Winterslow, Winterslow itself, and so across Winterbourne Down to the main London-Salisbury road, where you turn left and travel along it for about a mile and a half. The main road crosses the Roman road at Hitterist Bungalow, where a lane branches off to the right and follows the line of the Roman highway for a further mile, where it crosses A338, the main road between Salisbury and Marlborough. It continues across the road, then descends the valley of the Bourne towards Ford. Beyond here the modern road, which is now on the line of its Roman forerunner, climbs in a dead straight line up towards the mighty ramparts of Old Sarum, which it enters by the East Gate.

No one knows for certain just how old this great fortress is, but the type of earthwork suggests that it was occupied in the Iron Age, and some relics of that period have been found on the site. It may well have been one of the forts which Vespasian stormed on his way westward, and certainly Old Sarum can be identified with the Roman station of Sorbiodunum, which stood either on the hill itself or in the immediate vicinity. Few Roman remains have come to light on the hill itself, but this may be due to later levelling and rebuilding by the Normans, to whom most of the present mounds and ditches are attributed.

Thomas Hardy described a hilltop where Gabriel Oak, keeping watch under the stars, felt " the roll of the earth eastward as an almost perceptible movement ". At Old Sarum, as at Lympne in Kent, one feels the roll of the centuries too. Here the Roman legionaries who once looked out from this crest are one with Saxon, Dane and Norman; each a thread in the fabric of our past.

From the west side of the ramparts you can see the westward continuation of the Roman road passing through woods and across meadows. This section can be explored on foot or bicycle with the help of the Ordnance Survey Map, but shortage of time compelled me to skip it. Instead, after lunch at the ancient " Red Lion " at Salisbury, followed by an hour in the Cathedral, I took the A354 road (signposted Blandford and Weymouth) until it rejoined the Roman road which comes in from the right at an acute angle.

There was no mistaking it this time; a high-raised *agger* sweeping down from Old Sarum and, after crossing A354, thrusting on across the downland on its way to the west. A little further along, the main Blandford road rejoins it and for about a mile the modern road runs along the crest of the *agger* itself. Then I reached a point where the main road turned off at a slight angle to the north, but on the left I could see the Roman highway striding purposefully forward and climbing the opposite crest. It was a high, perfectly-preserved embankment, some 6 feet high and about 20 feet broad. This is the famous Ackling Dyke, one of the most impressive surviving stretches of a Roman road in the West of England.

The best place to see it is at a point about one-quarter of a mile along a by-lane which branches off southward from the Blandford road leading towards Cranbourne. Here it is best to leave the car and climb on to the bank beside the road. Looking eastward, you will see first the line of the *agger*, ruler-straight and very high, stretched across the open grassland and skirting a belt of conifers about half a mile away. Beyond that you will see the point at which it joins the modern tarmac road, which prolongs its course in precisely the same direction as far as the eye can see. To enhance the impression of age and mystery you will see on the left of the *agger* (looking north) a group of Iron Age burial mounds (tumuli) standing between the Roman road and the modern highway with its lines of telegraph poles. They were old even when Vespasian passed this way.

The lure of the remote past is something quite inexplicable to those who do not feel it; but this stretch of Wiltshire downland beside the Blandford road can stir the blood like the distant echo of trumpets. It is one with Mycenæ's Lion Gate, with the wild asphodel springing from the worn stones of Knossos, with the grey bulk of Tiryns in the morning light of the Peloponnese. Here you breathe the air, not of England, not even of Roman Britain, but of prehistoric Europe.

The walker can explore the length of the Ackling Dyke. He has the advantage over the road-bound traveller, though the latter can find compensation by following the side-lanes, which will lead him through villages of such enchantment as Tarrant Hinton, Monkton, Wimborne, and Witchampton, until, at a point a little to the east of Tarrant Rushton, he finds the *agger* arrowing across the high downs towards where the hill-fort of Badbury Rings breaks the skyline with its concentric embankments.

Badbury Rings can, of course, be approached quite easily along the main road from Dorchester, but I strongly recommend the approach from the by-lanes to the north-east. A study of the Ordnance Survey Map will show how this can be done, and even motorists can make the journey, though the lanes are narrow and twisting, and the last stage involves climbing the steep grassy slopes, which are treacherous in damp weather. But the rewards are manifold. The roughly metalled lanes creep up the folds of the chalk downs, always climbing, past half-hidden farms which seem to have been overlooked by the centuries. Clumps of trees accentuate the smooth swell of the downs, above which huge clouds hang like a ceiling, emphasising the curving line of the crests. Here is serenity; bird cries, a hopping pheasant, the occasional distant hum of a car. Even the great airfield at Witchampton seems to fit unobtrusively into the wide, tranquil landscape, its long, low hangars taking on something of the quiet solemnity of the beech-clumps, from which at a distance they can hardly be distinguished.

The best approach to Badbury Rings is from King's Down Farm. Take the right fork and climb the grass track which turns left after about 100 yards, following the line of the hill. The road swings upwards on the east side of the fort, which stands magnificently against the skyline, with its thick coppices of elm, ash, fir and dwarf oaks. On the west side, looking south-west, the *agger* can be plainly seen as a raised embankment striding across the smooth green turf towards where a line of trees marks the main road between Blandford and Wimborne Minster.

Badbury Rings is another of those great hill-forts built in the Iron Age by immigrants who crossed the Channel in search of new lands a few centuries before Cæsar invaded Britain. The successive lines of ramparts with deep ditches between are impressive, but perhaps not everybody realises why they were so constructed. In Cæsar's day the principal weapon of attack and defence was the sling. A good slinger could hurl a pebble with lethal effect across a considerable distance. But if he had to hurl his missiles uphill, against the force of gravity, he was handicapped; whereas his opponent, comfortably ensconced behind a high embankment up which his enemy had to climb, was at a decided advantage. *He* had gravity to help him. Hence these great embankments, one inside the other, presenting a formidable obstacle to the attackers. You scrambled up the first steep slope and there was a line of slingers at the top firing at you. If you managed to despatch them you had to plunge down the slope on the other side and then climb up to the next rampart. And there, on the crest, was another line of slingers, ready to plant a pebble smartly between your eyes as you panted up the rise. The Second Legion could not have had an easy time.

From Badbury Rings it is a short drive through Tolpuddle (of the " Tolpuddle Martyrs ") to Dorchester, through a lovely country of chalk downs, with clumps of woodland outlined against the clean, bare ridges. Dorchester (Roman Durnovaria) must, of course, be visited if only for the sake of its excellent museum, and it provides an ideal halting-place for the night. But for the purpose of this book I propose first to describe the great Iron Age fortress of Maiden Castle nearby, since, after seeing it, the visitor will be in a better position to appreciate the objects found on that site, and in Durnovaria itself, which now repose in the Dorchester Museum.

To reach Maiden Castle take the Weymouth road out of Dorchester. After less than half a mile a road leads off to the right across cornfields and arable land to the ramparts of the fort, which looks huge, though least impressive, from this angle. When I visited Maiden Castle in late autumn, the final approach, across grassland, was a mere quagmire, but I managed to keep the car going and so climb the turf slope to the north-west corner of the fortifications.

I have had the luck to see a fair number of the ancient monuments of Europe and Asia, but say without hesitation that Maiden Castle can be equated with the finest of them. It is quite the most stupendous prehistoric fortress I have seen, both in sheer size and in the ingenuity with which it is built. The amount of manpower represented by these colossal embankments, built in a series of concentric rings, enclosing an area two-thirds of a mile in length and one-third in breadth, overpowers the imagination. In this respect alone Maiden Castle can be compared with the Pyramids of Egypt.

The second impression is one of sheer functional beauty. Ovoid in plan, the successive lines of mighty ramparts, some of them over 100 feet high, follow the line of the hilltop, here and there bulging outwards in the form of buttresses, and at other places biting into the plateau in long concave curves. So sweet are the lines that they remind one of the functional streamlining of a ship or an aircraft, and the lovely symmetry of the east entrance, with its massive "hornwork", is clearly the work of a fine intelligence, a Vauban of the Iron Age. Here the approach path divides, and then has to outflank a second mighty breastwork before it pierces the inner rampart in two places. This is the fort which the Second Legion had to take before it could proceed with its conquest of the West.

The view from the top of the innermost rampart is superb, with Dorchester looking quite small on the north-west, and a widespreading patchwork of fields between, on which cattle grazed. Indeed, herds of fine Jerseys were grazing within the fortress itself, treading daintily along the sharp crests of the embankments, and sheep nibbled the turf between the worn grey stones of a Roman building near the centre of the great enclosure, probably a temple to Mars, and a kind of war memorial to the Legions which fell in the assault. The tinkle of sheep bells mingled with the cawing of rooks and the bubbling cry of the curlews. There was no other sound in this place which was once crowded with men, women, children and cattle.

The present-day atmosphere of the place is deceptive. The smooth slopes of clipped turf seem to have been there for ever. It is difficult to imagine the fortress when it throbbed with life; when the central area was a squalid, muddy compound crowded with primitive huts and thronged with women, children and beasts; when the ramparts were newly cut and crowned with vicious timber spikes; when the entrances were flanked by " gun-platforms ", where the slingers stood at the ready, their heaped piles of missiles at hand. This is not imagination. We know very accurately what Maiden Castle looked like from excavations carried out by archæologists, especially those of Sir Mortimer Wheeler, between 1934 and 1937.

It would be impertinent to attempt a condensation of Wheeler's brilliant little pamphlet on Maiden Castle prepared for the Ministry of Works and which can be bought on the site for 6*d*. Reading this you may feel the centuries roll back at the command of a great archæologist who is also a vivid writer. So I will skip the early part, in which he describes the history of the great fortress in Neolithic times (the New Stone Age) and content myself by quoting only from the section which deals with perhaps the most dramatic event in its history, the moment when the invaders, who were probably *Veneti* from Brittany, had established themselves on this hilltop, re-fortified it with all the skill and ingenuity of which they were capable, and stood watching the advance of Vespasian's Second Augustan Legion, 5,000 seasoned, disciplined men moving across the plain in battle order; that deadly, solid, slow-moving Roman infantry which had conquered their Gaulish ancestors and forced them to flee across the Channel. And here they came, grasping their slender throwing-spears, shields interlocked, corselets and helmets gleaming.

No written record of this battle exists; only the bare reference, in Suetonius, to the fact that Vespasian overthrew twenty British hill-forts in the west. But what Suetonius did not, perhaps could not, tell us, we now know, thanks to the archæologists whose spades cleaved the chalk of this peaceful Dorsetshire hillside and revealed secrets which had been hidden for eighteen centuries.

" Approaching from the direction of the Isle of Wight, Vespasian's legion may be supposed to have crossed the Frome at the Dorchester crossing and to have found itself confronted, some two miles away, by the sevenfold ramparts of the western side of the fortress-town, towering above the cornfields which probably swept then, as now, up to the defences. Whether any assault was attempted upon these gates we do not at present know; their excessive strength makes it more likely that Vespasian moved his main attack to the somewhat less formidable eastern end. What happened there has been revealed by excavation. First the regiment of artillery which usually accompanied a legion put down a barrage of ballista-arrows. The arrows have been found about the site, and buried amongst the outworks was a man with an arrowhead still buried in one of his vertebræ (to be seen in the Dorchester Museum). Following the barrage, the Roman infantry advanced up the slope, cutting its way from rampart to rampart until it reached the innermost bay, where some circular huts had recently been built. These were set alight, and under the rising clouds of smoke the gates were stormed and the position carried. But resistance was obstinate and the fury of the legionaries was roused. For a space, confusion and massacre dominated the scene. Men and women, young and old, were savagely cut down before the troops were called to heel. A systematic slighting of the defences followed, whereafter the legion was withdrawn, doubtless taking hostages with it, and the dazed inhabitants were left to bury their dead among the ashes of the huts beside the gates. The task was carried out anxiously and without order, but, even so, few graves were omitted those tributes of food and drink which were the proper perquisites of the dead. With their food vessels and trinkets, the bones, often two or more skeletons huddled into a single grave and many of the skulls deeply scored with sword-cuts, made a sad and dramatic showing—the earliest British war-cemetery known to us.

" After the battle the survivors were left in their dismantled town to continue their traditional mode of life as best they could until, with the conquest of lowland Britain and the consequent replacement of a native by a Roman economy, the new Roman town of Dorchester was ready some twenty or thirty years later to receive them. About A.D. 70 the population finally deserted its hill-top huts and moved down the valley, and the site of Maiden Castle reverted for a second time to pasture and tillage."

Roman order, organisation and discipline had overcome the wild courage of the Celt, as it was to do repeatedly in successive battles throughout the breadth of the British Isles. But that grim struggle at the East Gate must have lingered long in the memory of the Second Augustan Legion, and one may imagine the stories which may have been told and re-told by the veterans in the peaceful years which followed the conquest; of the wiry, desperate little men who poured down a deadly rain of sling-stones from the forbidding ramparts. Wheeler found great dumps of these stones, some of them comprising 20,000 selected beach pebbles, still in position near the platforms built at vantage points beside the main gates.

* * * * *

After Maiden Castle, Dorchester is something of an anticlimax. On the windy ramparts of the fortress you seem almost to catch the gleam of legionary standards. In Dorchester the turbulent past has been pinned under the glass cases of a provincial museum. Little remains visible of Roman Durnovaria. There is, admittedly, the Roman amphitheatre beside the Roman road where it leaves Dorchester on its way to Ridgeway Hill and Radipole Lake. Here, however, memories of the Roman city are confused with the earlier and later history of Dorchester. Originally the amphitheatre was a Sacred Circle of the late Stone Age. The Romans transformed it into a miniature Colosseum, where as many as 13,000 spectators could watch gladiatorial sports, and in its present form it is fairly easy to envisage the Roman arena, with its entrances (still preserved) on each side. But the environs do not encourage such imaginings. One side abuts on to a busy main road, the other overlooks the railway. In any case, it retains memories of more recent barbarities than those of the Romans; in the eighteenth century it was a place of execution, and here the young Thomas Hardy witnessed a public hanging. The last execution within its precincts was of an eighteen-year-old girl, Mary Channing, who was convicted of poisoning her husband. She was first strangled by the hangman and then burned at the stake before 10,000 spectators.

The only other relic of Durnovaria still *in situ* is a fragment of the Roman wall. It forms part of a garden wall in West Walks at the corner of Princes Street. At Colliton Park there is also the tessalated pavement of a large Roman house—dull, but quite well preserved.

But, as at Canterbury and Chichester, you have to go to the Museum to see the most evocative relics of Roman Dorchester. Like those two cities, it was a tribal centre, in this case the capital of the Durotriges, who had formerly occupied Maiden Castle.

The Dorchester Museum, in West High Street, contains one of the best collections of Roman antiquities in Great Britain. It is small, but well laid out and not overcrowded. You will find the Romano-British objects on the ground floor. Most visitors, I think, will find the Maiden Castle section the most interesting, particularly if they visit the Castle first. The story of the fortress, from Neolithic to Saxon times, is well told in a series of maps, diagrams and photographs with descriptive details, mounted on a revolving stand near the far end of the room. Here you can see pictures of the military cemetery near the East Gate, with the bodies of the slain as found by Wheeler. One of the victims has a cleft skull, and there is a grim close-up of a vertebra of one of the defenders with a Roman ballista bolt still sticking in it. In a nearby case you can see the actual skeleton. The bolt had entered the man's body *from the front*, which gives some idea of the penetrative power of these weapons.

Other objects on display illustrate the earlier history of Maiden Castle, which goes back to at least 2,000 B.C. Somewhere round about this date it seems to have been used as a cemetery. On the hilltop, between the later embankments, Wheeler found the remains of an enormous long barrow or burial ground measuring a third of a mile in length. Under its eastern end was the body of a man about thirty years old which, in Sir Mortimer Wheeler's words, " had been hacked to pieces immediately after death. After fruitless attempts to penetrate to the brain by means of circular incision in the skull, the base of the latter was cut through and the brain removed, apparently with some pieces of the skull adhering to it. But it was not merely the skull that was attacked. The long bones are covered with cuts and slashes, indicating thorough dismemberment prior to the careful collection and interment of the mutilated remains. The ritual eating of the brain and butchering and cannibalisation of the body are not without parallel; but whether in the present instance the intent was that the survivors should merely absorb the virtues of the dead it would be hazardous to guess."

Other objects displayed in the Museum show the kind of life lived within the ramparts by the later Iron Age people. At one period they lived in pit dwellings roofed with thatch, and spindle whorls are exhibited, showing that yarn was spun. They also kept sheep and cattle, grew crops (which they reaped with iron sickles). They stored their grain, carbonised remains of which can be seen. But to me the most astonishing fact about Maiden Castle is that its huge ramparts, some of them 100 feet high, were built not with spades (which were not introduced until the Romans came), but with *bone picks made from antlers*. These, apparently, were the only digging tools they possessed, and yet if Maiden Castle had been built to-day, with the aid of mechanical excavators and bulldozers, it would be still a remarkable achievement. Consider the amount of soil which one man could shift in a day with an antler-pick, and then look at those ramparts, and you may guess how many thousands of people must have lived on these Dorsetshire uplands in prehistoric times.

The Roman objects found in Dorchester follow the usual pattern; there are padlocks, door-locks with keys very like those used to-day; there are the usual feminine belongings—rings, eyebrow pluckers, hair-combs, nail-cleaners and glass beads, bronze bracelets and brooches. There are toys and games, including draughtsmen, and, presumably from the villas of the wealthier classes, some very elegant silver and glassware. In some ways the most dramatic find in Roman Dorchester was a hoard of Roman coins—22,000 in all—and ranging in date from the Emperor Caracalla to the Emperor Gallianus. They were discovered in 1936 at the back of No. 45 South Street, and probably formed part of a treasure in charge of some official. They can be seen in the Museum, near the door.

There are some interesting, if rather ugly, examples of "Kimmeridge ware" which are peculiar to Dorset. Kimmeridge shale, a soft stone, which is exposed at Kimmeridge Bay in the Isle of Purbeck, was used as early as the Bronze Age, and up to Roman times formed an important industry. Dishes, bracelets, spindle whorls, and even articles of furniture, were produced from this unattractive substance. Some of the exhibits in the Dorchester Museum—table-legs carved from grey-black shale in the form of animal legs—remind one of the worst examples of Victoriana. One admires the skill of the craftsman while deploring the taste of his patrons. But no doubt they looked well enough to the newly Romanised Durotriges, sitting in their comfortably heated villas within a few miles of the deserted hill-fort where their ancestors had lived in holes in the ground.

For current developments, see section on *New Discoveries*, p. 285.

CHAPTER EIGHT

ROMAN SOMERSET

FROM Dorchester my route lay along the Roman road which leaves the city on the north-west and runs past Yeovil to Ilchester, where it is crossed by the Fosse Way. My plan was to turn north-east along the Fosse towards Bath, making a detour to visit the Roman lead-mines near Charterhouse in the Mendips, and then resume course through Bath and so to the Bristol Channel. But before going on to Ilchester I made a detour—which I also recommend to the reader—along the Sherborne road to Cerne Abbas, one of the most delightful and secluded villages in the West Country. Here I was pleased to observe that the Cerne Giant still flaunts his virility to the world, as he has done for at least 2,000 years, though the postcards on sale locally persist in emasculating him. This great figure, cut out of the turf on the hill overlooking the village, may possibly represent Hercules (he has a club in his hand), though some archæologists believe that he antedates the Romans by many centuries, and may be a Fertility God of the Iron Age people who built the great forts, such as Badbury Rings and Maiden Castle.

At Ilchester, a Roman station, I joined the Fosse Way—the great road which ran from Lincoln to the coast of Devon, and was a frontier in the early years of the Occupation—and travelled along it for twenty glorious miles, dipping and swooping over the low, wave-like crests of the Somersetshire hills, dead straight for most of the way. I had no compunction about cruising along it at 80 m.p.h.; these roads were built for speed, and the Romans, an eminently practical people, would certainly have made the fullest use of motor transport had it been available to them. Ironically, the roads they built more than eighteen centuries ago are to-day practically the only highways left in these islands along which speed is occasionally possible and safe.

Just beyond the village of Street-on-the-Fosse the road takes a sharp turn to the right towards Shepton Mallet. At this point there is a signpost, one arm of which points left to Glastonbury, and the other due north along a secondary road. This road, which follows the line of the original Fosse Way, is the one we should take. If the traveller has any doubt, he can identify it by a row of grey-stone cottages on its left, one of which bears the name " Japonica ".

This secondary road crosses the main A371 and then, after about half a mile, passes under a railway bridge, before meeting A361 (Wells to Frome). The Roman road appears to go no further, but do not be discouraged. A slight turn right along the main road will reveal a tiny lane which leaves the road on the left and goes through the little village of Charlton, with its grey limestone houses and sturdy oaks. From the village the lane, now a narrow, grass-grown track, climbs a steep hill. I managed to traverse it for about half a mile, wheels brushing the nettles, until I was halted by a fallen tree. From here I continued on foot for about another mile until I had to return. But walkers can follow this deserted trackway for several miles, up and down hill, until at last it crosses the Roman road to the west, which is described later in this chapter.

It is hard to recognise in this deserted cart-track, half-overgrown with weeds, the lineaments of the great Fosse Way. But if you look carefully on your left after you have climbed the hill out of Charlton, you will see the faint remains of its *agger* running across the meadows, roughly parallel with the lane. The best time to see it is in the evening when the westering sun throws it into shadowed relief. It was near sunset when I last saw it, and I remember sitting on the fence beside the road and reading Tacitus's " Agricola " which I carried in my pocket. Agricola, later to become Governor of Britain and conqueror of the Caledonians, served as a junior officer under Suetonius Paulinus during Boudicca's revolt. He very probably rode along this very road, which is now a barely visible track, and if so, he too would have seen Glastonbury Tor, several miles away, a dark mound against the setting sun. Oaks would be growing in the fields just as they do now, and the young officer would have drawn his cloak more closely about his shoulders as the familiar evening dampness began to creep out of the earth. One wonders how those sun-loving Mediterranean people bore with our climate!

* * * * *

I stayed overnight at Wells, and in the morning travelled to Shepton Mallet via the main road and continued along A361 until, a little beyond the village of Doulting, I took the second road on the left, signposted Wells. This was part of the main Roman road to the west, which we saw leaving the western ramparts of Old Sarum, and which I had now rejoined. About two miles further on is Beacon Hill, marked by a line of giant firs. It is wise to halt here and explore the ground away to the left of the road, for this was an important road junction. Here crossed the Fosse Way, which we attempted to follow yesterday, and if you take your stand near the highest point of the tarmac road you will see, on your right, a narrow rutted lane, running at right angles to the modern road, and plunging downhill to the north. That is the Fosse Way on its way to Lincoln. On the opposite side it is more difficult to recognise, because the Forestry Commission has fenced off the road to protect its young conifers. But look carefully and you will see the gravel surface of the road going straight up the slope towards the crest of Beacon Hill. (Incidentally, what right has the Commission to fence off a public road which has been a right of way for nearly 2,000 years?)

However, the fence is easily climbed.

Beacon Hill itself is a mysterious place. On the crest,

under the trees, are several circular mounds, one of which presumably supported the beacon from which the hill gets its name. A little to the west of the hill, just beyond where the pipeline crosses a ditch, is another stone, evidently marking a parish boundary, inscribed " Shepton Parish 1706 ". From here look west across the field towards the main road, along which you have travelled from Shepton, and you will see three large tumuli near the hedgerow. Others are marked on the Ordnance Survey map, and the whole district would repay exploration by amateur archæologists with time to linger. There may have been some kind of Roman settlement at such an important road-junction, but I have not heard of any remains having been discovered.

The next part of the westward route requires careful navigation if one is not to stray off the true Roman line. From Beacon Hill continue along the Wells road, cross A37, and so on past Maesbury Castle (another ramparted Iron Age fort), which you will see on your right. Beyond here the road crosses a railway bridge, where you must take a very sharp turn to the right along a road signposted Priddy and Cheddar. Left again along B3135, and continue over another crossing near Whitnal Corner, where there are clusters of burial mounds (marked on the Ordnance Survey map). From here the Roman road runs dead straight for about five miles, crossing A39 about midway. Then continue along B3135 until, one mile after it crosses another main road (A39), the Roman road leaves B3135 on the left, rejoining it a mile further on. Just beyond the junction with B3135 there is a plantation of young trees on the right of the road near a modern red-brick house. Stop and look over a gap in the hedge, and you will see the original Roman metalling, clearly visible for about 70 yards, after which it disappears under the soil.

You are now approaching the Mendips, where the Romans mined their lead and silver. The road will take you straight to a pleasant inn, charmingly named the " Castle of Comfort ", and if you time your arrival correctly you can refresh yourself, as I did, with some excellent cider, and perhaps meet some of the enthusiastic speleologists (or should it be speleologues ?) who are attracted to this district—a happy hunting-ground for cave-explorers. They may even initiate you into the mysteries of such romantically named caverns as Swildon's Hole, Tor Hole and the Devil's Punch Bowl. The Mendips, like many limestone hills, are honeycombed with holes, galleries and caves, some of which were inhabited by primitive man; there are also mysterious rivers which plunge into the hillside and reappear miles away; for example, at Wookey Hole, near Wells.

When the Romans came this way the district must have been thickly populated, to judge from the many groups of Bronze Age tumuli with which it abounds. One of the finest of these groups is easily accessible from the "Castle of Comfort" and should not be missed. From the inn take the Wells road for about a mile, and at the cross-roads ("Miners' Arms") turn sharp right, continue for about one mile, then turn sharp left along a lane. After about one-quarter of a mile you will see a small gate on the left-hand side. From here you cross a wide field speckled with golden gorse to where the "Priddy Nine Barrows" ride the skyline. They are of the round type and have all been excavated, but they make a splendid sight under the wide sky, these graves of chieftains who died more than a thousand years before the Romans came. The invaders must have known well what these monuments were, for in their day this method of burial was still practised by some of the barbarians over whom they ruled; and in any case, every educated Roman would know his Homer, and had not the great poet meticulously described the building of such a barrow for the burial of Patroclus ?

Returning to the Castle of Comfort Inn, it is only a short run into the hills to the hamlet of Charterhouse. Although there is little to be seen there to-day, these few hundred acres of hummocky ground, pitted with bracken-choked holes, were the main objective of the Roman road we have been following from Old Sarum. For here lay the lead and silver mines, which were exploited by the Romans, no doubt using native labour, and the pits are the remains of the ancient workings. It must always have been a lonely, desolate place, and most people find it distinctly depressing, especially on those grey, rainy days when, as one writer has commented, " the miners' hearts, as well as their produce, must have been of lead ".

It is well worth travelling the few extra miles to see it, if only because it helps to fix in our minds an aspect of the Roman occupation which tends to be forgotten—the economic side. One of the main attractions of Britain to the Romans was its rich mineral wealth, and once installed, they lost little time in exploiting it. Remains of Roman lead mines occur in many parts of Britain; at Halkyn and Holywell in Flintshire, in the Derbyshire hills near Matlock, on the Yorkshire moors, and near the foot of the bleak Stiperstones in Shropshire. There is one place which I know well, for I used to live near it, where, many years ago, explorers found the skeletons of Roman miners, with their tools still beside them. This was in a hole in the hillside at Llanymynech, near Oswestry. I have also heard old inhabitants of the district tell of a blind fiddler who, like the Pied Piper, walked straight into the side of the hill and was seen no more. There may be a substance of truth in this legend, as Arthur Weigall (who also heard the story) suggested in his book on Roman Britain. The unfortunate fiddler may have fallen into one of the old Roman workings and been killed.

To return to the Mendip lead mines; these workings produced a great quantity of the metal, which was cast into " pigs " and exported, probably from a harbour now called Uphill, near the mouth of the River Axe. One of these " pigs " or blocks, bearing its mark of origin, was found at St. Valery, near the mouth of the Somme, stamped with the name of the Emperor Nero and that of the Second Legion—the troops which Vespasian led to the west. Could it be that detachments of this famous

Legion were responsible for guarding the mines and supervising the local miners? Or did they themselves mine the metal? The Roman legionary, we know, was expected to turn his hand to anything and the Legions included many skilled tradesmen in their ranks, just as a modern army does.

Lead-mining sounds dull, but it was not only the base metal for which the Romans were looking. In their days the only known method of producing silver was by cupellation from lead; lead was therefore a by-product of silver extraction and silver was needed in abundant quantities for coinage. This, as Professor Richmond points out, explains the rapid development of British lead resources:

> ". . . attested by the numerous date-stamped ingots, or pigs, of the metal. The Mendip mines were in production in A.D. 49, six years after the conquest, the Flintshire mines by A.D. 74, the mines of Nidderdale in Yorkshire, by A.D. 81. All these dated pigs, and most others, are from direct Imperial workings" (because the exploitation of metals in any province was almost exclusively a state monopoly) " but some undated examples from Flintshire, bear the stamps of lessees, all Roman mercantile citizens."

It may interest modern miners to know that the Romans had pit-head baths, and the regulations for the use of such baths were carefully set out. The miners of Charterhouse, or at any rate their supervisors, did not do so badly, to judge from the buildings and objects found during excavations carried out after the 1914–18 War. Well-built houses with good solid walls, window-glass, and well-made drains were discovered. The workers even had a small amphitheatre for their amusement in leisure hours, and the fleshpots of Bath (Aquæ Sulis) were only twenty miles away.

From Charterhouse the traveller can reach Bath quite easily along A368, which is entered at Blagdon and so through West Harptree and Marksbury, where A39 takes him straight to the city. Those who have time, however, should make a detour through the lanes to the secluded village of Stanton Drew (marked on the Ordnance Survey map), where, just behind the seventeenth century grey-stone manor house, in a 20-acre field, are the remains of three Neolithic stone circles, one large and two small. The stones, which appear to be granite or some other porphyritic rock, are not local, but probably were brought here from South Wales. Like similar circles at Avebury and elsewhere, these probably formed part of a temple, and when the Christians built their church here they may have chosen the site on account of its earlier religious associations.

The hoary old monoliths were in violent contrast with the rural serenity of the valley. Here, in this cup of the Somerset hills, 3,000 years of history stand juxtaposed. There is the Carolean elegance of the Manor House with its close-clipped lawns and rustling elms; there is the farmhouse with its barns and byres and cackling geese. There is the squat-towered medieval church, from which the bells chime drowsily across the quiet fields. But, thrusting out of those meadows, like the jagged teeth of some primeval monster, are these savage reminders of who knows what barbaric faith? It is like hearing Grainger's "Shepherd's Hey" rudely interrupted by Stravinsky's "Rites of Spring".

And so to Bath, perhaps the most precisely named of British cities. The British bathed in its medicinal thermal springs; the Romans, great bath lovers, turned it into a luxurious spa, which they dedicated to Minerva. In the Middle Ages, when cleanliness and godliness rarely met, the baths continued to be used for their curative powers. Becoming fashionable again in the seventeenth century, the city reached its peak of elegance in the eighteenth century under Beau Nash; and to-day, although industry has crept in, the city still owes its principal importance to the natural phenomenon which gave it birth—the hot springs which gush out of the rock at a temperature of 120° Fahrenheit.

Most people, I imagine, have heard of, if not seen, the Roman baths at Bath, and some may have thought that all Roman baths were like them; but this is not so. The Romans built baths all over Great Britain. You will hardly find a single town, camp, settlement or villa which did not boast one, but they were not like the great baths of Aquæ Sulis (the Roman name of Bath). The usual Roman bath is more like a Turkish bath, consisting of a series of heated rooms in which the bather sat and sweated, after which he took a cold plunge to close his pores. Then an attendant—or, if he was a rich man, his slave—massaged him with oil and scraped him down with a sharp instrument called a strigil, effectively removing the dirt, after which he was free to dress and go away refreshed to his evening amusement.

The various chambers, such as the *tepidarium* (warm room) and the *calidarium* (hot room), were heated by means of hypocausts, such as we saw at Canterbury and elsewhere. Hot air from a furnace was led under the floors and up the walls in hollow tiles, escaping under the eaves. The floors of the better-class establishments would be covered with tessellated pavements, which were easy to keep clean. The only immersion baths would be the small plunge baths already referred to.

Although the Romans popularised this type of bath throughout their Empire, they did not invent it; indeed, the primitive fathers of the Roman Republic were probably as grubby as our medieval forefathers. The institution of bathing is of Eastern origin, and also prevailed among the Greeks at an early period. The Romans copied it from the peoples whom they conquered, but once having adopted the practice, they spread it with their customary thoroughness and efficiency. During the first three centuries of the Christian era, they and their subject peoples—Rhinelanders, Greeks, Danubians, Spaniards, Gauls, British—sat sweating in their hot-boxes from the Black Sea to the Atlantic. Bath-houses in the first century, like Cadillacs and Coca-Cola in the twentieth, were the marks of a standardised culture-pattern of which other examples are not lacking.

Baths of this customary Roman type exist at Bath, and

can still be seen, but what makes the site unique in Britain are the large *swimming*-baths which adjoin them. They were built, of course, to enable residents and visitors to benefit from the medicinal properties of the water. The chalybeate springs are most useful in the treatment of gout, rheumatism and certain skin diseases. These remains—a great rectangular bath floored with original Roman lead, and two circular baths, with their accompanying suites of hot and cold rooms—are large enough to impress the imaginative visitor. Apart from Bath, the finest Roman sites in Britain are military; Hadrian's Wall, Porchester Castle, etc. Bath, a civil monument, is the only British site where the atmosphere of Roman luxury still lingers.

Partly this is due to the fact that two of these baths, the Great Bath and the Circular Bath to the north of it, are still filled with water which pours into the Great Bath from the same stone culvert which fed it in Roman times. This living water which gushes up from some mysterious source, deep under the earth, is a murky green from mineral salts. Vapour rises constantly from its surface, which is not still, but always gently moving, blurring the reflections of the Emperors whose statues look down from the parapet like figures in a dream.

Most archæologists deplore these figures, and the nineteenth-century " restoration " of which they form part. I do not share this dislike. The Victorian columns and walls are no doubt archæologically incorrect, but they do help the lay visitor to form a rough picture of the original effect of the Great Bath. As for the statues, they are not great works of art, but harmless enough in their setting, and probably little worse than the Roman originals.

You will enter the bath-building from its western end. As you descend the steps you see one of the two large circular baths which flanked the Great Bath. This one is still filled with warm water from the spring. Stand at its southern end and look north across it, and you will see an arch leading to the seventeenth century " King's

Bath " (still in use). This, of course, is the bath in which the fashionable world of Beau Nash used to bathe, and most people think of it as purely seventeenth or eighteenth century. In fact, that semi-circular arch leading to it is Roman, part of the original building.

The Roman baths were in use for more than three centuries, and were modified and reconstructed several times. This western Circular Bath is, for instance, a later addition. When the baths were first laid out there was an aisled hall at this end. When the bath was made, the Romans made a wall which cut off a corridor to the north of it, and a vestibule was created on the southern side. These have since disappeared.

Moving eastward you come to the Great Bath, floored with lead sheets, and filled from its north-western corner by the original culvert. You can see the hot water from the spring flowing into the bath as it has done since the first or second century. The iron in the water has stained the lip of the culvert rust-red. Near this culvert is the " diving-stone " which projects over the water. The feet of ten generations of Roman bathers have worn a groove along the side of the bath, and a deep hollow where they sprang into the water.

Further eastward, on the northern side of the Great Bath, you can see quite clearly the remains of two pavements, one above the other, evidence of rebuilding. Nearby, between the two central pillars are the remains of a fountain. The peculiarity of this is that it was a fresh-water fountain, whereas the water in the bath is fed from the warm saline spring. This cold water supply, which may have been made to cool and dilute the water, was probably fed from a cistern, or perhaps from the municipal water supply.

From the western end of the Great Bath you come to another Circular Bath, matching that on the eastern side, though this one is now dry. Perhaps one of these was reserved for ladies, for bathing and its social accompaniments was not exclusively a male privilege. One may imagine the gossip among the Julias and Octavias as they relaxed in the alcoves, while slaves massaged them with perfumed oils.

Though the remains are extensive, they form only a part of Aquæ Sulis. Many other rooms, and perhaps more baths, lie buried under more recent buildings—some, perhaps under the medieval Abbey, which abuts on to the site from the north.

There remains the Museum, which adjoins the Great Bath, and though small, is beautifully planned and lit. Here you can admire the vigorously carved head of the Gorgon, with hair wreathed like tongues of flame. It formed part of the pediment of the temple of Sul Minerva to whom the spring was sacred. Sul was probably the earlier British God of the place; the Romans, always tolerant and accommodating in matters of religion, found a way of combining the two. Aquæ Sulis means " the waters of Sul ". The Gorgon's head formed part of Minerva's shield. The treasure of the Museum, however, is a fine bronze head of the goddess herself, clearly of Italian origin and far superior to the dull provincial work which one finds on most Romano-British sites. Many gems and coins were found in the spring-head, evidently offerings to the goddess of the waters, but most intriguing of all was a curse written on a piece of lead and which has been translated as follows: " *May the person who has stolen (the heart of) Vilbia waste away like that dumb water. It may be Vinna, or Exsuperius, or Verianus, or Severianus, or Augustalis, or Comitianus, or Catusminianus, or Germanilla, or Iovila, . . . !* "

Do not ignore the tombstone inscriptions, even if your Latin is as rusty as mine; translations are provided, and from these you can study the names and occupations of some of the men and women who knew Aquæ Sulis and bathed in its waters; people such as Julius Vitalis, an armourer of the Twentieth Legion, who died in the ninth year of his military service, and one Tancinus, who came from Caurium in Spain. He had been a cavalry officer and died, aged forty-six, shortly after his retirement. Others came from Metz on the Rhine, Trier on the

Moselle, and Frejus on what is now the French Riviera. There were also, of course, native-born citizens, a Gloucester town councillor, and a sculptor from Cirencester. But they were all Romans, whatever their origin, and they knew and no doubt loved this gracious city beside the Avon as much as the retired officers who still come to live there to-day.

That is another secret of Bath's fascination—its feeling of continuity. Here, as in few places in Britain, or in the world for that matter, one senses a tenuous link with the Roman past. When you have completed your tour of the Museum, take lunch on the terrace overlooking the Great Bath, where the statues of Vespasian, Agricola and Hadrianus look down from their balustrade. Then wander through the glorious eighteenth-century Pump Room, with its gilt columns, superb candelabra and the sunlit alcove in which the King's Spring bubbles. Here, under the portraits of George III and Martha Blount (whom Pope loved), you can see through the crimson curtains the Abbey churchyard, with its row of elegant little shops which calls for ladies in hooped skirts and gentlemen with clouded canes and periwigs.

It is this echo of eighteenth-century style and elegance which links us with the fashionable Romans who came to Aquæ Sulis. It is a fading echo, of course, and in time it will, I suppose, die altogether. But there is something of Roman Bath which will never die. Bath will be kept alive by the never-ceasing spring which welled up out of the hill æons before the Romans came and will be flowing long after we are forgotten. It is this gentle sound of water which haunts the visitor as he wanders from room to room, along pavements worn by the feet of bathers who died eighteen centuries ago. After he has left Bath it is the sound he will remember longest.

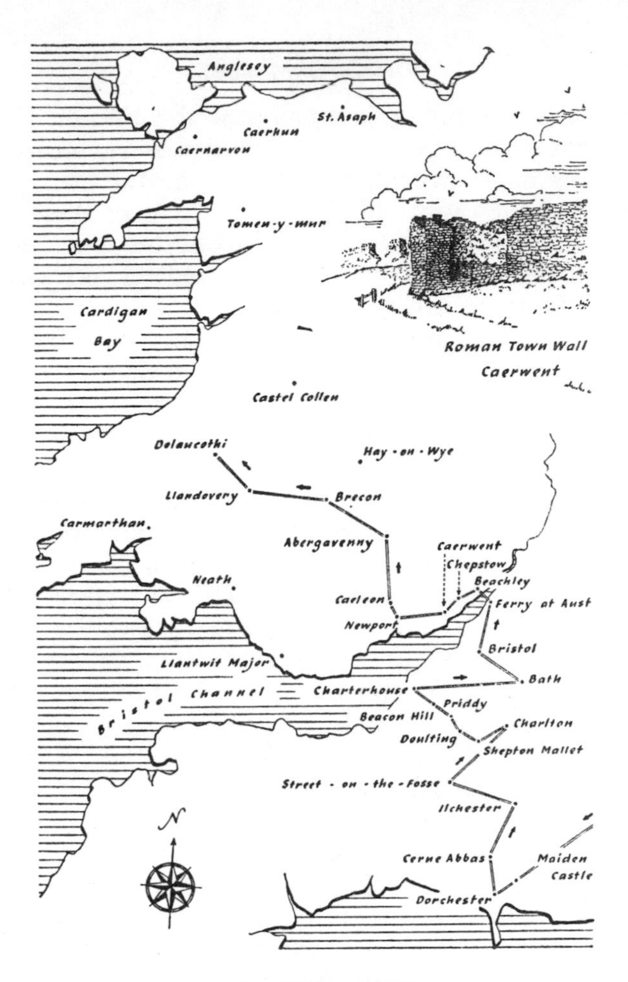

CHAPTER NINE

INTO WALES

FROM Bath I took the main Bristol road, passing the village of Bitton, and then on over Durdham Down, where part of the Roman road can still be seen. I threaded the suburbs of Bristol and came at last upon a winding lane which wandered through flat, charming country down to the Severn Estuary at Aust. It was pleasant in the evening with the sun shining through silver-tipped clouds over Sudbrook on the opposite bank.

There, where chimneys belched grey smoke into an opalescent sky, was the place where the Roman ships landed after crossing the Channel from the Somerset coast.

I parked my car behind the others waiting for the ferry to return from the Monmouthshire bank, and sauntered along the shore to get my ticket. Bars of rosy light lay across the slate-grey water, and across the mud-flats, where gulls left tiny footprints. It was very quiet. The great river moved silently towards the sea, and the hills of Monmouthshire opposite gradually lost depth and became a flat silhouette. Beside the landing-stage was a cheerful café, where the waiting motorists and cyclists consumed tea and buns. I wondered what the ferry was like in Roman times. Perhaps horsemen, chariots and waggons also waited in line, just as we were waiting. Perhaps the travellers lounged in some inn kept by a retired legionary who would swop news and gossip with them. Perhaps his grandfather had campaigned with Julius Frontinus and he would question the young soldiers about their campaigns and bore them with his reminiscences, while the boats came slowly across the estuary.

The ferry-boat came alongside the stage at Beachley. A few houses rose among the trees above the mud-flats, and Welsh voices floated out of the darkness; voices of another country, the land of the Silures. And it suddenly occurred to me that the Romans would have heard similar voices, speaking the same foreign language.

* * * * *

Mountainous Wales naturally presented the Romans with a much tougher problem than Southern England and the Midlands. I have dealt summarily with the conquest of Western Britain by Vespasian, and, if this were a history, I should proceed with the subjugation of the North, which was partly achieved before the conquest of Wales. However, as this book is designed to help travellers rather than students of history, and as South Wales is a natural step from Somerset, readers may bear in mind that the country I am about to describe came under Roman dominion a considerable time after Vespasian overran the West. However, before we begin our journey into Glamorganshire, before we look at Caerwent and Caerleon, it may be as well to look at the general pattern of the Roman conquest during the twenty to thirty years following the Claudian invasion, in order to see how South Wales fitted into this pattern.

After their defeat on the Medway, the British forces resisting the invasion split into two groups, one retreating northward the other westward. The leader of the first group, Togodumnus, had been killed, and his capital, Camulodunum, was taken by Claudius. The other body of Britons was led by that redoubtable figure, Caratacus, the Caradoc of Welsh legend, who continued to trouble the Romans for nine years. After his initial defeat, he took refuge with the Silures, a tribe occupying roughly the area now represented by Monmouthshire, Glamorgan and part of Carmarthenshire. It provided him with ideal country for guerilla warfare.

Meanwhile, as Vespasian and the Second Augustan Legion advanced westward, the Fourteenth and Twentieth, with their auxiliaries, moved north-westwards, probably as far as Wroxeter, near modern Shrewsbury, along the line of the Watling Street. From Colchester (Camulodunum) the Ninth marched northwards and eventually occupied Lincoln. Thus in the first four years the invaders overran the whole of what is now Southern England and the Midlands and consolidated a line stretching from the Trent to the Severn, the line later followed by the Fosse Way. This frontier line was drawn by Ostorius Scapula, who was Governor of Britain from A.D. 47 to 51–2. There the invaders paused for a while, while the conquered tribes were disarmed. Some of them, notably the Iceni of Norfolk, resisted disarmament, and with some small neighbouring tribes, gave battle, probably at a place now called Cherry Hinton, near

Cambridge, where the earthwork known as the War Ditches show signs of slaughter which some archæologists suggest may date from this period.[1]

But the Welsh tribes remained unconquered and gave continuous trouble to the Romans, and also to the British tribes who had accepted Roman sovereignty, such as the Dobunni of Gloucestershire, whose capital was at Cirencester. That is why the first standing legionary fortress in the south-west was established at Glevum (Gloucester) at the crossing of the Severn, to protect the Dobunni from their wild neighbours in the Forest of Dean and the mountains beyond.

After campaigning against the Deceangli of Flintshire, Ostorius Scapula turned his attention to the Silures, among whom Caratacus had taken refuge. Realising that if he was defeated, his retreat to the north would be cut off, the British chieftain shifted his field of operations to Powys, where another tribe, the Ordovices, were resisting the invaders. Unwisely Caratacus abandoned his guerrilla tactics and sought a pitched battle, in which he was soundly beaten. The site of this historic battle has long been a subject for debate among archæologists and historians. Years ago I was taken by an old Welsh gentleman, who could trace his ancestry back to Vortigern, to a place called Criggion, on a bend of a river roughly midway between Shrewsbury and Llantsantffraid in Montgomeryshire. This, my old friend assured me, was the site of Caratacus's last stand, and he went to great lengths to prove it to me by quotations from Tacitus, by the lie of the land (which, he was convinced, exactly fitted the Roman historian's description) and by references to local tradition. Whether he was right or not is anybody's guess, and I expect archæologists would not accept his argument. Personally, I hope he was right, because the site—though somewhat marred nowadays by wireless masts—has a natural majesty which satisfies the imagination. But it has rivals, of which the strongest is Caer Caradoc, near Little Stretton, in Shropshire.

[1] Winbolt, S. E., " Britain under the Romans ".

Caratacus managed to escape, but unhappily put himself under the protection of a woman, Queen Cartimandua of the Brigantes, a powerful northern tribe. She handed him over to the Romans, who, after taking him to adorn a triumph in Rome, generously pardoned him.

But the Silures of South Wales continued to harass the Romans, cutting off foraging parties, surrounding and destroying the forts of the Auxiliaries, taking prisoners and stirring up the conquered tribesmen to revolt. When Ostorius Scapula died in A.D. 51 or 52 they were still unconquered. A. Didius Gallus, successor to Ostorius was little more successful. Veranius Nepos might have done better, but died prematurely. The next Governor, C. Suetonius Paulinus (A.D. 58–61) turned his attention to North Wales. It was he who destroyed the Druid stronghold in the Isle of Anglesey, a centre of British resistance, and then had to dash south to quell the revolt of Boudicca (Boadicea). But that must come later in our story.

The man who finally subdued the unruly Silures was Sextus Julius Frontinus (A.D. 74–78), more than thirty years after the Claudian invasion. It says much for the toughness of the Welsh tribesmen that by this time much of Northern Britain had been conquered, yet the Silures still held out in their mountains. Logically, as Professor Richmond points out in his book "Roman Britain", Wales should have been conquered first, but political events determined that this order should be reversed. When, at last, Julius Frontinus was free to commence the long-delayed operation against the Silures, "he decided to use sea force and occupy the rich and fertile sea-plain of Glamorgan. Once a foothold was here obtained the immediate result was the conquest of South Wales. Forts at the river mouths ensured command of the littoral and the river valleys could be used to penetrate and outflank the Black Mountains and to force open the gateway to Brycheniog by way of the upper Wye and Usk. The importance of the Usk valley as an arterial route was emphasised by the foundation at its mouth of the legionary fortress at Caerleon, (Isca Silurum) which for long remained the seat of the south-western command."

* * * * *

There is a good fast road between Chepstow and Caerwent. Take the main Cardiff road for the first part of the journey, and turn off to Caerwent at the signpost. At "The Coach and Horses" turn left along a lane and you will see, on your right, one of the finest Roman monuments in Wales—the original city wall, still standing almost to a height of more than 10 feet, at some parts to 12 feet. Park your vehicle and scramble up the grassy slope and on to the top of the wall. You can walk along the top for most of its length. At the bottom of the lane a stile leads to a footpath which follows the wall where it turns westward. This section overlooks a pleasant valley of brown ploughland and green meadows where cattle graze. Woods cover the far slopes and, apart from a modern housing estate which overlooks the eastern side of the wall, the old capital of the Silures still stands in open country.

Along the impressive length of the southern wall of the city, great bastions project at regular intervals, and at one point there is one of the original gateways, partially blocked. Although the land inside and outside the wall is private property, visitors are free to walk the length of the wall itself, thanks to the Ministry of Works, which has charge of the monument.

As at Dorchester, Caerwent was built on the standardised Roman pattern to accommodate the tribesmen (or their descendants) who had once occupied a neighbouring hill-fortress. Just as the Durotriges inhabited Maiden Castle before they moved down to Durovernum, so the Silures seem to have occupied a hill-fort at Llanmelin Wood, a mile to the north-west. They also had a "promontory fort" at Sudbrook, which we saw when we crossed the Severn from Aust.

Venta Silurum, the ancient name of the city, was founded round about A.D. 75. It means "the market town of the Silures ". It covered 44 acres, and, as usual, was divided in half by a main street running east to west. There were also two other roads running east and west and four more running north and south. Thus the town was divided into twenty blocks or *insulæ*. The visitor will see very little of the city which the Silures knew, save for the great wall, and the small excavated area to the north of the modern road through the village, which follows the line of the main east-west road through Venta Silurum. Only on the wall itself, rising starkly from the smooth turf, and buttressed by its out-thrusting bastions, will he obtain any impression of what the city was like, and that, inevitably, will be a partial and therefore misleading impression.

If you live in London you will think of the city as you know it to-day. Leicester Square will mean the great cinemas, and the offices of the Automobile Association; you will not think of the square as Dr. Johnson knew it, surrounded by the elegant, red-brick mansions of the nobility, with a palace on the northern side. When you think of the Strand you will see the Law Courts, modern shops and offices, and the Savoy Hotel. You will not see the great mansions of the Elizabethan aristocracy with their gardens stretching down to the river.

Four hundred years separates us from the period when the Earl of Essex, Queen Elizabeth the First's favourite, built the Water Gate which still stands at the bottom of Essex Street. Yet, if in a thousand years from now, London lies in ruins, a visitor looking at the foundations of the Water Gate, built in the time of Elizabeth the First, might possibly confuse them with the ruins of the Savoy Hotel built more than four centuries later.

This is the problem which confronts us to-day when we look at Romano-British towns like Caerwent. The earth bank on which the wall is built may date from the first century A.D., but the stone wall above it was probably built more than a century and a half later.

Again, more than 100 years—three generations—separates the builders of the original wall from those who built its protective bastions. When the first wall was built Rome was strong and the citizens may have felt reasonably secure. But a century later Irish raiders might slip past the Roman fleet and ravage the towns near the coast. So the citizens built these great polygonal bastions, six on the south wall and probably the same number on the north, to provide flanking fire against an enemy creeping up towards the wall, and to make platforms for field-guns—the *ballistæ*—which could hurl a heavy stone missile some quarter of a mile.

A century later, the enemy actually succeeded in breaching the walls and attacking the town; and when the defenders had at last driven them off, they tipped some of the bodies of the slain into one of the bastions, along with the debris, so that, eighteen centuries later archæologists found " a complete skeleton and several skulls. . . ." which had been " tipped into the bastion together with building stones and other Roman materials, debris possibly cleared up after some enemy raid on the town in the fifth century."

In the first and second centuries Venta Silurum was a proud city. There was a market-place enclosed on three sides by colonnades, a great Basilica or Town Hall approached by a fine flight of steps, a great Bath Building with its suites of rooms, several fine temples (one outside the city walls) and elegant mansions with tessellated pavements and rooms built around a central courtyard, centrally heated by hypocausts, and with verandahs opening off them. It was during this period that the citizens set up, on an important site, a memorial inscription to a distinguished official, one Claudius Paulinus, who had been Legate of the Legion at Caerleon, then Legate of Aquitania, after which he was Legate of the Upper Province of Gaul.

Yet, a century and a half later, some of these fine houses were in ruin, so that squatters were free to occupy them. Above the ruins of a fine courtyard-type house of the second century, archæologists found the stone hearths of these squatters, actually built on top of the ruined walls. In one house they had dug an iron-smelting pit into the mosaic pavement of a once-splendid house. Such discoveries tell their own grim story, a story of decay of once-proud towns due to taxation, "the abandonment by Rome of the policy of fostering towns, the hostility of the peasantry, and inflation. . . ."

North-east of the Forum, or market-place, the inhabitants began to build an amphitheatre, for gladiatorial sports, in the fourth century. It was built over the ruins of houses, on top of a road, suggesting that the population was decreasing. But for some reason the amphitheatre was never completed, and by the middle of the fourth century A.D.—300 years after the Claudian invasion—"many of the houses of Caerwent were ruinous and had collapsed down to ground floor level, and by the end of the century the basilical hall of the baths was in decay." [1]

In this way, by patient excavation and research, the archæologists can extract from mute stones the story of the rise and fall of cities, and partially fill in the large gaps in the chronicles of Roman historians. In this we amateurs of archæology are fortunate. When such great antiquaries as Leland came to Caerwent 400 years ago they could only speculate on the significance of the ruins which they saw. To-day we can buy for a shilling an accurate but simply-written pamphlet in which the results of years of excavation and study are summarised and expounded for our benefit.

Returning to "The Coach and Horses", turn left along the road through the modern village, which overlies the main east-west road of the Roman city. A hundred yards along it you will see on your right a large section of Venta Silurum, which was excavated in 1947–48 and which has been left uncovered. The western side is bounded by Pound Lane, which also follows the line of a Roman street for about 70 yards. Here you can see the foundations of two large Roman houses. Both were considerably altered in the four centuries during which

[1] "Caerwent, Roman City," by O. E. Craster, Ministry of Works Guide, 1951.

Venta Silurum was occupied. No. XXVI. N (see Plan in Ministry of Works guide) began as two " strip " houses, 7 feet long and 24 feet wide, separated by a 5-feet wide passage. The front part of the houses were shops, facing the main street, with living rooms at the back. This was in about A.D. 100. More than a quarter of a century later, one of these houses was knocked down and a new wing built, divided into three large rooms, one of which had tessellated pavements, and the other a mosaic pavement laid down in about A.D. 200. Eventually this house developed from two shops to a fine town house of three wings facing on to an open courtyard, with a colonnade and a double entrance. But later still, in the fourth century A.D., this town mansion fell on bad times and was occupied by manufacturers, who built a forge and a tempering trough in the west wing. A modern parallel would be a fine Queen Anne house, in a market town like Worcester, now occupied by a firm which makes wireless components in what was once the dining-room.

And so to Caerleon, one of the finest Roman sites in Great Britain, equal in importance to its sister sites of Chester and York, but less built over. To reach Caerleon, continue along the main Cardiff road to Newport, where turn off to the right. The site of the fortress, though somewhat marred by industrial development, is still lovely, overlooking the River Usk, with low hills on three sides. Unfortunately, not all of the site is open as an Ancient Monument, though the great amphitheatre and barracks are controlled by the Ministry of Works.

Geoffrey of Monmouth, the Welsh historian, makes it the setting for the crowning of King Arthur. " On one side," he wrote, " the city was washed by that noble river, so that kings and princes from the countries beyond the seas might have the convenience of sailing up it. On the other side, the beauty of the meadows and groves, and the magnificence of the royal palaces with gilded roofs that adorned it, made it even rival the grandeur of Rome."

Sir Mortimer Wheeler, who excavated the amphitheatre, has written a fascinating little guide to Caerleon which can be bought on the site. In it he points out that when Geoffrey knew Caerleon in the twelfth century, the city must still have had a fair show of ancient architecture. Even the less imaginative Gerald of Barry, who saw it in 1188, writes of—" immense palaces formerly ornamented with gilded roofs in imitation of Roman magnificence . . . a town of prodigious size, remarkable hot baths, relics of temples and theatres all enclosed within fine walls, parts of which remain standing. You will find on all sides, both without and within the circuit of the walls, subterraneous buildings, aqueducts, underground passages; and, what I think worthy of notice, stoves contrived with wonderful art to transmit the heat insensibly through narrow tubes passing up the side of the walls."

Seeing such remains, and comparing them with contemporary buildings, cultivated men such as Gerald must have despised their Norman masters, huddled round the open hearths of their draughty, insanitary castles.

The fortress was begun round about A.D. 75, when Julius Frontinus began the conquest of the Silures. It was an oblong enclosure of about 50 acres enclosed at first by an earth bank crowned by a timber stockade and protected by an outer ditch. Some twenty-five years later, however, the Romans revetted the bank with stone and built permanent barracks of masonry. Caerleon could accommodate between 5,000 and 6,000 men, the full strength of the Second Legion Augusta, one of the three legions which were permanently stationed in Britain. The other two were the Ninth, at York (later replaced by the Sixth) and the Twentieth, at Chester. We shall visit both these cities in the course of our tour, but Caerleon is the best preserved. Before we examine it, however, I propose to devote part of my next chapter to a sketch of the Roman Army in general, so that when we visit Caerleon we may have a clear picture of the kind of men who lived in it.

CHAPTER TEN

THE CAMP OF THE LEGIONS

THE Roman Army was the world's first professional army in the modern sense. Except in times of emergency, it was recruited on a voluntary basis; men joined it because it offered them regular pay, a good life, and a career. Recruits signed on at the age of about twenty and retired in their middle forties with a substantial gratuity. In theory, the legionaries had to be Roman citizens before they could be accepted, though this rule was modified in later years. The auxiliaries were not Roman citizens, but were granted Roman citizenship on retirement, and as such citizenship carried substantial privileges, it provided another inducement to join the Roman Army.

If a young man of good family wished to join up, he usually armed himself first with a letter of introduction. Here, for instance, is such a letter, dated the second century, A.D., in Mr. M. R. Watson's translation:

" To Julius Domitius, tribune of the Legion, from Aurelius Arcaleus his orderly, greetings.

" I've already recommended my friend Theon to you, and now again I beg you, Sir, to keep him before your eyes, as though he were me; he is the sort of fellow you ought to like, for he has left his family and affairs to follow me and has looked after me in every way. So I beg you to accept this introduction to you so that he can tell you everything about our business. Keep this letter before your eyes, Sir, and imagine I am talking to you."

Physical fitness was, of course, essential. Vegetius, a Roman official, wrote in the fourth century, a book in which he tried to lay down the principles of recruitment and training of the Roman Army in the great days which had passed.

" Whoever is going to levy recruits," he wrote, " must look at the face, the eyes, and the whole shape of the man, to see whether he will make a good fighter. So a young man who would be thought suitable for warfare should have shining eyes, an erect carriage, a broad chest, muscular shoulders, strong arms, long fingers, a modest belly, feet and calves sinewy. . . ."

Training was rigorous. Battle courses are no new thing. Here is Vegetius describing how an infantry soldier should be trained for combat.

" Single stakes six feet high are fixed in the ground. The recruit attacks them as if they were an enemy, with a wickerwork shield, and a wooden sword. He attacks as though against the head and face, against the flank, the knee and the legs; withdraws, comes up from the side, slinks up as though it were a real enemy, threatens him with his wooden sword, using all the strength and skill needed in real battle."

And much more in the same strain. Vegetius also has sections on marching, or as he calls it " the military pace " and lays down that a march of twenty Roman miles must be complete in five hours, at the normal pace, and twenty-four at the faster rate.

The Roman Army was regularly paid. An actual example of a Roman soldier's pay-book was discovered at Alexandria in Egypt, dating from A.D. 83–84, about the time when Caerleon was built and occupied.

In the first century A.D. a private soldier's pay was 225 denarii per annum, paid in three instalments, but the Emperor Domitian (A.D. 81–96) raised this to 300 denarii a year. The pay could be supplemented by loot and by Imperial bounties. In Egypt, however, the troops seem to have been paid in drachmæ, the local currency, and received 248 drachmæ for each pay-period. But there were a number of compulsory stoppages, as follows:

Bedding	10	
Food	80	
Boots and straps . . .	12	
Annual Camp Dinner .	20	(in the first pay-period only)
Burial Club	4	(in the second period only)
Clothing	60	(in the first period, 146 in the third)

Out of 248 drachmæ due to him in the first pay-period, our soldier got only 66. In the second he received 142. This was the balance he withdrew, leaving the balance in the Army Savings Bank to accumulate. There was a very sound reason for this, which Vegetius explains: ". . . from the bonuses which were issued to the troops a half-share was retained with the Colours and preserved there for the men themselves, to prevent its being wasted by the other ranks through extravagance or the purchase of useless articles. For the majority of men, and in particular those who are poor, are in the habit of spending all that they are able to acquire. This putting aside of money, however, is in the first place shown to the men themselves to be advantageous; for since they are maintained at the public expense, their personal savings are increased with every bonus by their half-share."

One of the most fascinating documents I have come across is an Army Duty Roster, dating from the reign of the Emperor Domitian, over 1,800 years ago. It, too, was found in Egypt and gives the duties of various soldiers for the first ten days of October. The document has been damaged so that some of the entries are missing, but enough survives to give us a vivid idea of the duties of a private soldier in a permanent camp.

A " Century " was a unit of 80 men (not 100) under the command of a Centurion; the names of some of these, e.g. Helius, Decrius, Serenus, are given. Scholars differ in their translation of certain words. For example, the duties of Marcus Arrius Niger from October 5th–10th can be read " camp streets ", but this almost certainly means " barrack fatigue ". Here is a translation of part of the document, for which I am indebted to Mr. M. R. Watson (*see following page*). The monotonous repetition of " barrack fatigue " after the name Marcus Arrius Niger will have a familiar ring to modern soldiers. One wonders what Marcus had been up to!

The Roman Army had ranks of seniority, some of which have approximate equivalents in a modern force.

NAME	OCTOBER 1	2	3	4	5	6	7	8	9	10
G(aius) Domitius (C)e(ler)									Leave by permission of Prefect	
G(aius) Aemilius Vale(ns)	Uniform of Helius						?	Armoury	Bath-house fatigue	
G(aius) Julius Valens	Sand	?	Ditch-ing	Boots	Armoury		Bath-house fatigue	Batman	Duty in century	Bath-house fatigue
L(ucius) Julius Oc(ta)via(nus)	Sand				Duty in century	Bath-house fatigue	H.Q. guard	Street duty	Duty in century	?
P(ublius) Clodius (S)ecun(dus)	Camp-market duty ?						Gate guard	Cen-turion's boots	Helius' boots	Helius' boots
M(arcus) Arrius Niger			Duty in century		Barrack fatigue	Barrack fatigue	Barrack fatigue	Barrack fatigue	Barrack fatigue	Barrack fatigue
L(ucius) Sextiliu(s) G(e)rm(a)n(us)	Gate guard	Regi-mental colours	Bath-house fatigue	?	Duty in the Century of Decrius					
G(aius) Julius F....	?	Windows ?			Duty in the Century of Serenus					
Q(uintus) Cassius Ru(f)us	The island									
G(aius) Julius Long(u)s Sipo	Camp-market duty ?					In the century of Helius				Duty in the century

Starting with the lowest-ranking soldier they ran as follows:

Miles gregarius	Private. Also bore the slang name of *caligati*—" the booted ones."
Immunes	Probably equivalent to a lance-corporal. The *immunes* were soldiers who were immune from ordinary fatigues. Compare *gefreiter*—" freed man " —in the modern German army. They could be clerks or orderlies.
Tesserarius *Optio* *Signifer*	Roughly equivalent to sergeants. The *signifer*—the name means " he who waves the Standard "—would be a signaller in a modern army, but he also had administrative duties rather like those of a Company Quartermaster Sergeant. He was roughly equivalent to a warrant officer. He was also responsible for the Army pay-chest and banked the money deposited by the troops in the army savings bank.
Beneficiarius	A sergeant promoted on the recommendation of a particular officer.
Cornicularius	Head of the office staff, higher than a *Beneficiarius*, but still below the rank of *Centurion*.
Centurion (*commissioned officer*)	Company commander, in charge of a " Century "—80 men at full strength. Some rose from the ranks but the greater number were commissioned directly. There was also a senior centurion, known as the *Primus pilus*, equivalent to a full colonel or brigadier. Unlike the lower ranks, the centurions wore shoes instead of boots and carried swagger-sticks.

From *miles* to *centurion* we can find approximate parallels with modern army ranks. It is only among general officers that the Roman Army parts company with modern practice. The senior ranks of that army were filled by men to whom military command was only part of their duties and responsibilities. Under the Roman Empire there was not the distinction which exists to-day between military and civilian life. There was what one might call " the senatorial career ", which included both civil and military command. The Roman system required a high-ranking officer to be more than a professional fighting man. He had also to possess a sound knowledge of law, finance and administration, and be able to govern a province. As for his military ability, a soldier friend of mine, a great admirer of the Roman

Army, put it to me in this way—" they picked their men in their teens and then trained them to be generals, not platoon commanders. They gave them their divisions before their arteries had hardened."

As you travel in search of Roman Britain you will often find in museums, and elsewhere, memorial tablets concisely setting out the successive steps by which a high Roman official attained his exalted rank. These terse inscriptions, of which hundreds have been found in Europe and throughout the Empire, can tell us a great deal about " the senatorial career " and of how the Romans picked and trained the men who ran the Empire. A young man of good birth—the son of a Senator (roughly equivalent to a member of the House of Lords)—would begin his career in his late teens as an official in some minor Government post in Rome. In his early twenties, he would be appointed Military Tribune to a Legion, to get his first taste of soldiering. The post of Tribune was not unlike that of a liaison officer or A.D.C. at formation headquarters. This was a try-out job in which the young man would be under the observation of his seniors, who would judge whether or not he had the makings of an officer. If he was keen and able, and liked the military life, he could learn a great deal about the art of war, and some Tribunes commanded quite large bodies of troops. On the other hand, he might prefer the life of a " base-wallah " (to use a 1914–18 phrase). Whichever course he adopted, his conduct would no doubt be noted by his superiors and reported to Rome.

After a few years with a Legion the young man would return to Rome to take up a number of civilian administrative appointments of increasing responsibility, some in Rome itself, others in the Provinces. He would become a *Quæstor* or Financial Officer at twenty-five, a *Prætor* or Judge at thirty, until, at about the age of thirty or thirty-five, he would command a Legion, equivalent to a modern division. It is fair to say that at any given moment in the Early Empire a majority of divisional commanders would be under forty; young, vigorous men.

The rest of the Senatorial career will be dealt with later; the point to remember here is that when a Roman officer was sent to command a Legion he would come to it with some experience as a junior staff officer fifteen years before, and with a great deal of civilian administrative experience, but with no other military background. This was because the duties of such a commander in an occupied country like Britain were administrative as well as military.

The efficiency of the Roman Army depended to a great extent on the non-commissioned officers, from *immunes* upward, and the *centurions*, the lowest rank of commissioned officer. These were professional soldiers, permanently employed, and the success of the army in holding the frontiers of the Empire, and keeping the peace for 300 years, was due to their iron discipline and superb training. The barbarians to whom the Legions were opposed often had great courage and superior numbers, but they were not professional armies and their arms and equipment were far behind those of the Romans.

When the fighting was done, the function of the Legions was to hold the frontiers or *limes*. On the frontier itself there would be a screen of forts, manned by auxiliary troops and lined by military roads for the rapid movement of reinforcements to threatened areas. But behind this screen were the permanent headquarters of the Legions, of which Caerleon was one. The Romans called it *Isca*, from the Celtic name of the Usk River. Paradoxically, the later Welsh preferred to call it Caerleon, a derivation of the Latin phrase *Castra Legionis*—the " Camp of the Legions ".

The Legion which occupied it for 300 years was the famous Second Augusta, or " Augustus's Own " because it was probably founded by Octavian, afterwards called Augustus. Its emblem was the Capricorn, a mythical creature, half-goat and half-fish, which was the legionary badge. It is worth memorising this emblem. You will find it stamped on roofing-tiles at Caerleon and at other places in our island, because, although Caerleon was the permanent base of the Second Augusta until it was transferred to Rutupiæ (Richborough) in the fourth century, it sometimes operated in other parts of Britain; for example, it helped to build Hadrian's Wall. Later the Legion adopted a second badge, the Pegasus or winged horse, still worn to-day by a famous British regiment.

Regimental pride was encouraged in the Roman Army, and no doubt the legionaries who wore the badge of the Capricorn or the winged horse were as proud of their emblem as the Parachute Regiment is of theirs. Equally, one may be sure that like modern soldiers the men of the Second Augusta affected superiority over those of the Sixth and the Twentieth "Valeria Victrix", an affectation which would be reciprocated by the men of those legions.

We have already encountered the Second Augusta in our tour of the West, where it conquered under Vespasian. Before coming to Britain it had served in Spain from 30 B.C. to A.D. 10. Later it moved to the Upper Rhine and fought against the Germans. In A.D. 17 it was moved to Strasbourg (Argentoratum), remaining there until the invasion of Britain. Its emblem has been found near Charterhouse, in the Mendips, described in Chapter Eight, where it probably supervised the lead mines, if it did not operate them itself. In A.D. 50 it crossed the Severn and began operations against the Silures, though it also sent a detachment to Italy to fight in the civil war of A.D. 69. Eventually, under Julius Frontinus, the Silures were finally subdued and the Legion built its permanent headquarters beside the Usk.

The best way to visualise the original appearance of Caerleon is to climb Christchurch Hill on the south and look down on the loop of the Usk. There, on a slightly sloping stretch of land, protected on one side by the river, the Legion built its camp, surrounded by a protective wall and ditch, curved at the corners. It was a strong site, standing adjacent to the mountain zone, on a navigable river estuary, and, as Dr. Nash-Williams wrote in his invaluable little handbook to Caerleon, "accords closely with the recommendations of the Roman manuals on field fortifications. In its original form," he goes on, "it comprised a rectangular enclosure of fifty acres, defended by a ditch and palisaded clay bank. The buildings inside the enclosure were of wood, though substantially built, with clay, timber, or concrete floors, glazed windows, and tiled roofs. For the next twenty years (after A.D. 75) we picture the Legion living under active service conditions, strenuously engaged in the manifold tasks of frontier organisation. . . . With the final consolidation of the Welsh frontier towards the close of the first century, the work of rebuilding the fortress in stone was put in hand."

The skeleton of this stone-built fortress still exists beneath the houses, churches and shops of modern Caerleon. At various periods from 1849 onwards parts of the foundations have been excavated. Sir Mortimer Wheeler and the late Mrs. Tessa V. Wheeler did extensive work there from 1926 onwards, and every year from that date up to the outbreak of the Second World War a new section of the town has been systematically excavated, photographed and planned, mainly under the direction of the late Dr. V. E. Nash-Williams, Keeper of Archæology of the National Museum of Wales, whose recent death was a great blow to British archæology. When I visited Caerleon in 1955, Dr. Nash-Williams, in heavy gum-boots and working clothes, was deep in the mud with his youthful staff, revealing yet another section of the ancient Legionary headquarters, more than two-thirds of which still lie hidden.

As he had recently returned from North Africa I suggested that the scanty remains of Romano-British towns must be disappointing in comparison with the better-preserved ruins of Europe, Africa and Asia. It was an inept remark to make to an archæologist, and fully merited the swift rebuff.

" Nonsense," he said, " in Southern Europe and in North Africa you are not far from the heart of the Empire. Here in Britain you are on the frontier. Here you can see just what the Romans were capable of when they were up against it." And he went back to his digging.

That remark is the key to any true understanding of Roman Britain. If we think of the country as a self-contained entity, its Roman remains may mean much or little, depending on how interested one can get in a few stones in a field. But if we think of Britain as a frontier—just as the Rhine and the Danube and the Euphrates were frontiers—then we see Britain as the Romans saw it, as the northern bastion in the Imperial defence system. During the comparative peace between the first and the fourth centuries—incidentally the longest period during which the Mediterranean world has known peace—the Roman Empire might be compared to an egg, with a soft core, but a hard shell.

Outside the shell were the barbarians, the Asiatic peoples east of the Euphrates, the peoples beyond the Rhine and the Danube, and the Celtic tribes north of Hadrian's Wall. Within that shell—which enclosed a quarter of the world—there was peace and order. The shell itself was the Roman system of frontier defence, a network of interconnected forts manned by auxiliaries, backed by the ultimate power of the legions in their permanent bases behind the Euphrates, the Rhine and Danube, in Egypt, and in Northern and Western Britain. How important these islands were to the Roman defensive system is proved by the fact that throughout the Occupation three legions were stationed in Britain. The only other province of the Roman Empire which had three legions permanently based there was Syria. Northern Germany had two. And yet within the whole of Gaul, comprising modern France, there were no permanent troops; only 500 police at Lyons guarding the Mint.

For this reason, command of Britain or Syria were the

two " plum " jobs of the Roman Army, and some of the Legates of Britain were remarkable men. For Britain was the northern frontier of the Empire and the men who ruled it were the guardians of the Roman Peace.

With these facts in our minds, a visit to Caerleon can be a rewarding experience; without them it may not mean very much, because, apart from the great amphitheatre—the finest in Britain—and the fascinating little museum, there is not much of ancient Isca visible above ground. Where possible, the Ministry of Works has preserved parts of the ruins, e.g. the Roman barracks in Prysg Field, and part of the defensive walls in Broadway Field, but most of the foundation walls uncovered by archæologists during the past thirty years have had to be reburied.

The best way to follow the layout of the Roman settlement is with Dr. Nash-Williams' little book, " The Roman Legionary Fortress at Caerleon, Monmouthshire ",[1] usually available at the local museum. It contains three excellent detachable plans, one of which shows where the Roman buildings lie in relation to the modern town. With this plan it is not difficult even for the amateur to get a good idea of what Isca was when the Second Augustan Legion occupied it.

You will probably approach modern Caerleon from the bridge over the Usk. The line of the High Street is roughly parallel to the Roman road which entered by the south-east Gate until it was crossed by a transverse road running at right-angles to it, emerging from the north-eastern and south-western gates; one end of this road is represented by the Broadway and the other by the straight section of Backhall Street. After passing along the High Street, bear right along Museum Street, past the churchyard. The Church stands approximately in the centre of the Roman fortress town, and it is as well to take your stand here and study the plan.

You are now on or near the line of the *Via Principalis*—the main street of Roman Caerleon—and if you had

[1] Published by the National Museum of Wales, 1952. 5s.

been standing here in the time of, say, Hadrian, you would have seen in front of you to the west the Headquarters Building of the Garrison. It had a paved courtyard in front—which gravediggers in the churchyard have often struck—and this was surrounded by a colonnaded walk, beyond which were ranges of small rooms—the armoury and arsenal of the Legion. Further west was a large aisled hall and then more rooms, offices, staff-rooms, and the regimental chapel and strong rooms. The Commanding Officer would have his office in this block, with his staff; and no doubt there would be army clerks and other minor officials producing what in the R.A.F. we used to call " bumf ". Here our friend, Marcus Arrius Niger, or his equivalent in the Second Legion would be put on a charge; here part of his hard-earned pay would be banked for his own and the Empire's good, while he gambled away the rest in the bath-house outside the city walls. And here also clerks would draw up duty rosters like the one I have quoted.

This great Headquarters building was about 250 feet square, and near it was another of equal size, possibly the *quæstorium*, used for the disposal of prisoners, hostages and booty. A third great building, with sides 230 feet long, stood more to the north-east. It had a central block of rooms with a courtyard behind, and the whole was surrounded by corridors leading to ranges of large and small rooms. Dr. Nash-Williams thought that this may have been the *fabrica*, the Legionary workshop, full of carpenters, builders, smiths, wheelwrights, the tradesmen-soldiers of the Legion, of whom there were many.

These Legionary fortresses kept closely to a standard pattern; that is why it is sometimes possible to deduce the purpose of a building even when only part of it can be excavated; by noting its position in relation to the other known buildings and comparing it with similar structures in other Legionary forts. For instance, there was one at Neuss, in the Rhineland, which was thoroughly excavated between 1888 and 1900, and which bears some resemblance to the Caerleon structure. The fact that the Romans used standardised methods can be a great help to archæologists.

Two other streets ran parallel with the *Via Principalis* on its western side. Beyond the westernmost street, between it and the enclosing wall, were rows of barracks. Similar barrack blocks existed on the northern and southern flanks of the central block of buildings, and more again to the east of the *Via Principalis*. So that if you could look at Roman Caerleon from the air you would see something resembling a modern factory site—parallel rows of single-storey buildings with tiled roofs surrounding a central area of larger buildings around courtyards; the whole neatly enclosed by a high wall with a rampart walk for the sentries, and crossed by streets laid out in a rectilinear pattern. This is the standard layout of a Roman camp, large and small. You will find it again and again, especially when you visit the northern frontier along Hadrian's Wall, and behind the Antonine Wall in Scotland.

Retracing your steps along Museum Street and the Broadway (which follows the line of the *Via Principalis*) you will pass over the site of the Roman south-west gate and find yourself outside Roman Caerleon. Near this point are the two best-preserved relics of the ancient city, the amphitheatre and the barrack-blocks in Prysg Field, both admirably preserved by the Ministry of Works.

The amphitheatre was excavated by Sir Mortimer Wheeler in 1928, at the charge of the *Dail Mail*. Most Romano-British towns of any size included such buildings; they were built outside the city walls—as at Dorchester and Winchester—and used for animal-fights and gladiatorial sports. The Caerleon amphitheatre is by far the finest and best-preserved in Great Britain, a stone-built oval structure surrounded by a seating bank and eight vaulted entrances. Two of these entrances show remains of boxes for important spectators, of which the Camp Commandant would be one, and there was accommodation for 6,000 persons. Now, a Legion normally consisted of 6,000 men, and Dr. Nash-Williams has suggested that " the significant correspondence between the amphitheatre's seating capacity and the nominal strength of a Legion suggests that its primary purpose was to serve as a training school (*ludus*) for regimental drill and sword-exercise ".

Amphitheatres represent the least attractive aspect of Roman civilisation, and I would like to believe, with Dr. Nash-Williams, that the Caerleon example was used mainly for military purposes. But one has one's doubts, walking over the clipped turf of the arena, and looking up at the great earth banks where tiers of seats once stood. Did they once echo to the shouts of 6,000 spectators as animals fought or were baited, or prisoners tortured? One thinks of attendants sprinkling sand over freshly spilled blood, while others dragged the corpses of the slain out through the huge entrance-gates. We know such things happened in Rome. Did they also happen in Monmouthshire, where the friendly hills look down on the Usk? I have little doubt that they did.

Structurally the building is magnificent, and there is a human touch in the presence, at four points, of stones inscribed with the names of the centuries (or companies) who built that section of the wall. In the arena wall near the south-east entrance is a stone with the words:

C. C(ENTURIA) FVL(VL) MAC(ERI)

" the century of Fulvius Macer (built this) ". On the western side of the northern entrance is another stone inscribed:

F. COHO(RS) VIIII

meaning " the ninth cohort (built this) ". Other inscriptions are as follows:

C(ENTURIA) SADI TIR(ONIS)

" the century of Sadius Tiro built this " (on the arena wall south of the middle entrance on the western side).

COH(ORS) X, C(ENTURIA) FLAV(I) JULIAN(I)

" the tenth cohort, the century of Flavius Julianus (built

this) ", (on the arena wall to the north of the same entrance as the above).

A cohort, incidentally, consisted of six centuries, or 500 men at full strength. There were ten cohorts to a legion, but apparently there was no cohort commander, at least not in a legion. Mr. Birley, a leading authority on the Roman Army, told me that in his opinion a cohort was simply a position on the parade-ground.

You will cross the site of the parade-ground as you leave the amphitheatre and cross the field to the east. Away on your right is a well-preserved section of the ditch which protected the city, and beyond it, part of the wall. In this south-western corner of the ancient city lies Prysg Field, the largest part of Isca which is open to the public. Here you can see the well-preserved foundations of rows of barrack-blocks where the men of the Second Augusta lived, and a stretch of the south-western and north-western defences and their adjuncts.

The barrack buildings are in pairs (*strigæ*) and each could house a single company of men with their centurion, who had more spacious quarters at the western end. If you take your stand on the defensive wall at the western end and look down on the foundation walls of the barrack-blocks, it is not difficult to visualise their original appearance. They would be of one storey, long, narrow buildings, 250 feet long and 40 feet wide, with red-tiled roofs and rows of doors along the side, opening on to a colonnaded street serving two blocks. Nearest to you are the quarters of the centurion, or company commander, a suite of rooms, one of which was furnished with a paved floor and stone gulleys—an ablution room. These rooms would be occupied by the company commander and his non-commissioned officers, the *Cornicularius*, *Beneficiarius*, *Signifer*, *Optio*, *Tesserarius*, and so on. Beyond lie the privates' quarters, twelve double cubicles, each consisting of a small outer room where the men kept their arms and equipment when off duty, and a larger living-room behind it.

The barracks were well built, " of good mortared

masonry with tiled, paved or cemented floors, glazed windows, and red-tiled roofs ". They were larger and probably more comfortable than the barrack-blocks of to-day. In some of them the archæologists found a number of lance and spear-heads, an identity disc for attaching to equipment, and three dies for stamping tiles and the like " which bore the names of centurions whose companies had presumably occupied the buildings in which the objects occurred " (Dr. Nash-Williams).

An intriguing find was " an iron finger ring set with a sard intaglio which has been identified as of Hellenistic origin and was thus already an antique when it was lost at Caerleon ".

Between the barracks and the defensive wall of the fortress are remains of the cook-houses, aligned along the back of the ramparts as a precaution against fire, and, in the south-west angle of the fortress, remains of a latrine. These were well-built stone structures with roofs, and were equipped with paved floors, seats and a flushing system. Everywhere you will notice the well-made, stone-built drains which led to underground sewers. The water-supply came partly from wells within the fortress and partly from water-mains connected perhaps to an outside aqueduct. Well-made lead pipes of 7-inch bore have been found carefully laid along the edges of streets at a depth of from 3 to 4 feet.

Before leaving Caerleon, it is essential to visit the museum in Museum Street—one of the finest in Britain —containing most of the objects found in the legionary fortress during the past 100 years. All the remains of Roman Caerleon have been on public view for many years; before many years have passed another Caerleon will have been brought to light, though whether it will be left uncovered has yet to be decided. Three years ago the Caerleon Town Council purchased the old race-course, with the intention of turning it into a sports ground. With an intelligence and public spirit rare among official bodies, it first asked that the site should be archæologically investigated. Archæologists have long believed that, in addition to the fortress, there must also have been a large civil settlement for the families of the legionaries and for time-expired veterans. Thanks to the gesture of the Council, and the skill of Dr. Nash-Williams and his assistants, this settlement has now been discovered, and with each season's work it becomes clearer that it is one of the great finds of the century.

So far, only modest excavations have been carried out, but from these it seems probable that the settlement covered more than 100 acres and may have housed 12,000 people—twice the size of the garrison. If the settlement can be fully excavated and preserved it may be the only complete one existing, except perhaps for Lambæsis in North Africa. The area lies between the fortress and the river.

Even the sight of the small area so far uncovered stirs the imagination, for I think there can be little doubt that this, and not the fortress itself, is the Caerleon which Gerald of Barry saw and described 800 years ago—" a town of prodigious size, remarkable hot baths, relics of temples and theatres enclosed within fine walls . . . subterraneous buildings, aqueducts, underground passages. . . ." Dr. Nash-Williams pointed out part of a massive boundary wall which runs parallel with that of the fortress, suggesting that what has now been discovered is not a random agglomeration of buildings, but a planned settlement. Evidence inside the wall confirms this. There is a heavily metalled straight street, edged with a large culvert, and substantial stone buildings, all residential in type, some with shop frontages. The strength of the footings of the walls suggests that these buildings may have been of two storeys. They were floored with concrete slabs, and sometimes with red, white and blue tesseræ, and the side walls were decorated with painted plaster. Somewhere in the enclosure the archæologists hope to discover the temple of Diana, which is known to have existed, because its dedicatory inscription was found in the seventeenth century. Other inscriptions imply the presence of shrines dedicated to Mithras and the Syrian god Dolichenus.

It is believed that the civil settlement was begun in about A.D. 100 and was occupied for some 200 years. Here lived the wives and children of the legionaries; already the excavators have found, in the silt of the culvert, part of a woman's necklet of fine gold wire, a man's silver signet ring and a gold ear-drop. Generations of time-expired legionaries would have settled here with their British wives, and brought up children, some of whom perhaps would themselves join the Legion in which their fathers served.

When the first of those retired veterans settled in their pleasant new town beside the Usk, they would tell their sons about the battles fought against the Silures, in the mountain passes which by then would be policed and controlled by the auxiliaries in their high forts. But that was a recent campaign in the history of a legion already a century old. Perhaps, sitting in a corner there would be a very old man who might recall to his boastful son an earlier campaign, when he, as a young man, marched with Vespasian up to the ramparts of Maiden Castle and felt the sling-stones of the defenders ring on his shield.

But that would be ancient history when Caerleon was built.

CHAPTER ELEVEN

IN THE MOUNTAINS

I LEFT Caerleon in the late afternoon, and drove to Newport; then along a winding road which follows the Usk past water-meadows and low hills. Ahead lay the mountains, outlined against a red sunset. Near Abergavenny there is a high, steep-sided peak, like a volcano, which stood out strangely in the fading light. There was something sinister about it, and I wondered what the Second Legion thought of this wild land when they marched through it nearly 2,000 years ago.

They knew Abergavenny as Gobannium (notice how the old Latin name is still there, thinly disguised) one of a chain of auxiliary forts which stretched from Caerleon up into the mountains of Breconshire. There is nothing Roman to be seen to-day, but it is a pleasant town, one long street of purplish granite buildings, beyond which the road winds on into the mountains. This was the way the Romans came, following the Usk. For some miles beyond Gobannium the landscape is gentle and undramatic, but the mountains ahead gave promise of sterner country.

It began at Brecon, a little town built along one street, which was thronged with young soldiers wearing the shoulder flash of the South Wales Borderers. It is a garrison town, just as it was in the second century, when an auxiliary cohort was stationed here. Part of the walls of their fort, excavated by Wheeler, can still be seen near the church. In the dining-room of the hotel where I stayed the night sat four Syrian officers, presumably under training at the nearby barracks. Their swarthy Semitic faces seemed outlandish in that little Welsh town, until I recalled that there were Syrian auxiliaries in the Roman Army too. Some Syrian bows were found not long ago at Caerleon.

The following morning was bright after a rainy night, and the mountains of Breconshire rose splendidly ahead as I drove along the steeply climbing road, past Y Gaer (another auxiliary fort) and Y Pigwyn, where, on a mountain top, there is a Roman marching camp, first built by the invaders in about A.D. 52. It was occupied for a time, deserted, then re-occupied for a second time, so that archæologists, when they dug the site, found the remains of two camps, one built inside the other. But there is practically nothing of the fort to be seen to-day.

The road coiled and uncoiled through country of increasing grandeur, until I came at last to Llandovery, surely one of the most beautifully-situated towns in Wales. Welshmen who go in search of their Roman towns have one inestimable advantage over the traveller in England. The remains they look for may often be scanty, except at sites such as Caerleon and Caerwent, but they will rarely have to make a dull journey.

Beyond Llandovery, near the borders of Carmarthenshire, is one of the most interesting Roman sites in the British Isles; interesting, though not spectacular. These are the ruined workings of the Roman gold mines at Dolau Cothi, near the lovely River Cothi, which foams and tumbles over the rocks at the foot of its valley. One of the reasons for the Roman invasion was to exploit Britain's mineral wealth, and many mines have been found in Britain; we have already seen the lead mines in the Mendips; and there are other workings in Flintshire and Montgomeryshire, and copper mines in Anglesey. But gold mines were rare, which is why this example is one of the most important archæological sites in the country.

The workings are not easy to find; they lie on the right bank of the river near a place called Ogfau, which means caves. As they are on private land, it is best to make inquiries locally and try to get the landowner's permission to visit them. The tunnels penetrate some distance into the mountainside. Outcrops of auriferous pyrites were attacked to a depth of about 30 feet, and then by underground workings which included two drainage channels.

An aqueduct more than five miles long brought water from the Cothi to the workings. After removing the ore the miners pounded it on stones, some of which have been found bearing cup-shaped marks made by the pounding. Presumably the miners would be native workmen under Roman supervision, but their comfort seems to have been studied; the excavators found remains of a well-constructed building which seems to have been the pit-head bath!

How were such mines operated? Who ran them? What were the working conditions of the miners? By a fortunate chance a document has survived from Roman times which can answer some of these questions for us. It is a lease drawn up in connection with a Roman mine at Vipasca in Spain; its official title is *Lex Metalla Vipascensis*, and there is little doubt that the lessees of mines in Britain would be governed by similar conditions.

The owner of the mines was the Imperial Government, who leased them to an operator under the terms of a strict legal agreement. One interesting section of this lease is headed " Of The Bath Management " and lays down rules for the use and maintenance of the baths attached to the mine. It reads:

> " The lessee of the baths or his partner shall entirely at his own cost and charge warm and keep open the baths which he shall thereby hold in lease until the following 30th of June, from sunrise to noon for women and from 1.00 p.m. to 8.00 p.m. for men, subject to the Procurator in charge of Mines " (i.e. the Government's representative). " He shall properly furnish water running into the tank, over the heating chambers up to the highest mark, and to the plunge-bath, for women as well as for men. The lessee shall charge each man half an *as* " (a small coin) " and each woman an *as*. Freedmen and slaves of the Emperor who shall be in the service of the Procurator shall have free entry; so shall miners and soldiers. The lessee, his partner or his agent at the termination of the lease shall hand over in good and serviceable repair the equipment of the Baths and everything which has been assigned to him, except that which has been worn away by age."

Those who have had to sign modern tenancy agreements will immediately recognise some familiar phrases! The agreement goes on:

> " The articles which he shall use he shall properly wash, dry and coat with fresh grease once every thirty days. If any necessary repairs

shall make impossible adequate use of the baths the lessee shall deduct from the contract price an amount proportionate to the loss of time. . . . The lessee shall not be permitted to sell wood, except the ends of branches which are not suitable for burning." (The point here was that the Government supplied the fuel.) " If he violates this rule he shall pay 100 sesterces to the *fiscus* of the Imperial Treasury for each sale. If these baths shall not be properly opened for service the lessee shall pay to the Procurator for Mines a fine of not more than 200 sesterces each time it shall not be open for service. The lessee shall have wood in reserve sufficient to last for (   ) days." (Here a blank is left to be filled in.)

Another section of the lease is headed " Of The Tax On Mining Dumps and Rock Piles " and begins:

" He who within the boundaries of the mining district of Vipasca shall clean, crush, smelt, break up, separate or wash silt of copper dumps, or dust from dumps, or shall undertake work of any nature whatsoever in the quarries, shall declare within a period of three days the number of slaves and freedmen whom he is sending to this work, and shall pay to the lessee, on or before the last day of the month (   ) sesterces. . . ."

" Mines of silver shall be exploited in conformity with the regulations laid down in this Law. The price of these mines shall be maintained in accordance with the edict of the liberal and sacred Emperor Hadrian, namely that the usufruct, that portion which belongs to the Treasury, shall belong to him who shall first put up the price of the mine and present to the Treasury 400 sesterces."

Apparently such mines could be leased to a company of shareholders, for another clause in the agreement runs:

" As to those *coloni* (tenants) who undertake the expense of a mine in which many partners are interested, there shall be the right in law of regaining from their partners that which shall appear to have been asked for in good faith. The *coloni* may sell at as high a price as possible shares in the mines which they have bought from the Treasury and for which they paid the full price."

This evidently means that a tenant could sell his share at its commercial value, irrespective of what he originally paid for it.

Particularly interesting to modern miners are the regulations governing the safety of the workers, and the manner in which the mine is to be worked.

" All mines shall be properly propped and supported, and in place of old material the tenant shall substitute a new prop. No one shall injure the pillars or props. The person who works a copper mine shall avoid the ditch which carries the water from the shaft. He who works a silver mine shall avoid the tunnel which carries the water."

Practically the only part of this 1,800-year-old agreement which sounds strange in our ears is the sentence:

"Those to whom the ore belongs shall convey it to the smelter from sunrise to sunset. . . . If an ore-thief be a slave the Procurator shall beat him and sell him, with the condition that he be kept perpetually in chains and shall not be allowed to live in a mining-camp."

Dolau Cothi was the farthest point to which I penetrated on this Welsh journey, but before I set off for Gloucestershire, I stopped at Cardiff and visited the National Museum of Wales. This Museum, in its spacious building overlooking the University grounds, is a treasure-house of Romano-British antiquities, and no visitor to Roman Wales should fail to see it. For some reason, many of the richest sites in Wales present nothing to the eye. A few broken walls, perhaps, or some grassy mounds. In the Museum, however, you can see the objects found on these sites, imaginatively presented together with photographs and drawings of the sites when they were being excavated.

In my opinion, the Romano-British collection in the National Museum is a model of how such antiquities should be presented. The only snag—if it is a snag—is that the *pre*-Roman objects, of the Iron Age and Bronze Age are so much more attractive than the Roman ones.

What a splendid artistic tradition was unintentionally destroyed by these efficient, orderly, unimaginative people! Look at the lovely Iron Age ornaments in the Museum—the harness mounts of gilt-bronze with enamel panels, worthy to adorn the chariot horses of Boudicca, the bronze terrets decorated with quatrefoils of red and yellow enamel, the suave shapes of Celtic swords and shields, the vigorous *living* line of their ornamented pottery. Compare these with the mechanically repetitive patterns of Roman bronze-work and their dreary red-glazed "Samian" ware with its monotonous designs.

One has to admit that there was something middle-class about the Romans. . .

When, sated with Celtic individualism, one turns to the Roman section and sees above glass cases the names of sites one has visited, interest returns. Here, from Caerwent, is a fine silver standard-head once borne by a *signifer*, and near it the bone dice with which he may have played. There is a bronze mirror once used by some elegant British lady in her fine house.

In another case are the finds from the Dolau Cothi mines, including a wooden panning ladle found some 100 feet underground, and part of a wooden water-wheel used in the operations. Archæologists also found, on the same site, gold necklaces, wheel-shaped clasps and gold bracelets. But the Roman speaks to us most clearly through his practical objects—a milestone, for example, found near Port Talbot, bearing an inscription to "the Emperor Cæsar Flavius Valerius Maximus—the invincible Augustus. . . ." And then there are the epitaphs, sternly brief: "Here lies Cantusus. His father was Paulinus."

On my way back to Gloucestershire I stopped again at Caerleon and talked to Dr. Nash-Williams. He sat in his wooden hut at Caerleon, wearing dungarees and muddy gum-boots, talking about Roman Wales, to the study of which he devoted most of his working life. On a bench near him lay a pile of oyster shells, dug up in one of his recent excavations. "You usually find them on Roman sites," he said "the Romans loved oysters."

Knowing that on this particular journey I should not be able to see all the Roman sites in Wales, I asked him if he could summarise the most interesting and important Roman remains, so that even if I was not able to visit them I could at least mention them, with his recommendation. He thought for a few minutes and then gave me the following information which I will summarise briefly.

In North Wales one must see the Roman fort of Segontium, near Caernarvon. It was founded in about A.D. 80 and designed to house a detachment of 1,000 men;

as at Caerleon, the first buildings were of wood, replaced at the beginning of the second century by permanent stone structures. It was an auxiliary fortress, connected with the Legionary headquarters at Deva (Chester), which was to North Wales what Caerleon was to the southern part of the country. Though naturally much smaller than Caerleon, it was built on similar lines, with a Via Principalis, a Commandant's House, granaries and barracks, the whole surrounded by a strong rampart and ditch. The Museum is one of the most interesting in Wales. Segontium can be reached easily from Caernarvon. It was excavated by Sir Mortimer Wheeler and is now in the custody of the National Trust. North Wales, the territory of the Ordovices, was finlly subdued by Agricola, successor to Julius Frontinus, in A.D. 78.

Opposite Segontium are the Menai Straits and the Isle of Anglesey, stronghold of the Druids, which was stormed and taken by Suetonius Paulinus, as described in a later chapter. In Anglesey there are a number of fine prehistoric monuments, such as the Burial Chambers at Bodowyr, Presaddfed and Lligwy, also standing stones at Penrhos-Feilw, hill-forts at Caer y Twr and Caer Leb, and the famous Holyhead Mountain Hut Circles. There is also, at Caer Gybi, the remains of a Roman fort, about one and a half miles west-north-west of Llanidan Old Church. It was built in the late third or early fourth century as one of the defences against sea-raiders, like the Forts of the Saxon Shore in England. Anyone contemplating a tour of Anglesey will be well rewarded. I went there a number of years ago, and it brings vividly to mind the kind of people to whom the Romans were opposed, and the country in which they lived. When you go take the " Annals of Tacitus " with you, and read that wonderful passage in which he describes the moment when the Legions came face to face with the Druids and their fanatical followers: " Among them were black-robed women with dishevelled hair like Furies, brandishing torches. Close by stood Druids, raising their hands to heaven and screaming dreadful curses."

Other sites in North Wales are Tomen-y-mur, in Merionethshire, another auxiliary fort. Though much of the earthwork is mediæval not Roman, the wild landscape alone is sufficient justification for a visit. Tomen-y-mur, like Segontium, Canovium (Caerhun) and Varae (St. Asaph), were all links in a chain of auxiliary forts forming part of the Roman defensive system of North Wales, for which Deva (Chester) was the Legionary base.

In South-Central Wales there is the fort at Castell Collen, in Radnorshire, deep in the heart of the mountains. Like the others, it was an auxiliary establishment, begun as a timber structure and reconstructed in stone in the time of the Emperor Trajan. Mr. Leslie Alcock, of University College, Cardiff, who has been excavating there from 1954 to 1956, found the remains of the south gate which had two projecting guard chambers, an unusual feature for a fort of this early date (the first part of the second century). He and his helpers also found, outside the wall of the fort, well-preserved remains of the garrison bathhouse, with its hot and cold rooms, and walls standing to a height of 5 feet in places. The stokehole and furnace-room were there, and in another room was a masonry bench 3 feet wide, with narrow slots passing through the wall behind it. Mr. Alcock, who very kindly supplied me with a summary account of his discoveries, suggests that these may be " weep-holes " and that the concrete bench is where the bathers sat while cooling off in the *frigidarium* after their sweat-bath. The water they splashed about, he suggests, may have drained off through these holes.

Excavations, which are on private land, are still going on, but some of the remains have had to be re-covered as they lie under valuable farming land. It seems doubtful, therefore, if this fortress will remain permanently on view. The same is true, unfortunately, of many other Roman sites in Wales, such as Caersws in Montgomeryshire, at the meeting of the Carno and the Severn, which was the focal point of the mid-Wales Roman road system; also Gelligaer, in Glamorganshire, and Llantwit Major (a villa), though this lovely site, on the coast some fifteen miles from Cardiff, is worth a visit for the sake of its beautiful setting. Something pretty grim happened there in the early third century. Archæologists found the bodies of forty people who had evidently been massacred. But part of the villa continued to be occupied afterwards. There was also an important Roman settlement at Maridunum, on the site of modern Carmarthen, also at Brecon, where the stone rampart of the fort can be seen, and at Clyro, a marching-camp in Radnorshire about half a mile from Hay-on-Wye.

An interesting point is that some Welsh place-names are derived from their Roman predecessors, e.g. Laughor, possibly the ancient Lucarum, and Neath, which may be on or near the site of the fort of Nedum, mentioned in the Antonine Itinerary. The recent discovery of Roman remains near Neath may help in this identification. In 1949 the Neath Borough Council took over some ground for a housing estate. Mr. Stanley Thomas, a local engineer, noticed fragments of pottery thrown up by the mechanical excavator. He put the fragments in a paper bag and sent them to Dr. Nash-Williams. The first piece to fall out when the bag was opened dated from before A.D. 75, i.e. the period when the Roman invasion of Wales was at its height. The archæologist hurried to the site and the borough council obligingly suspended the work until the site could be carefully examined. Excavations began, and soon afterwards part of the gateway of a fort was revealed. It can still be seen near the side of the road between Neath and Swansea just after you pass the river bridge. Thus a layman discovered the long-lost site of Nedum and added another chapter to the history of the Roman occupation of Wales.

I am aware that some of the sites I have mentioned lie far apart, and a few are difficult of access. To those who wish to visit them—and there must be many—the best advice I can give is that they buy the excellent Map of Roman Britain, newly published by the Ordnance Survey Department, and, with the additional help of a modern map, discover the sites for themselves. I would only add a word of warning. Your search will take you through some of the finest scenery in the British Isles, which should be sufficient reward, but when you finally track down Gelligaer or Castell Collen, don't be disappointed if you find only a grassy mound or some broken walls. Try to people those walls with the men from Spain, Germany and France who fought their way, eighteen centuries ago, through the same mountain passes you have crossed, at a time when every defile might conceal an ambush ; and their successors who occupied the forts intermittently for 300 years. They came as conquerors, but they settled, married Welsh wives, and in the end became guardians of the conquered against fresh invaders.

Paradoxically—and I write as an Englishman—it is the English and not the Romans who provide the foreign element in Britain. We, and the Danes, were the latest to arrive. We did most to obliterate the old Latin culture which the Romans brought with them. But the Welsh, descended from the Celtic tribes who once occupied the whole of Britain, first fought the Romans and then intermarried with them, so that to-day there must be many men and women living near Caerleon, and Carmarthen and Caernarvon, who are descended from the legionaries and auxiliaries who fought under Julius Frontinus and Agricola.

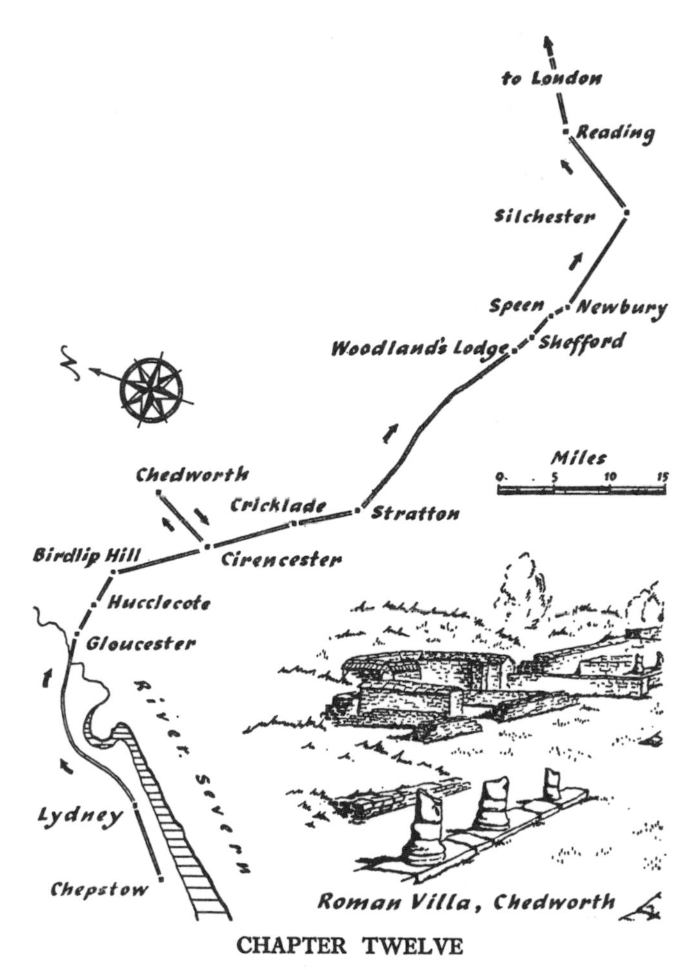

Roman Villa, Chedworth

CHAPTER TWELVE

GLOUCESTERSHIRE AND BERKSHIRE

FROM Caerleon the quickest way to return to London would have been via Bristol and Bath, but this would mean re-covering old ground. Instead, I planned to visit Gloucester (Roman Glevum), then cross the Cotswolds to Cirencester (Corinium), and finally complete the trip by following the original Roman highway which runs south-eastward across the Berkshire Downs to Silchester (Calleva Atrebatum) and London. I must also admit to a more personal motive. Gloucestershire and the Cotswolds particularly, were the playgrounds of my boyhood and I never resist an opportunity of seeing them again.

Leaving Chepstow, I followed A48, with the Severn on my right and the Forest of Dean on my left. I passed Lydney Park, where Sir Mortimer Wheeler discovered the greatest of all Romano-British temples, a centre of healing and pilgrimage, dedicated to the Celtic god Nodens, and equipped with an elaborately appointed hotel as well as the temple and priests' houses. All this was built in the fourth century A.D. within a prehistoric earthwork, above the remains of an early Roman iron-mine. One of the pleasantest traits in the Roman character was its readiness to accept other people's gods—though they drew the line at the Druids and their cult of human sacrifice.

This part of England, the lower Severn Valley and the Cotswold Hills, is thickly scattered with Roman villas, large and small, as will be seen by studying the Ordnance Survey map of Roman Britain. Many of these were excavated many years ago and then re-buried, so that little or nothing can be seen of them to-day; others would undoubtedly repay re-excavation, if facilities and money were available. More undoubtedly remain to be discovered.

At Newnham the river runs alongside the road, and there is a ferry. From here you see, away to your right, the high rampart of the Cotswold Edge, rich territory for those who seek our prehistoric and Roman past. Within a few miles of each other, on the wolds and in the hidden valleys, lie Uleybury Camp and the great Long Barrow, near Dursley; Woodchester, Witcomb, Bisley and King's Stanley with their Roman villas, and many other remains. But to reach them you must first cross the river, at Gloucester.

Here the Second Augustan Legion established the first standing Legionary fortress of the west, during the early stage of the conquest; later, as we have seen, they moved to Caerleon. The fortress stood on the western fringe of the territory of the Dobunni, a powerful Celtic tribe whose land fronted that of the Silures across the river. This was one of the reasons why the Romans established a strong military base here, long before they began the conquest of Wales. They called it Glevum.

Later it became a *Coloni*—a colony for time-expired veterans like Colchester. Nothing remains of Roman Glevum save the layout of the main streets, which intersect where their Roman predecessors did. Near these cross-roads, in the centre of the town, traces of the Forum have been found, and the ruins of the *Prætorium* or Headquarters House. From time to time, during building operations, fragments of foundations and pavements have been discovered under the modern buildings; for example, a fine tessellated pavement was found under the Bon Marché stores.

The lack of visible Roman remains need worry nobody except the archæological purists. Unlike Wroxeter and Silchester, which are dead cities, or Caerleon, which dwindled into a village, Glevum has gone on living and growing. Most of us would gladly exchange the Prætorium for the splendid Cathedral, that ponderous Norman shell encased in a casket of delicate Perpendicular masonry and enriched by some of the finest medieval glass in England.

But it is well worth while to visit the Museum, where are collected some of the most interesting Roman and pre-Roman antiquities found in Gloucestershire. It is an old-fashioned building, not too well lit, but the Museum authorities have made good use of it. There is no overcrowding, the fault of many provincial Museums, and the Roman and Celtic objects are well displayed. There is a particularly interesting display of Samian ware, with a map indicating the places in which it was manufactured. Much of it came from Legoux, near the modern town of Clermont-Ferrand, and La Graufesenque, between Arles and Montans. Many of the pots bear the makers' stamps, and these help archæologists to date the layers in which the fragments were found, e.g. Solinus of Legoux (A.D. 138–180) and Genialis of La

Graufesenque (A.D. 54–79).

Coins have never greatly interested me, but there was a display in the Gloucester Museum which amusingly illustrates how the Emperors used coinage as instruments of propaganda. The reverse side of these coins were used to convey ideas which the rulers wished to spread among the people, e.g. the Emperor's achievements, like the conquest of Judea, and such conceptions as "a peaceful Empire", "the world set to rights" and abstract ideas like loyalty, victory and freedom.

Then there are the inscribed stones found in Gloucestershire. The finest is a tombstone showing a helmeted cavalryman, with spear in hand, riding down an enemy who has long hair and brandishes a broadsword. This particular officer, an auxiliary, came from Macedonia. The inscription reads:

> " *Rufus Sita, horseman of the VI Cohort of Thracians*, 40 *years of age*, 22 *years of service. His heirs, in accordance with his will, have caused* (this monument) *to be made. He lies here.*"

The stone was found near Wooton, Gloucestershire, over a century ago. There is also a charming votive tablet showing a soldier with spear and shield standing under a triangular pediment. The much-worn inscription has been translated: " *Vettinius gave* (this tablet) *made by Juventinus, to the god Romulus.*" A third inscription, found near Cirencester, reads: " *Philus, son of Cassavus, of the tribe Sequirai, lies here. He died aged* 45."

Among the many domestic objects displayed, I noticed a set of surgical instruments, with a probe and spatula, found at Kingsholme (the Legionary fortress), and an infant's feeding bottle complete with teat. Even more touching was a little terra-cotta doll, with jointed arms and legs, found in a Roman villa. There are also some well-preserved examples of " hipposandals "—probably ox-shoes—and, from Stinchcombe Villa, near the village of Stinchcombe, a set of women's toilet implements, including ear-prickers, eyebrow-tweezers, and a *ligulæ* for extracting cosmetics from phials.

Among the most recent discoveries is the fine mosaic pavement found under the basement of the Bon Marché store in Gloucester itself, and some rather elegant Roman jars from Ifold villa, near Painswick.

These and other things found scattered over Gloucestershire all testify to a high standard of material civilisation among the Romanised Britons who lived here nearly 2,000 years ago. But their art is unimpressive, especially when one compares it with such objects as those of the famous Birdlip Grave, found in 1879. In that year a road-mender with the appropriately rural name of Barnfield found three burials beside the Crickley to Birdlip road. The graves were grass-covered and had limestone slabs. In them lay the skeletons of three people, two men and a middle-aged woman. The woman was probably an important member of the Dobunni tribe, and she had with her a superb bronze mirror with an incised design inlaid with red enamel. It measures about 1 foot in diameter and the style of the decoration is typical of the Bronze Age at its best. It is a superb work of art, the product of an aristocratic culture which had attained a high degree of sophistication. In the same grave were a silver-gilt brooch, a necklace of amber beads (obviously imported) a bronze bowl of lovely shape, bracelets and bronze tweezers. The skull of the high-born lady who owned these lovely things grins down at them from a shelf at the top of the showcase—a somewhat macabre sight—but it is a well-shaped skull; she may well have been a very attractive woman.

When you set out from Gloucester to Cirencester, along A417, you can look forward to an exhilarating drive, for this is one of the finest examples of a Roman road in Britain, still in use as a main highway. Go straight through Hucclecote, past the factory, and on to a point just north of Great Witcombe, where the modern road turns left for a short distance. But don't allow yourself to be diverted. Carry straight on along that secondary road to Great Witcombe, near which are the remains of a large Roman villa, signposted as an Ancient Monument. There is more than usual left to see; the site is worth a visit if you have the time.

Returning to the main road, the rampart of the Cotswold Edge lies straight ahead; up, up you climb along the steep flanks of Birdlip Hill and then for eight glorious miles you switchback over the wolds, riding high on a broad *agger* about 25 feet wide and 6 feet high. I traversed it on a wet, windy day, when the clouds hung low over the wide fields; the wet tarmac streamed ahead and the hiss of the tyres mingled with the engine's strident beat. Then, near Brimpsfield, there was a slight change of alignment, after which the ancient road carried me straight into Cirencester, where the church tower stands high above the buried ruins of Corinium.

This was the commercial centre of the Dobunni tribe, but, unlike Glevum, modern Cirencester occupies only a small portion of the much larger Roman town. This is unusual in the west. The Roman road passed under the site of the fifteenth-century church, which must be seen.

After lunch I visited the Corinium Museum, which is quite the most beautiful building of its kind I have seen, though that of St. Albans runs it close. You approach it through a pillared portico leading off Park Street, next to the headquarters of the British Legion, and not far from the high walls of Bathurst Park.

It is a rectangular, flat-roofed building, lit by windows in the ceiling and on each side. The floor is occupied by several huge tessellated Roman pavements, beautifully revealed by the roof-lights. One of them, known as the Dyer Street pavement, has a hunting scene, with hunting-dogs in the central medallion, a winged sea-dragon and a sea-leopard pursuing a fish. Another pavement, from the same area, represents the Seasons. It is an enormous thing, consisting of nine medallions, each measuring 5 feet in diameter, but only five remain perfect. Three of the Seasons survive, Autumn, Spring and Summer, represented by the goddesses Flora, Ceres and Pomona; there is also a medallion showing Silvanus sitting backwards on an ass, and holding a wine-cup. On the centre medallion of one of the longer sides Actæon is being changed into a stag by the angry Diana; the stag's horns are sprouting from his head, while his hounds attack him.

This is one of the most pleasing tessellated pavements I have seen anywhere in Europe. The pattern is clear and beautifully executed, the colours are clean and refreshing, and not glaring as in some pavements. It must have belonged to a large and luxurious mansion. The third pavement, discovered in 1825, is more damaged than the others, but in the centre can be seen Orpheus charming the beasts, and wearing a Phrygian cap. Around him are two concentric circles, the central one showing birds—a duck, goose, hen and peacock—the other filled with animals—a lion, panther, tiger and leopard—all walking with measured tread to the sound of Orpheus' lyre.

After the grim fortresses of Wales, it is refreshing to find these remains of opulent and civilised homes, the products of the secure and peaceful life which the presence of the Legions made possible. It is fascinating also to realise that elements of Hellenic culture had penetrated to these remote Cotswold valleys more than fifteen centuries before the Stuart noblemen adorned their mansions with pictures depicting the same classical myths.

Those who believe that civilisation runs in cycles will find ample support in the Corinium Museum. Corinium in its prime must have been a magnificent city. The Museum contains massive, finely carved capitals which must have surmounted columns of great height. One of them dominates a plinth at the upper end of the Museum and its size speaks eloquently of the magnitude, as well as the splendour of the Roman buildings. Corinium was, in fact, the second largest city in Great Britain. It was the capital of the Cotswolds, the centre of the wool industry and stood in one of the richest areas of Roman Britain.

There was probably an auxiliary fort in the neighbourhood. There is a tombstone of one Sextus Galerius Genialis, a cavalryman serving in the Thracian auxiliaries, and another to Dannicus, a cavalryman serving in the Indus auxiliaries in Albinus' troop. This man, according to the inscription, was a Raurecan from North-West Switzerland, and died after serving sixteen years in the Army. Another tombstone commemorates a lady, Julia Castor, who died aged thirty-three; it was set up by her husband. The lettering is perfect and no part of the inscription is missing.

The pottery displayed at Corinium is above the usual standard, some of it is very beautiful, painted and glazed, and includes black and white bowls imported from the Rhineland. Fragments of gaily-painted wall-plaster, with red, yellow and pale blue flowers, give some slight idea of the interiors of the homes in which the richer citizens lived. Another case gives prominence to women's objects; rings, glass phials for toilet preparations, nail-cleaners, mirrors, eyebrow tweezers, brooches for holding cloaks, bodkins of bronze and bone, bronze bracelets of the expandable type and, of course, spindles and spindle-whorls.

Before you leave this absorbing collection don't omit to see the famous " Corinium acrostic ". This consists of five Latin words roughly inscribed on a piece of tile. It reads:

ROTAS
OPERA
TENET
AREPO
SATOR

which can be translated " Arepo the sower guides the wheels with work ". It can be read left to right as well as from top to bottom and from bottom to top. It may have been a charm. But all the letters of the formula are contained in the first words of the Lord's Prayer—Pater Noster—and the acrostic may possibly have been a secret sign used by the early Christians when Christianity was a forbidden religion. Undoubtedly there were Christians in these Romano-British towns. There is a small building at Silchester which may have been a Christian church, and at Caerleon, in 1954, Dr. Nash-Williams discovered a clay oil-lamp with a dotted pattern on the base which has been recognised as a secret symbol used by the early Christians to reveal their faith to their fellow-converts.

Before turning my wheels towards London, I made one minor foray along the Fosse Way (A429) north-eastwards of Cirencester, in order to visit one of the finest Roman villas in England. About eight miles along the Fosse is the tiny hamlet of Fosse Bridge, in the valley of the Colne. Here I turned left, along narrow dusty lanes, to the village of Chedworth, a sleepy little village of yellow limestone, one of scores of such hamlets which lie enfolded in their secret valleys—Coln St. Denis, Coln St. Rogers, Winson, Ablington—the names themselves spell peace.

They all seem the same—there is usually a Carolean manor-house enclosed in its garden of clipped yews, a couple of public-houses, and a street of cream-coloured houses where women sit gossiping in the sunlight, and an old man trudges behind a chestnut mare; dream-like places of enchantment where the roar of the main road seems centuries away and nothing appears to have changed since the time of George III. An illusion, of course; there are television aerials on the lichened roofs, and if you visit the pub in the evening the conversation is as likely to turn on Lady Barnet's earrings as the price of heifers at Cirencester market. None the less, these villages are the nearest approach to an escapist's paradise one is likely to find in twentieth-century England, and provide a suitably romantic approach to Chedworth's Roman villa, which is not only more complete and better-preserved than most, but occupies a site of unusual beauty.

More than twelve Roman villas have been discovered within a ten-mile radius of Cirencester, and there were probably many more. They stood near the three important highways which radiated from the town, Ermine Street, Akeman Street and the Fosse Way. There was also a fourth road, called the White Way, which ran northwards close by Chedworth and onwards to Bredon, in Worcestershire.

Chedworth Villa was discovered by a ferret. Nearly a century ago Mr. James Farrer was digging for a lost ferret in Chedworth Woods, on the property of his nephew, the Earl of Eldon, when he came upon some fragments of Roman paving which aroused his curiosity. Trial diggings disclosed walls and more pavements, and the young Earl, whose interest was aroused, agreed to finance a full-scale excavation. Not only did Mr. Farrer excavate one of the best-preserved Roman villas in Britain, but money was spent in building protective sheds above the pavements, run-offs to shield the excavated walls from the rain, and a fine Museum to house the objects found on the site. Then the villa was opened to the public, though remaining under private ownership until it was acquired by the National Trust.

Lanes signposted " To the Roman Villa " lead you gently along the foot of the wide Colne valley, through meadows golden with buttercups, beside a river as clear and sparkling as any nymph-haunted Hellenic stream. No doubt the Colne had its naiads in Roman times, and dryads lived in Chedworth Woods. One imagines that they still linger near the ruins of the temple which Farrer discovered by the river.

You climb a few hundred yards up a small side-valley and at your right, on a level space backed by woods, lie the foundations of the villa, built around three sides of a clipped lawn, overlooking gardens and orchards which fall gently away to the valley-bottom. At Chedworth on a drowsy summer's day, when the wind gently stirs the overhanging woods, and birds flit across the lawns, one feels very close to that ancient civilisation.

" This was (ever) among the number of my wishes; a portion of ground not over-large, in which was a garden, and a fountain with a continual stream close to my house, and a little woodland beside. . . ," wrote Horace from his rural retreat in the Sabine Hills. " There is a range of hills," he wrote to a friend, " broken only by a shady valley; not so shady however but that the rising sun can shine on its right slope, and the setting sun warms its left. The climate would delight you. Even the sloes and ruddy cornels bear their fruits more abundantly here than elsewhere; and the oaks and ilexes feed my herds with their acorns, and rejoice me, their master, with their shade. In fact, you might imagine a slice of leafy Tarentum had been transported hither. There is a stream too, abundant enough to give name to a stream. . . ." Apart from the orientation—Horace's villa evidently faced south—the poet's description of his country retreat near Rome almost exactly fits the site of Chedworth. Also, by a coincidence, a silver spoon found on the site of the Chedworth villa bore the name Censorinus, who may have been one of its owners. Now, one of Horace's friends was named Censorinus, and I remember as a boy being very excited by this discovery, until I found out that Chedworth Villa was not begun until the end of the second century A.D. when Horace had been dead nearly 200 years.

I shall not give a detailed description of the villa, because a well-written little National Trust guide can be bought on the spot, but among the things not to be missed is the well-preserved suite of rooms in the west wing, facing down the valley. Here one gets a vivid idea of what such country houses were like when occupied. You will see the Triclinium or dining-room, with its tessellated pavement representing the Seasons—Winter as a cloaked man holding a hare, Summer as a cupid, and Spring as a girl bearing a basket of flowers. The lower part of the walls still exist, with their hollow flue-tiles to carry the warm air from the heated areas beneath the floor, and two projecting pilasters between which, probably, a curtain was stretched to divide the room.

Along the courtyard side of this west wing runs a corridor leading to other rooms, of which the northernmost are the baths. Here you can see at a glance how the system worked. First you enter the Undressing Room or *Apodyterium* which once had a set of cupboards in which the bathers hung their clothes. From here they stepped into a paved passage which probably had a bench along one wall. Here the bathers waited their turn to enter the first chamber, the *calidarium* or hot-room, over a stone threshold worn deeply by the feet of generations. In this room the whole of the area beneath the floor was occupied by heating flues, which also ran up inside the walls. Most of the mosaic floor is well-preserved, apart from a break at one end, below which you can see the hypocaust. Next to this was a still hotter room, the floor of which has disappeared, and a peculiar curved projection which may have been a hot immersion bath, though it is thought that at a later date it was converted into a basin or *labrum*, from which warm water could be thrown over the bather. Near this point you can see the arched doorway (restored) which may have been the entrance from the outside for the stoker. At the northern end of the paved corridor is a perfectly preserved cold plunge bath with steps leading down to it, and the original lead drainpipe still in position.

Now leave the west wing and cross the grass at the north-west corner of the enclosure. Here is an octagonal basin of stone, the *Nymphæum* or water-shrine, behind which rise the woods. It had an apsidal chamber at the west end, in which was found a small uninscribed altar, doubtless to the deity of the waters. The basin could contain about 1,500 gallons, insufficient for such a large villa, so it seems certain that there would be other reservoirs, probably above the slope on the northern end.

In describing Bignor in Sussex, I mentioned that Romano-British villas were not merely country retreats, but the residential and administrative centres of farming estates. Sometimes manufacturing was carried on within them. This evidently happened at Chedworth, where the north wing (in the last days of the villa) was given over to processes connected with cloth-making. " Its features," says the Guide " are to-day unevenly preserved, and water rather than fire has disfigured them. The entire north wing with its furnaces must have remained working almost to the end of the villa's habitation. It probably fulfilled several different functions at various times, and its isolation from the other two wings confirms the suggestion that part of it was used for fulling and dyeing." The house had passed to an absentee owner who did not live there but put it to profitable use.

A deep square chamber at the north-west end was evidently a furnace, with the draught channel still visible. Three long iron " blooms " or anvils were found here, suggesting that this was at some time a smithy. Further east are two large dipping tanks, semi-circular in shape, which, when first found, were coated on the inside with pink cement like similar tanks found at Pompeii. In these basins men and boys would tread out linen, cloth or any material which required cleaning or fulling. There is also a square rinsing tank, and a chamber with an apsidal end with substantial stone supports for the floor. It may have once housed the fullers' presses.

Little of the south wing is left except for the remains of the domestic kitchens which were near the living-room. There is a story, which I have not heard confirmed or denied by archæologists, that on the Chedworth site there still exists a species of edible snail which is not a native to Britain, but which the Romans are known to have relished. No doubt they raised sheep and cattle for food, and may even have grown vines on the slopes of the hills. They certainly imported wine from Gaul. The great jars (amphoræ) in which it was shipped have been found in London and elsewhere.

The little Museum, like that at Corstopitum in Northumberland, is far more fascinating than most of the larger town Museums, because you come straight to it from the site on which its contents were found. It contains a fine model showing the original appearance of the villa, and even the most mundane domestic objects—such as locks and keys, carpenters' and smiths' tools, pottery and glassware, gain in interest because you are standing in the place near which these things were made and used.

Nevertheless, I feel that for most visitors the memory of Chedworth which will live longest is the site itself, the rustling woods through which winds the bridle-path to the White Way—the path which Censorinus and his family must often have used—the mellowed walls of Cotswold stone, the pillars which once supported a shady verandah, and the gardens sloping gently down to the river. Was there perhaps a fountain like the one of which Horace sang . . .

> " Thou too among famed fountains shall be known,
> When I thy holm-oak sing, whose branches wave
> Above thy rocky cave,
> Whence leap thy babbling waters down."

. . . and did Censorinus sometimes recall the poet's lines as he sat beside it on a summer day ?

* * * * *

From Chedworth I idled back along the lanes until striking the Fosse Way at Fosse Bridge. I could of course, have turned left at this point, followed the Fosse for a few miles and then turned right on to the main A40 road, which goes through Northleach, Witney, Oxford, and so to London. Alternatively, one could return to Cirencester and drive to London through Swindon, Hungerford, Newbury and Reading. However, I was determined to follow the original Roman road to London as far as possible, and a close study of the Ordnance Survey map revealed that a large part of it still existed. Moreover, a considerable section—that which crosses the Lambourne Downs in Berkshire—was marked as a secondary road, which gave promise of a less tedious trip. This is the route which I finally took and I was well rewarded by a most interesting journey, first along the main trunk road until it foolishly left the Roman line (taking with it the bulk of the traffic) and then along the true Roman road which, though it assumes various shapes, sizes and numbers, carries one straight across the Berkshire Downs to Spinæ (Speen, near Reading). It passes through attractively unfrequented country and pleasant villages which the main road misses.

The route is as follows: Cirencester, through Cricklade, to Stratton St. Margaret, just north of Swindon. A mile beyond this point the main road makes an abrupt turn to the right and this is where you desert it. Carry straight on along the secondary road which follows the Roman alignment, and keep doggedly to this line whatever the signposts may say. Sometimes the old road narrows to a mere lane, at others it expands to its original breadth, but it hardly ever deviates from a straight line. However, there is a point beyond Wanborough where the road switchbacks over chalk downs and winds considerably. This was evidently one of those places at which, the old road having decayed, the Anglo-Saxons had abandoned it; but I was certain that bits of it must still survive, so I kept a sharp eye open for them. I was right. Just beyond a crossroads look out for a signpost marked Russley (left) and Baydon (right). Stop at this road-fork and walk back down the hill along which you have come. Count seven telegraph posts and halfway between the seventh and the eighth posts from the road fork a wire fence on the left of the road is bent at a right-angle, forming an " L ". If you stand at this point and look back towards the road junction, you will see a wood a couple of hundred yards away on the right. You will then see the *agger* of the old Roman road as a raised bank, going towards and into the wood. Now turn your back and look in the opposite direction across the modern road. If you sight between the eighth and ninth telegraph posts, you should detect a strip of lighter green going across the fields. This marks the line of the Roman road, clearly visible when I saw it in the autumn, though it might not be so clear in the summer. Here the voice of Rome speaks clearly, for whereas the " modern " Anglo-Saxon road meanders in a leisurely fashion up the hillside, the Roman road can be seen running as straight as a die through the wood and beyond it.

Now return to the fork and take the right-hand road towards Baydon. As you climb Baydon Hill you will see the *agger*, which is quite high at this point, running beside the modern highway. At Woodlands Lodge the modern road wiggles to the right, but soon returns to the line of the Roman highway. Then for mile after mile it goes straight on, at times quite narrow, but very straight. It is an unclassified modern road, but the surface is excellent and it keeps its alignment wonderfully. Sign-posts to right and left point to Lansdown and Marlborough, but keep straight on, unless you want to pause at one of the delightful little inns with which the road is thoughtfully provided.

At Shefford you cross A338—the road from Wantage to Hungerford—but take the narrow lane opposite which follows the Roman alignment, passing north to the church at Woodlands. About a mile beyond Shefford the lane suddenly takes a sharp left-hand turn, and here there is a gate leading to a sloping field. Keen *agger*-hunters can here see where the Roman road continues quite clearly as a low bank running up the slope of the meadow, to rejoin the modern lane further on. After a few more straight miles through pleasant country, you strike the main A4 road just outside Speen (Roman Spinæ), and here you get your last glimpse of the *agger* away to the left of the main road, keeping you company as you drive through Speen into Newbury.

CHAPTER THIRTEEN

THE TOWN IN THE WOODS

I HAD one last visit to make before returning to London, and that was to Silchester, Calleva Atrebatum—" the town in the woods ". In Roman times the road I had followed from Cirencester ran straight into Calleva, which was one of the most important road junctions in the country. But, unlike Cirencester, Winchester, Dorchester and other Roman towns, Calleva was deserted after the occupation and now lies buried under the Hampshire fields. It has dwindled into a mere hamlet and the five great roads which once streamed into it now stop short, so that one must find one's way along lanes so narrow and devious that they seem to have been designed to conceal the old capital of the Atrebates rather than reveal it.

Silchester lies approximately in the centre of a diamond-shaped area of land, bounded on the west by A33 (Reading to Basingstoke) and on the east by A4 and A340 (Reading to Aldermaston and Basingstoke). From London the best approach is via Reading, but I came to it via Newbury, first along A4, then sharp right along A340 for about four miles, when I plunged into the lanes on the left, which carried me into a countryside which seemed utterly remote from that seen from the crowded trunk road. It was an autumn evening, and mist rising from the still valley-bottoms clung to the fields; the dark clumps of woodland seemed to absorb the growing dusk as blotting-paper absorbs ink. Again I marvelled that in this overcrowded island there should exist, not far from London, a landscape so detached from our strident twentieth-century world. Even the names on the sign-posts were not marked on my map, and it was only by a fortunate accident that I came upon one bearing the name Silchester.

I knew I was approaching one of the most important road junctions in Roman Britain, where stood the large and flourishing city of Calleva Atrebatum, guarded by mighty walls and enclosing 80 acres of buildings—mansions, tradesmens' shops, public baths and *basilicæ*—a town from which five great roads had radiated like the spokes of a wheel. Yet there was nothing in this miniature landscape of small fields, hedgerows and tiny hamlets to suggest such a place. Then I saw the name SILCHESTER on a metal plaque such as one sees at the approach to important towns. I drove on through the narrow lanes, under the damp branches of ancient trees, but saw no sign of a village, or even a hamlet. There was only ploughland, meadows with grazing cattle and an occasional lonely farm-house.

Again I came upon a metal plaque with the name SILCHESTER. Surely I was approaching it now? But still there were only the fields and the darkening sunset. Then, just as I had begun to give up hope, I saw the dark outline of a high wall rising above the hedgerow on my right and running parallel with the lane. I got out and looked more closely. Yes, it was a Roman wall. I was at Silchester.

I followed the wall to the north-east corner, then turned right until the wall ended. Here, beyond a deep ditch, rose a fine twelfth-century church, its new whitewash picking up what remained of the evening light. A path led me through the churchyard to the fields beyond. There was a large poultry farm nearby, and the murmurings of hundreds of geese rose from the huge pens. But apart from the great wall stretching away to the north there was absolutely nothing to be seen of Roman Silchester.

Underneath the fields lies the best preserved Romano-British town in the British Isles. In 1864, the Reverend J. G. Joyce began systematic excavations on behalf of the second Duke of Wellington. He worked there for fourteen years, disclosing streets of houses, the market-place, baths, shops and temples. From 1890, the Silchester

Excavation Fund took over and worked there for nineteen years. More and more of the city was uncovered, photographed, drawn and planned. In 1909 the work ceased. Twenty-nine years later, Mrs. M. A. Cotton carried out important work at Silchester on behalf of the Ministry of Works, when she established the date of the defences and street plan; and within the last few years Mr. George C. Boon, working on a small scale and within a modest budget, has proved that a Celtic settlement existed here in pre-Roman times. All this is very valuable archæological information; but the fact remains that no one has seen Roman Silchester as a whole for nearly fifty years. Why?

The answer, given by Mr. Boon himself in his " New Guide to the Roman City of Calleva Atrebatum ", is that " the city occupies part of Manor Farm, and thus the working arrangement had to be that the area leased for excavation each year should be restored for cultivation afterwards ". The Forum-Basilica, he admits, " with one or two other buildings which Joyce had uncovered, did remain open from about 1875 to 1909, when structural deterioration forbade longer exposure ".

From a purely local standpoint this may seem an adequate answer, and I can understand that Mr. Boon and his fellow-archæologists working at Silchester must accept the existing situation, whatever their private opinions may be. There are some archæologists who would rather that sites such as Silchester were kept as they are, and not excavated, preserved by shelters and opened to the public. There are other equally distinguished scholars who take the opposite view, in the belief that the more the public can see of Roman Britain the more likelihood there is of public support for future excavations. I do not know to which school Mr. Boon and his colleagues belong, but as an outside observer with a deep interest in archæology and some experience of presenting it to the general public the situation seems to me absurd.

Looked at from a national standpoint is it not ridiculous

that one of the finest Romano-British sites in Britain, a site unencumbered by modern buildings, where excavations have proved that a great city exists, should be permanently buried? If you wish to find out what lies under these Hampshire fields, you have to read the excavation reports of the Reverend Joyce and the Silchester Excavation Committee, and examine their photographs. Here was a city of some 80 acres, systematically laid out with a rectilinear street plan, containing within its walls a great Forum, or market-place, a Town Hall, public baths, temples, street after street of villas and shops, some with fine tesselated pavements, and what may be the earliest Christian church in Great Britain.

The city was laid out round about A.D. 90–120, although the site was occupied by the invaders shortly after the conquest. By the end of the first century, in accordance with the Roman policy of building towns in Britain, the city was begun, and the Forum, Basilica, Baths and Temples were built. The Forum was overlooked on one site by the Basilica, or Town Hall, 234 feet long, 58 feet wide and 60 feet high, with two rows of Corinthian columns 27 feet high. It must have looked like a cathedral. Not far away were the great Public Baths, with a portico 65 feet long. Then there were temples, two of which now lie under the churchyard. In the foundations of a third, excavators in 1907 found the name CALLEVAE inscribed on a stone, thus confirming the identity of the city, the name of which was known from the Antonine Itinerary.

Next to the Forum was an apsidal building with nave and aisles, which is very similar to early churches in other parts of the Roman Empire. It may be a Christian church, though it is similar in plan to two temples found in Rome which were devoted to pagan mystery-cults. If it was Christian, it must date from the period following the Edict of Toleration issued by the Emperor Constantine in A.D. 313.

Calleva was divided into thirty-seven *insulæ* or islands, separated by a carefully planned system of streets, most of which have been traced. Along these streets were the mansions of the richer citizens, public buildings, smaller houses, and many shops. Some of the houses, writes Mr. Boon, " consisted of rows of rooms, connected by open corridors, ranged round two or three sides of a court. In the largest we can recognise the dwellings of the tribal councillors, or decurions. The houses mostly had flint wall footings with tile quoins, a half-timbered superstructure, plastered and painted within and outside, and tiled roofs. Hypocausts, heating systems and mosaic pavements were found in many of them. Domestic water supply came from wells, and sewage disposal was by cess-pit."

What kind of people lived in the city of Calleva Atrebatum? Mostly British tribesmen, the Atrebates, who had emigrated to Britain from Gaul round about 50 B.C. It now seems certain that they occupied the site before the coming of the Romans, and probably threw up defensive earthworks. When the Romans persuaded the conquered Atrebates to build a city on the Roman plan, they probably utilised the existing defences—which would account for the polygonal plan.

After the conquest the old tribal aristocracies would be allowed to retain some of their power, and the magistrates of the town would be drawn from the wealthier classes. But, of course, they would wear Roman dress and would have to merge their old tribal customs with those of Rome. " Life," writes Mr. Boon, " would be in the main comfortable and peaceful during the Hadrianic and Antonine heyday. The cultural standards of the inhabitants were doubtless not high, but from chance scrawls which have been preserved we can judge that they were mostly literate, and *wrote* Latin even if they did not speak it habitually."

The city was occupied for at least 400 years, during which its defences were altered several times. At first there was an outer earthwork—parts of which can still be seen—thrown up a few years after the Conquest. Then, about 120 years later, in the Antonine period, the inhabitants made a bank and ditch to replace this outer earthwork, and reduced the city area to about 100 acres. The reason for this is unknown, but it may well have been a precautionary measure taken when the Brigantes, a Northern British tribe, revolted about A.D. 154–8. Some time in the Third Century the present stone wall was built.

Though Calleva seems to have been occupied, in part, right down to the end of the Fourth Century, there was a severe decline in the third century, of which one sees evidence in cities all over the Empire. The Roman State was becoming top-heavy, burdened by an army of civil servants which tried to wring from the exhausted Provinces more than they could yield. As always in such cases, there was corruption and bribery. Civil war added to the confusion; high taxation led to inflation, and the richer citizens began to desert the cities, probably to escape the rapacious tax-gatherers. This happened at Silchester as in other places. Yet coins found in the Forum area seem to indicate that the machinery of local government went on functioning to the end.

In the fifth and sixth centuries, Saxon settlers from the Thames Valley began to threaten the area, and from this period may date the earthwork on Padworth Common, two miles away. Finally, the city was deserted, grass grew over the ruined walls, and from that date to this it has never been occupied. Even its identity was lost until, in the nineteenth century, archæologists began to dig there.

I would not like it to be thought from the fact that there are so few visible remains that Silchester does not repay a visit. This would be a superficial judgment, and grossly unfair to the devoted people who have dug the site, and set up the fascinating little Museum nearby. It contains a small but interesting collection of Roman antiquities of the type with which the reader will by now be familiar—fragments of tessellated pavements, ornaments, brooches and inscriptions, of which the most moving is a small fragment of limestone bearing the name CALLEVAE—a pathetic contrast with the proud city which it commemorates. An old Curator with a welcoming smile and a soft Hampshire accent showed me round, and opened albums of photographs of the excavations at which he assisted more than fifty years ago.

When you leave the Museum, follow the lane for half a mile, when you will see the great wall on your right. Where this ends, near the site of the East Gate, enter the churchyard and cross the fields past the poultry farm. If you take with you the " Guide to the Roman City of Calleva Atrebatum ", which you can buy for a shilling at the Museum, you will be able to trace the outline of the ancient city, and identify the Outer Earthwork, the Severan Wall, the ditch of the Antonine rampart, and the ruins of the North Gate. Near the church you will recognise the ruins of the amphitheatre, which, as at Caerleon and Dorchester, stood outside the wall. From the church you may follow the drove-road across the centre of Calleva to the high hedge which follows the line of the ancient ramparts. The North and South Gates can easily be identified as gaps in the trees and undergrowth which hide the backing mound of the wall.

Personally, I feel that the best time to see Calleva Atrebatum is in the late evening, as I saw it after the long drive from Gloucester. From the churchyard, looking west, the ground fell away in a gentle slope from west to south. If I had been standing on that spot in Roman times I would have been looking across the roof-tops of Calleva. Near the centre of the drove-road would have stood the columned portico of the Basilica fronting its great square, and from it would have radiated well-paved streets of substantial houses, some enclosed by gardens, others, the streets of tradespeople, huddled tightly together. There would be the sound of children's voices, and dogs barking. Smoke would be rising from the chimneys, and the silhouette of the sentry would be moving slowly along the top of the ramparts.

I saw it on a melancholy autumn evening, with mist rising from the fields and a few birds calling from the high trees. The atmosphere was mysterious, almost eerie. Unlike Lincoln, Gloucester, York and Chester, where the medieval and modern have almost erased the memory of the Roman remains beneath, Roman Silchester lies only skin-deep. One is aware that only a thin covering of turf and soil covers the bones of the Roman past.

They are still there—the mansions with their richly-coloured pavements, the streets of shops, the Forum, the Basilica, the temples and baths and paved streets. And while it may be all very well for romantics to exercise their imaginations by repeopling fields and hedgerows with streets and houses, I could not help feeling that here, if enough people wanted it—there could be a British Pompeii. It is all there, waiting to be uncovered.

Calleva Atrebatum lies under valuable agricultural land, and no one wishes to interfere with food production. Also it is private property—and the proprietor's rights must be respected. But if the Government wanted it for a military airfield, or a town council wanted the land for a new housing estate, can one doubt what the answer would be? Is it mere sentimentalism to suggest that the revelation of our country's historic past might have at least an equal claim to consideration?

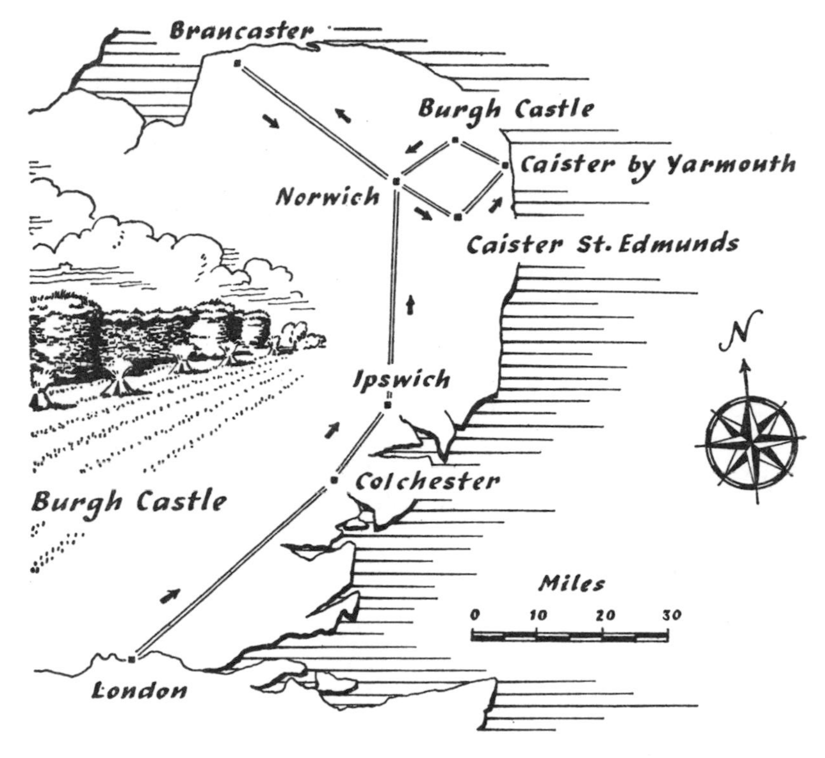

CHAPTER FOURTEEN

THE MARCH TO THE NORTH—I

UP to this point our journeys in Roman Britain have been confined mainly to the civilian south and west. From now on, except for this and the concluding chapters, we shall be visiting the military area to the north, which included Scotland, Northern England, and parts of the East Midlands. I have left this section to the last for the reason given in the early part of this book—that I would try, as far as was possible, to relate our tour to the successive stages of the conquest and occupation. The South, West and parts of the Midlands were over-run in the early stages; Ostorius Scapula established a provisional frontier from the Severn to the Humber about five years after the landing, but the progress of the Romans northward was much harder and slower. The Romans did not reach the line of Hadrian's Wall until the early 70's A.D. The wall itself, between the Tyne and the Solway, was not begun until 112 A.D., and the Antonine Wall, which joins the Forth to the Clyde, was not built until A.D. 140. These, however, were permanent fortifications. Agricola penetrated into Scotland many years before they were built; even so, the battle of Mons Graupius, in which he defeated the Caledonians, was not fought until around A.D. 84, forty-one years after the Emperor Claudius landed in Kent.

Roman remains in the north of England are sparser and more widely scattered than in the south; moreover they are mostly military. The Ordnance Survey Map of Roman Britain shows this clearly. South of the Fosse Way there are many civil settlements; large and small towns and clusters of country villas, especially in the Cotswolds. North of the Fosse you will see a few big towns, legionary bases like Chester, Lincoln and York, posting stations along the military roads, but the rest are forts; forts behind the Antonine Wall, forts behind Hadrian's Wall, forts along the coast and in the mountains of Wales. To the Romans North Britain must have been what the North-West Frontier of India was to the British Army. Even to-day the north of England is, in general, a sterner, wilder country than the softer landscape of the south. There are parts of it, in Yorkshire, County Durham and Northumberland, which must have looked much the same to the men of the Roman Army marching north to the Wall.

The journey begins at Colchester, which Claudius entered in triumph at the head of the Ninth Legion. From here the Legion and its auxiliaries moved slowly northward, occupying Lincoln before the end of the reign of Claudius (A.D. 54). This city, which the Romans called Lindum Colonia, became the headquarters and base of the Ninth Legion and remained so for some time. Meanwhile, the Fourteenth " Gemina " and the Twentieth " Valeria Victrix " were advancing north-west along the line of the Watling Street, while Vespasian led the

Second Augusta into the west.

The advance of the Ninth Legion was probably by Cambridge (Durolipons) and Icklingham (Camboritum). However, on my outward journey I deliberately avoided the southern part of this road in order to include East Anglia, which in Roman times was the territory of the famous Iceni tribe. Boadicea (Boudicca) was for a time their queen.

From Colchester I first took the main A12 road to Ipswich, then turned on to A45 as far as Claydon where I joined A140 which led me straight to Norwich. North of Yaxley this road follows the Roman alignment, and if you look at the map you will see that a southerly prolongation of this northern stretch will lead not to Ipswich but to Camulodunum (Colchester).

At Norwich itself there was only a small Roman village. The Roman city was Venta Icenorum—" the town of the Iceni "—now called Caistor St. Edmunds. You can find it by turning right from the main A140 road about three miles south of Norwich. The lane is signposted Caistor; after a short distance the lane crosses a small stream, after which you take the right-hand fork. About 200 yards beyond this junction you will see the grass-covered mounds of Venta Icenorum high on the right-hand side of the lane. Between the church and road is a long, high bank which marks the east wall of the city. Go through the church gate and mount the bank. To the right the north wall of Venta strides across the fields, and from this vantage point you can trace the outer limits of Boudicca's city which, like Silchester, is now completely hidden under fields and hedgerows. On the west side is the gap in the bank where the west gate stood, the gate through which in Roman times, the great road entered along which you travelled from Colchester. Its *agger* is visible at several points, bulging out of the meadows. There is nothing else to be seen. The site was excavated twenty years ago. Unfortunately the results of the excavation have never been published.

The story of Boudicca's revolt is well known. She was

the wife of the King of the Iceni, Prasutagus. Like Cogidumnus, King of the Regnenses of Noviomagus (Chichester) (see Chapter Six) he became a client-king under Roman overlordship, and when he died bequeathed half his property to the Emperor. The rest he divided between his two daughters, but for some reason Boudicca herself does not appear to have been a legatee. One wonders why.

As there was no male claimant to the throne, there could be no question of the kingdom continuing. The Romans had had trouble with another British queen, Cartimandua of the Brigantes (she who handed over Caratacus). Then the Roman treasury agents in Britain acted very clumsily. They began carving up the legacy of Prasutagus and revoked the grants which Claudius had made to the tribal chiefs. Tacitus wrote scornfully:

" Kingdom and household alike were plundered like prizes of war, the one by Roman officers, the other by Roman slaves. As a beginning, the widow Boudicca was flogged and their daughters raped. The Icenian chiefs were deprived of their hereditary rights, as if the Romans had been given the whole country. The king's own relatives were treated like slaves."

So the Iceni rose in terrible anger, and with them rose the Trinovantes of Essex, whose capital was at Colchester. Here the Romans had established a *Colonia* for their retired soldiers.

" The settlers," wrote Tacitus, " drove the Trinovantes from their homes and land, and called them prisoners and slaves. The troops encouraged the settlers' outrages, since their own way of behaving was the same—they looked forward to similar licence for themselves. Moreover, the temple erected to the divine Claudius was a blatant stronghold of alien rule, and its observances were a pretext to make the natives appointed as its priests drain the whole country dry." (In Chapter Five I described the foundations of this great temple which still exist under Colchester Castle.)

Led by Boudicca, the rebels moved on Camulodunum.

"Delirious women chanted of destruction at hand They cried that in the local senate-house outlandish yells had been heard; the theatre had echoed with shrieks; and at the mouth of the Thames a phantom settlement had been seen in ruins. A blood-red colour was the sea, too, and shapes like human corpses left by the ebb-tide were interpreted hopefully by the Britons and with terror by the settlers."

There were only 200 Roman soldiers in Camulodunum. Another 200, inadequately armed, were sent by Catus Decianus, the then Procurator (Financial Officer). All were slain. P. Petilius Cerialis, Legate of the Ninth Legion, then at Lincoln, marched south in the hope of saving the city but by sheer numbers the British overwhelmed these seasoned troops and slew 2,000 of them—one third of their total strength. Cerialis and the cavalry escaped. Catus Decianus—whose avarice and cruelty were partly responsible for the revolt—managed to sneak away to Gaul. Having no defensive walls, Camulodunum soon fell. The city was plundered, the inhabitants butchered and the new-built temple of the divine Emperor went up in flames. Then the Iceni and the Trinovantes, led by the Queen, moved towards St. Albans (Verulamium) and Londinium, which by this time had grown into an important commercial centre.

Suetonius Paulinus, Governor of Britain at this time (about A.D. 60) was far away in Anglesey, where he had destroyed the Druid stronghold. He sent a message summoning the Second Augusta from Gloucester, and then, at the head of a small body of troops, moved by forced marches south-eastward along the line of the Watling Street, which is now the Holyhead road. His small force, presumably of cavalry, hurried down through what are now Shropshire and Cannock Chase, and over the Dunstable Downs to London. But the enemy were near in enormous numbers, and the Governor realised that he had no forces capable of resisting them. The Second Augusta had not moved. Its acting commander feared he might share Cerialis's fate and disobeyed orders.

Suetonius's own troops were far behind. He decided to abandon the city.

" Unmoved by lamentations and appeals " writes the Roman historian, " Suetonius gave the signal for departure. The inhabitants were allowed to accompany him. But those who stayed because they were women, or old, or attached to the amenities of the place, were slaughtered by the enemy. Verulamium suffered the same fate. . . ." He adds that: " The British didn't take or sell prisoners, or practise other war-time exchanges. They could not wait to cut throats, hang, burn and crucify—as though avenging, in advance, the retribution that was on its way."

The words of Tacitus wipe away the centuries and reading him one feels transported not only to the scene but the very instant of the action, especially when he describes Boudicca rallying her followers before the final battle.

" Boudicca drove round all the tribes in a chariot with her daughters in front of her. ' We British are used to woman commanders in war ' she cried. ' I am not fighting for my kingdom and wealth now. I am fighting as an ordinary person for my lost freedom, my bruised body, and my outraged daughters. Nowadays Roman rapacity does not even spare our bodies. Old people are killed, virgins raped. But the gods will grant us the vengeance we deserve. The Roman divisions which dared to fight us are annihilated. The others cower in their camps, or watch for a chance to escape. They will never face the din and roar of our thousands, much less the shock of our onslaught. Consider how many of you are fighting, and why! Then you will win the battle, or perish. That is what I, a woman, plan to do! Let the men live in slavery if they will! ' "

It was a brave speech—if she actually delivered it—but unavailing. The Britons had become over-confident, trusting in their numbers to such an extent that they even brought along their families to see the anticipated victory. But the Romans had chosen the battlefield, and their disciplined formations won the day. Boudicca's forces were pinned helplessly against their own luggage-lines which cut off their retreat. The defeat became a massacre in which, according to one account, 80,000 Britons were slaughtered. Boudicca fled, and died soon afterwards, some said by taking poison.

Suetonius had triumphed, but the Romans had suffered a severe shock. After the recall of the Governor they adopted a more liberal policy which may have been inspired by Julius Classicianus, the new Financial Officer who succeeded Catus Decianus. The wife of Classicianus, Julia Pacata, was herself the daughter of a Celtic chieftain of the Rhineland, and their memorial stone was found near the Roman wall on Tower Hill, London, where a duplicate inscription can still be seen.

* * * * *

Although Norwich has no Roman ruins, it has a splendid Museum—one of the best in the country—a model of what a County Museum should be. The Roman collection is in the gallery devoted to objects dating from the Neolithic (New Stone Age) to early Saxon times. The objects are very clearly and intelligently displayed, so that the visitor, by moving from case to case, can follow the history of Norfolk from some 2,000 B.C. to the seventh century A.D. Thus the Roman period falls naturally into its appropriate place, and this is particularly important because, in such a context, one can study the culture of the Celtic peoples which the Romans conquered.

For instance, there is a fascinating collection of silver coins of the Iceni tribe. The Iceni were great horse-breeders (like the people of " horse-rearing Argos " in Greece) and the rich, flat landscape of Norfolk seems entirely appropriate to such a pursuit. It is not difficult, even to-day, to imagine the Iceni exercising their mounts over open country, and perhaps practising those astonishing cavalry charges which impressed Julius Cæsar. Inevitably one thinks also of Boudicca, with her long flowing hair and her chariot with knife-blades fixed to the axles.

" In stature she was very tall," wrote Cassius Dio, " in appearance most terrifying, in the glance of her eye most fierce, and her voice was harsh; a great mass of the tawniest hair fell to her hips; around her neck was a large golden necklace. . . ."

In the archæological collection of the Norwich Museum are some heavy gold necklaces, or " torcs ", shaped like horseshoes which may have come from Ireland.

In 1946 a great hoard of Roman coins was found at Caistor-by-Yarmouth. They are so perfectly preserved that the portraits of the Emperors and their wives can easily be studied. The Museum authorities have placed beside them photographic enlargements which are in themselves a tribute to the ancient craftsmen who could make a die (in reverse) so accurately that the resultant impression when enlarged, presents a vivid and lively portrait. One can recognise Nero's puffy jowl, Vespasian's pugnacious profile with its bruiser's chin, the grave face of Septimius Severus who had the task of reconquering northern Britain after the Caledonians broke through the frontier defences, the mad profile of Commodus (180–192) whose skill in archery was such that it was said he could shoot off the head of a running ostrich.

Here also is the elegant Faustina, wife of the philosopher Emperor, Marcus Aurelius and the Empress Lucilla, whose portrait in profile bears an extraordinary resemblance to the image of Queen Elizabeth II as shown on our modern coinage.

Other recent finds on view are a magnificent ceremonial cavalry helmet of gilded metal, dredged from the River Wensum at Worthing, Norfolk, in 1947. It has an eagle's beak on the crest, and a design of sea-dragons embossed on each side. Notice also the figures XII roughly scratched on the shoulder-piece.

Equally impressive in a different way is another recent discovery—the famous Snettisham treasure—which was found in 1948 during deep ploughing. It consists of three hoards of gold ornaments, including " torcs "—horseshoe-shaped necklaces—and gold and tin coins and other objects dating from between 100 B.C. and A.D. 100.

One can spend several profitable days exploring Roman East Anglia, using Norwich as a base. For example, there is Brancaster on the coast between Burnham Market and Hunstanton. Here stood Roman Branodunum, one of the forts of the Saxon Shore where a garrison of Dalmatian cavalry was stationed for a time. Portions of the fortress can still be traced. Then there is Castle Acre, a Roman station about five miles north of Swaffham, one mile west of the road between Swaffham and Fakenham—A1065. You reach it via a by-road which branches west from A1065 at Newton.

There is little to see at Castle Acre itself but it is on the line of the main northern Roman road in East Anglia, which ran from Chelmsford (Caesaromagus) by way of Ixworth, and from there to Holme-next-the-sea, a total distance of ninety miles. Margary says that this road may well have been of equal importance to the London—Colchester road. The Saxons called it Peddar's Way and the Romans evidently designed it to give direct access to the coast at the Wash. From Castle Acre you can follow this road nearly to the coast if you are prepared to walk part of the way over a grass-grown track. The stretch between Anmer and Fring is particularly fine—a ruler-straight embankment marching across a wide, flat landscape above which the sea-birds cry. It is clearly marked on the $\frac{1}{4}$-inch Ordnance Survey Map (Sheet 9) and well repays exploration, though I do not recommend it to motorists.

Another coastal fort, similar to Brancaster but better preserved, is Burgh Castle, which can be reached easily from Norwich via Yarmouth. It lies a few miles inland from Gorleston, and overlooks the River Waveney. The north and east walls still stand to a considerable height, although the west wall has gone and the south looks as if it will soon follow it. From the battlements you can look out over the fields of waving wheat where once a Roman cavalry regiment—the Stablesian Horse—used to exercise. One wonders what may still lie under those fields if money could be found to finance an excavation.

East Anglia has yielded thousands of Roman objects; over 100 sites have been found in Suffolk alone. For example, at Ickingham a hoard of 400 coins was discovered, and at Benacre 920 silver coins in a leaden box. The famous statue of Nero now at the British Museum was discovered at Barking Hall. In the same Museum there is a superb service of pewter plate, also from Ickingham.

But perhaps the most wonderful discovery of all was the Mildenhall Treasure, found at Mildenhall, Suffolk, in 1946. This splendid group of silver tableware has survived almost unharmed some sixteen centuries since its burial during the turbulent closing years of Roman rule in Britain. It consists of a great circular dish with friezes enclosing a lively scene showing the triumph of Bacchus over Hercules, silver platters with a scene of dancing satyrs and mænads, a small dish with a flange and circular panel ornamented with *niello*, bowls (one with an ornamented cover), ladles, goblets, and spoons of exquisite design and workmanship. This silver plate, among the richest ever found in Britain, is now one of our national treasures, and is on exhibit at the British Museum.

It is, however, not of local manufacture, but appears to have been imported from various places; the dish and two platters from some Mediterranean factory, the niello dish from the east, and other pieces from Gaul. Unlike the Traprian Treasure, a pirate's hoard which we shall see in Edinburgh, the Mildenhall silverware seems to have been buried by its owners during the troubled period of the later fourth or early fifth century.

From Norwich I drove to the recently excavated Roman town of Caistor-by-Yarmouth, over a flat landscape of great cabbage fields, grazing meadows, and occasional lonely farms under a wide sky. This is real farming country where the only heavy transport one sees are farm lorries. At the red-brick village of Acle I turned left and followed A1064 through Burgh St. Margaret and Filby to Caistor, which is clearly signposted. It is a small seaside village of one main street, but is obviously developing rapidly as an appendage of Yarmouth—three miles away. Turn along the lane by the church and after about 100 yards you will come to a group of newly-built villas on both sides of the road. Behind the fence on the right-hand side, where the building estate ends, lies the south part of an important Roman city. It was found by accident, by workers who were digging the foundations of the new houses.

Then Mr. Charles Green and his helpers made excavations on the north side of the road and revealed the south wall of the city with its footing, and the foundations of the south gate with what appears to have been a small tower on the west side, probably for storm warnings.

So far only a small portion of the site has been excavated. This seems to have been the artisans' quarter, but under the cabbage field to the north lies the rest of the city, so far unseen and unknown. Here, perhaps, the excavators will find the dwellings of the richer inhabitants of Caistor. In the part so far excavated you can see the foundations of granaries with a hypocaust for drying the grain; also a smithy and a finely built stone water-tank.

When I visited Caistor in the late autumn of 1955, the Ministry of Works was preparing the site for public exhibition, and by the time these words appear in type the visitor will have the benefit of an illustrated leaflet with a plan, and also a museum for the display of the objects found on the site. Some of these are likely to be macabre judging from what I saw in the Curator's temporary hut. There, arranged in fruit-boxes and paper-bags, were the bones and skulls of men whose bodies had been found under what is now the trim little building estate. Some of the skulls were pierced with holes, such as might have been made by weapons, and one had been hacked across the crown perhaps by a sword or axe.

The Curator, Mr. Bullock, showed me photographs of

the burials as they were found. They were nearly all tall skeletons and lay in shallow graves, without coffins, all aligned in approximately the same direction. This, apparently was the cemetery of an Anglo-Saxon settlement which grew up in the ruins of the Roman town. Anglo-Saxon hearths have also been found in the filled-up ditches outside the town hall.

Most recently Mr. Green has found graves which have been described as " pseudo ship burials ". They were, says Mr. Green, " little ' houses of the dead ' which seem to have projected above the soil and to have been made out of pieces of the sides of clinker-built boats ". The boats must have been in the nature of beach skiffs about 15 feet to 20 feet long. Above the head of one grave was found a coin of Egbert, grandfather of Alfred the Great, which suggests an eighth-century date, some 400 years after Britain ceased to be Roman.

Although later visitors will have the opportunity of seeing the Caistor exhibits properly displayed, I am not sorry I saw Caistor in 1955. For, alas, even the most beautifully arranged museum display cannot recapture the excitement and wonder of a " dig " in progress. During that brief period the long-dead city seems to stir in its sleep. The objects lie on or near the places where they were found, just where they were left by their last users. When they find their last resting-place in glass cases—the pottery artistically grouped, the cosmetic pots carded and labelled, the skulls in neat rows with a museum number on their foreheads—then the site seems truly dead. Its inhabitants have gone for ever, and there remain only a few walls dividing the well-clipped Ministry of Works grass.

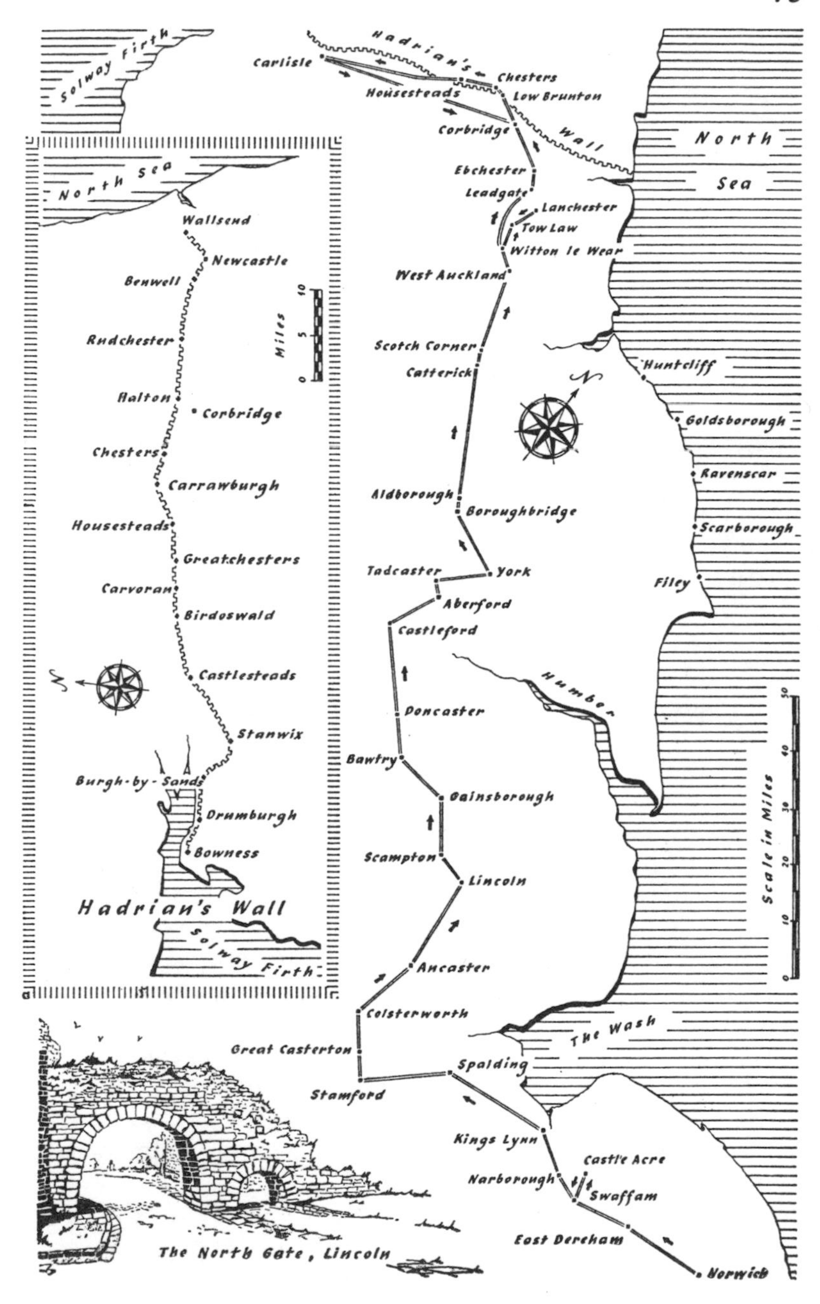

The North Gate, Lincoln

CHAPTER FIFTEEN

THE MARCH TO THE NORTH—2

FROM Norwich I wanted to get rapidly to the line of Ermine Street, the Roman road to the north. My route lay through East Dereham, Swaffham, Narborough, King's Lynn, Spalding, and so to Stamford, which lies on the Ermine Street. This is a fascinating, if somewhat circuitous journey, and travellers with more time than I had might find it worthwhile to explore such places as Castle Rising, a possible Roman station north of King's Lynn, Castle Acre, which can be reached from Swaffham along A1065 (and Peddar's Way mentioned in the last chapter) and something mysteriously marked on the Ordnance Survey map as " Roman Bank " which can be seen at various places to the north of King's Lynn to Spalding road (A17 and A151). I have no idea what the reader will see there, but it might be worth finding out!

For those who wish to stick to my own route, I can promise ample reward. For this is Constable's country, a land of huge brown fields, oaks twisted by the winter gales and haystacks as big as barns. Beyond East Dereham, where big white Georgian houses stand alone in their ample grounds, and Swaffham, a lovely village with a superb church of flint and limestone, the country becomes broader and flatter, as it nears the Fen Country. In the church walls one sometimes sees red Roman tiles peeping out of the medieval masonry, but the names on the signposts are stubbornly Saxon, names ending in " ham " and " ing "—Dereham, Swaffham, Tuddenham, Wendling. The men in the winged helmets had their way here.

But the Romans also left their mark in the Fen Country. They were familiar with this type of land in the Mediterranean, and knew its agricultural value. Fifteen centuries before Oliver Cromwell and other seventeenth-century speculators began to drain the Fens the Romans cut a series of big canals, of which the most notable were the Cambridgeshire and Lincolnshire Car Dykes; the last-named is over seventy miles long.

Professor Richmond, in his "Roman Britain", writes: "In conjunction with the rivers, which in many places followed different lines from those of to-day, these canals served both for drainage and for transport. As drains, they acted as water-catchers, trapping the flow of the adjacent uplands and keeping it out of the Fens; and they were also linked with a complicated series of minor cuts which drained the fens themselves. As canals, they linked the Fenland with the Witham at Lincoln, the Witham in turn being linked by means of the Fossdyke with the Trent. Access was thus obtained to the Humber and the Ouse, so that, as Stukeley long ago remarked, it was possible to proceed by inland waterways from the Fens to York. Stukeley further perceived that the importance of the connection lay in the opportunity which it offered for the transport of the Fenland produce to military supply-depots."

Who supplied the labour force for these great works? The answer seems to be "the Iceni". The canals date from the period following Boudicca's revolt of A.D. 61 and, says Richmond, "there can be little doubt that the conquered rebels were thereafter condemned to labour at the new works and were thereafter drafted to the new agricultural reserves thus created, working it upon terms much more favourable to Rome than to themselves."

I stopped for the night at the George Hotel in Stamford, a fine stone-built town with many noble churches. The "George" is one of the finest coaching inns in England, built around a square courtyard, and cleverly combines "olde worldery" with a touch of the Ritz. Next day I set off northwards along Ermine Street under a huge lapis-coloured sky. This part of the Roman highway has been in use for nearly twenty centuries. It is still one of Britain's " great " roads, though now hopelessly inadequate for the traffic it has to carry.

A few miles beyond Stamford on the Grantham road lies the greystone village of Great Casterton, though " Great " is a misnomer. It is a tiny hamlet lying in a hollow, and every day thousands of heavy lorries thunder down the slope rattling the window-panes of the village, and then grind up the opposite bank on their way to the North. But Great Casterton has a place in our history, for here stood one of the Roman stations which were built at regular intervals along the Ermine Street, places where the Imperial couriers could change horses and travellers refresh themselves. If you turn off right at the village and travel along a narrow lane for about 100 yards you can see, on your right opposite the school, the bank and ditch which protected this Roman settlement.

Mr. Philip Corder excavated the site as part of a scheme for training young archæologists, sponsored by the University of Nottingham. They began by examining the walls and ditches which surrounded the Roman town, and were able to establish that the wall—parts of which are buried—was built nct earlier than the end of the second century. But during the fourth century—a century and a half after the first defences were built—the inhabitants carried out drastic alterations. In Corder's words, "in front of the wall there was an enormous ditch dug round the town, 60 feet wide and quarried right out of the rock. The rock that was dug out was used to fill the ditch that ran immediately in front of the town wall."

Mr. Corder thinks that the Romans wanted solid foundations for artillery at the points where the walls changed direction; this artillery would consist of *ballistæ*, a kind of spring-guns like large catapults which were able to enfilade the front of the wall. A wide ditch was made as an essential part of the defensive scheme.

These *ballistæ* fired stones about the size of cricket balls.

Though ruined Roman walls may not be very impressive in themselves, they can, when seen in their historical context, tell an interesting story. And if it is asked how archæologists can date such walls with precision, the answer is just as interesting. Romano-British masons seem to have been careless with their coinage. Sometimes a *denarius* would slip out of a workman's pocket and lodge itself in a crack in the masonry. Subsequently, it would get sealed up, only to be found eighteen centuries later by archæologists, who, by looking at its date would know when the wall was built or repaired. Mr. Corder found several such coins sealed in the layers of chippings and stone left by the Roman masons.

North of Great Casterton lies one of the most thrilling sections of the Ermine Street, full 30 feet wide, very high and very straight. Just beyond Colsterworth look out for the railway bridge which crosses the road. Just beyond this there is a sharp turn right signposted Ancaster. Follow this and you will rejoin the original Roman road which goes almost straight into Lincoln, the railway following it for some little distance on the right.

When you reach the Blue Harbour Inn be careful not to take the right turn to Donnington, but to continue straight on towards Ancaster. Beyond this point you see the *agger* as a high bank on the right side of the road, until, just before reaching a twin line of electricity pylons, the modern road mounts the *agger* and for many miles rides along its crest, giving a magnificent view of the Lincolnshire Wolds on each side.

At Ancaster the road is crossed by A153 which runs between Sleaford and Grantham. Ancaster is a pleasant grey stone village on a broad, straight street, with a handsome fifteenth century church, just beyond the crossroads. Opposite the church, on the right-hand side of the Ermine Street, lie the evident remains of the Roman settlement, with its broad, deep ditch enclosing a quadrangular area.

At the far side of Ancaster the road makes another turn due north, on low ground in this instance, and is again magnificently raised all the way to Bayard's Leap. (Who, I wonder, was Bayard ?) The *agger* is particularly well seen here, being about 40 feet wide and 4 feet high. After Bayard's Leap, the modern road leaves the Roman line for some miles, but the old Ermine Street continues as a wide drove road still known as High Dyke, with the *agger* plainly visible in the middle.

Here it is well to consult the ¼-inch Ordnance Survey map, which clearly shows how the Roman road keeps to the high ground right into Lincoln and beyond. North of that city it goes on in a dead straight line right to the Humber. On the north bank of the river the Ermine Street shifts its alignment a little to the west and then shoots off towards York. Some day, perhaps, the old road will come into its own again; a bridge will be built across the Humber, and once again the Ermine Street will become the main road to the north, as it was nearly 2,000 years ago. Then, incidentally, Lincolnshire will become what it was in Roman times, a busy region in the centre of the country's main artery. A single impassable break in a road can change the whole history of a county for centuries.

The section of the Ermine Street between Bayard's Leap and Lincoln is one of the most interesting stretches for the walker or cyclist, though except in dry weather I would not recommend it to the average motorist. It can be negotiated, however, under suitable conditions by cars with a fairly high ground clearance, and the driver who has the patience to potter at 15 m.p.h., dodging the ruts, will be rewarded by a view of the Ermine Street raised high on its embankment, the contour of which can be plainly seen stretching away to the north over miles of ploughland. After about one and a half miles this trackway suddenly becomes a tarmac road again for a short distance. Walkers and cyclists with plenty of time to spare can easily traverse this stretch into Lincoln itself, and I cannot think of a better way to enter that great city. However, I must admit that I have also approached it in a very different manner, at high speed along the Fosse Way from the direction of Newark. The last ten miles into Lincoln were glorious. For ten miles the Roman road switch-backed over the broad fields, soaring and swooping. Names flashed by on the signboards—Willoughby-on-the-Wolds, site of the Roman Vernemetum, Castle Hill (ancient Margidunum) and East Stoke, where the road comes down to the edge of the silver Trent; here in Roman times was a bridge, and a settlement called Ad Pontem.

A county signboard flipped past with the word "Lincolnshire". Then, faint and far off at first, the towers of Lincoln Cathedral, rose high and serene against a grey sky. I cruised into the outskirts of the city, past suburbs, petrol signs, roundabouts, garages, transport cafés and lorries.

The road narrowed; ahead lay the steep hill on which the Cathedral stands, towering above the grey roofs. I steered into the nearest alley and began to climb towards the Cathedral, higher and higher, until at last, near the crenellated walls of the Castle, I managed to squeeze the car into a narrow gap.

I searched for the Newport Arch, the Roman gateway into Lincoln; a broad semi-circular arch of grey stone wide enough (if the pavements were removed) to take two cars abreast. Beside it was a small tunnel, also Roman, for pedestrians. Lorries, cars, cyclists swept under it, the oldest town gateway still in use in Britain; the same gateway under which the veterans of the Ninth Legion marched some seventeen centuries ago.

And that is practically the only tangible relic of Roman Lincoln—Lindum Colonia—which the visitor can see still standing. As soon as you leave it the Middle Ages press down upon you with their twisting, unsymmetrical streets, their pointed gables and Gothic fussiness. At Caerleon one can feel oneself in touch with the Roman past. In Lincoln it is almost impossible. For one thing the Cathedral dominates everything, and he would be a very insensitive man who could keep his nose to the earth when above him rises one of the loveliest buildings in the world. Wherever you go the central tower challenges you. You crane your neck to see to the top; you try to count the innumerable gargoyles which climb the sides; your eye is lost among the twisting convolutions of the tracery. You say to yourself " first quarter of the thirteenth century, Geometrical, on a Romanesque base."

And then the bell strikes the quarter, deep and sonorous and solemn—and detached. Seven centuries look down at you across a gulf which you cannot bridge. The bell booms out again, and all the guide-book twaddle is engulfed and swept away by the sound.

It is best, therefore, to get Lincoln Cathedral out of your system before you begin looking for Roman Lincoln. Sate yourself first with the Angel Choir, the thirteenth-century glass, the superb censing angels on the spandrels of the clerestory, the Langland Chapel and the Lincoln copy of the Magna Carta. Then, and only then, you may be ready to look at what remains of Lindum Colonia.

The British tribe which occupied what are now Leicestershire and Lincolnshire were the Coritani. They were probably less advanced than their eastern neighbours, the Iceni, whose coinage they used—when they used coinage at all. Their capital was Ratæ (modern Leicester) but their territory stretched north of Lincoln and eventually abutted on to that of the Parisi tribe of south Yorkshire. The loyalty of the Coritani was doubtful, which may have been the reason why the Romans quartered the Ninth Legion at Lincoln, near the eastern end of the Severn-Trent frontier. They called the town Lindum and it became a base for future operations in the north.

Later it became a *Colonia* like Colchester, though smaller, occupying forty acres against the latter's hundred. Glevum (Gloucester) was another Colonia of the same size as Lincoln, in fact they are so alike that the same contractor might have built them. Both, says Professor Richmond, resemble such foundations as Timgad in Africa, " a small and purely Roman unit whose lands were carved out of the native territory and whose town plan and building were ostentatiously and deliberately Roman in all their features. Their *territoria*, it should be noted, are in the lands of allied tribes, the Coritani of Lincolnshire and the Dobunni of the Cotswolds, but they are terrain of such a character which would be useless unless Roman enterprise drained and developed it. Their loss might thus ultimately be envied, but could not be immediately regarded as a hardship; and this suggests that the Romans had duly noted the feelings aroused by harsh expropriations as Camulodunum."[1]

The Colonia of Glevum was for veterans of the Second Augusta. That at Lindum was for men of the Ninth Legion.

Archæologists digging at Lincoln have found that at the beginning of the third century the town was extended to more than double its original size. It was no longer confined to the hill-top but came down to the River Witham, where remains of handsome and lavishly decorated buildings have been found. But, just as at Caerwent, Silchester and other towns, the troubled and unstable conditions of the fourth century left their mark on Lindum; the fine monumental buildings were dismantled, and replaced by small structures—workshops and traders' establishments—which in turn were riddled with medieval cess-pits.

Nothing of this can now be seen except the Newport Arch, but in the little Museum near the foot of the hill you can see some of the many objects which have been discovered not only in Lincoln but in Lincolnshire itself. The Museum is housed in a long, columned thirteenth-century hall which used to belong to the Franciscans, and is well laid out in view of the restricted

[1] " Roman Britain," by I. A. Richmond (Penguin Books).

space. The Roman section has charts and diagrams, and brief, pithy descriptions setting out the history of the city, illustrated by photographs of the excavations which are still proceeding. Nearby are glass cases containing smaller objects, and at one end, under the medieval vaulting, are milestones, tessellated pavements and memorial inscriptions.

Some of these things were found many years ago, others only yesterday. Recently, for instance, a small boy, who, for some mischief or other, was being chased by the Keeper of the Arboretum, stumbled and fell clutching at a handful of soil. When he got up he was holding in his fist a fine Roman brooch with enamel decoration. It was lying under an inch or so of soil.

Not long ago a man was digging out ferrets in the " Barrow " at Risenholme when he came upon a stone slab. It covered a Roman funerary urn. Many such urns have been found in the Roman cemetery outside Lindum Colonia. In the town area itself archæologists have found glass bottles, terra-cotta lamps, beads, counters, dice (with the dice-box), toilet implements; much of the daily apparatus of living. Most of these can be seen in the Museum.

Apart from Lincoln, the main centres of population in Roman Lincolnshire were Ancaster, Caistor and Horncastle. Ancaster, through which we passed on our way from Stamford, may have been Causennæ, mentioned in the Roman route-books. Caistor and Horncastle stand at the north and south of the Lincolnshire wolds; at Caistor are remains of massive walls, dating from the third century, when both towns formed part of the defences against the raiders.

There are many other Romano-British sites in Lincolnshire, concentrated mainly on high ground, and ranging from large farmsteads to simple dwellings. These are marked on the Ordnance Survey map of Roman Britain, together with some of the minor roads which linked the main highways. But be forewarned against disappointment. Nearly all these sites have been re-covered after excavation. Tracing them on a map and then seeking them by car, bicycle or on foot can be an absorbing pastime which will often take you through little-known country and lead you to places—not necessarily Roman—more interesting than the ostensible object of your journey. But when at last you have tracked down your villa or fort, you may find that your main reward will have been fresh air and exercise—both for your limbs and your imagination.

CHAPTER SIXTEEN

EAST OF THE PENNINES

Two Roman roads left Lindum Colonia for the north. One went due north to the Humber, and thence north-westward to Eboracum (York). The other took a more westerly course to Segelocum, where it crossed the Trent; then across the Idle, and at Bawtry, turned north-eastward for Isurium (Aldborough), Cataractonium (Catterick), and thence to Corstopitum (Corbridge), the supply-base behind Hadrian's Wall.

I drove out of Lincoln for the north through the same gateway which the Romans used—the ancient Newport Arch. At first, Ermine Street goes almost due north, needle-straight for nearly ten miles, following a slight ridge, with the Trent about eight miles away on the left. At Scampton, from which the " Dam-busters " flew, extensions to the airfield have pushed the road out of its original course, though the Roman highway is still there, under the airfield. At one point a cutting 5 feet deep had to be made across the line of the old road. The construction was similar to that of a section excavated at Ware, in Hertfordshire, some time ago, i.e. it is 60 feet wide to the inner edges of its side-ditches with a central roadway about 24 feet wide, with a hard surface and two side portions, each about 20 feet wide, with a softer surface. In fact, it was a three-tracked road with a carriageway for wheeled traffic and pedestrians, and side-tracks with a soft, sandy surface for horses and cattle.

Before reaching the other big airfield at Kirton-in-Lindsey, I turned off to the west towards Gainsborough. But the Roman road to York goes straight on past Kirton, passing midway between Scunthorpe and Brigg until it reaches the Humber. From the north bank of the

Humber it bears north-west and carries you straight to York (Eboracum), another legionary fortress which was occupied by the Ninth Legion after it left Lincoln.

However, to reach this section of the road I would have had to make a wide detour to the east and cross the Humber at Hull, which I wished to avoid; so reluctantly I left the Roman route and drove westward through Gainsborough and then along a winding road to Bawtry, where I struck the Roman highway again, now disguised as the Great North Road.

The original Roman route can be traced from Scampton airfield through the villages of Stourton, Marton, to Littleborough-on-Trent (the Roman Segelocum) where there must have been a ford in Roman times, if not a bridge. On the west bank of the Trent more narrow lanes lead through Sturton-le-Steeple and North Wheatley, to Clayworth, Everton,[1] and Bawtry.

Here the Ermine Street takes a northward angle and passes through Danum (modern Doncaster), a busy, grimy town choked with traffic, for the Great North Road passes straight through it, and workers cycling home from the locomotive works thread their way past huge lorries, against a grim backcloth of smoking chimneys and a leaden sky. A touch of relief is provided by an old notice on the Parkinson shop, proudly informing the world that the firm was " suppliers of butterscotch to Queen Victoria and Her Royal Highness the Duchess of Kent ".

Beyond Doncaster the road alternates between winding and straight lengths, which switchback over country of increasing barrenness. There are fewer trees, the grass seems sparser and less luxuriant. The trees are windbent and the air seems colder. Away to the west I could see the chimneys of the big Yorkshire wool towns —Sheffield, Barnsley, and the crest of the Pennines beyond. More than ten generations of Roman soldiers knew this country, and in spite of the industrial towns

[1] The author wishes here to make a purely personal salutation; a branch of his family came from this village.

which have scarred its face, one can still feel the harshness and grandeur which must have impressed those men from sunnier lands as they marched north to the Wall, " 24 miles in eight hours, neither more nor less, head and spear up, shield on your back, cuirass collar open one hand's breadth, and that's how you take the Eagles through Britain."

So wrote Rudyard Kipling in a brilliant passage from " Puck of Pook's Hill ", in which he describes a young officer taking his men to the northern frontier in the later, declining days of the Empire.

" Of course, the further north you go the emptier are the roads. At last you fetch clear of the forests and climb bare hills where wolves howl in the ruins of our cities that have been. No more pretty girls, no more jolly magistrates who knew your father when he was young and invite you to stay with them. No news at the temples and way stations except bad news of wild beasts. That's where you meet hunters and trappers for the circuses, plodding along with chained bears and muzzled wolves. Your pony shies at them, and your men laugh. The houses change from gardened villas to shut forts of grey stone, and great stone-walled sheepfolds guarded by armed Britons of the North Shore. Amid the naked hills beyond the naked houses, where the shadows of the clouds play like cavalry charging, you see puffs of black smoke from the mines. The hard road goes on and on, and the wind sings in your helmet plume, past altars to legions and generals forgotten, and broken statues of gods and heroes, and thousands of graves where the mountain foxes and hares peep at you. Red hot in the summer, freezing in winter, is that big purple heather country of broken stone."

If we keep this picture in mind we shall still be able to discern the lineaments of the Roman north, even where they are masked by pit-dumps and factory chimneys.

Beyond Castleford the highway becomes a real Roman road again, arrowing on in a straight line to Boroughbridge. However, I left it just two miles north of Aberford and took the right-hand fork to Tadcaster (Calcaria) and so to York.

Here we are in the territory of yet another British people, the Brigantes. They were the largest tribe in Britain, and their territory included not only north and west Yorkshire, but also Lancashire, Westmorland, Cumberland and County Durham.

" This great area, sundered by the Pennines and their spurs into numerous divisions, each large enough to maintain powerful war-bands, must always have owed its cohesion to mutual advantage and to local balances rather than to inflexible domination from a single centre; in other words, Brigantian power was an overlordship, embracing numerous powerful sects, rather than a direct and immediate autocracy."[1]

In the early years of the invasion the Brigantians gave the Romans much trouble, particularly their Queen Cartimandua and her consort Venutius. At first Venutius had been loyal to Rome, but after his divorce from Cartimandua he made war on her, and on the Romans. The Queen countered neatly by capturing Venutius' relatives. But, says Tacitus, " her enemies, infuriated and goaded by fears of humiliating feminine rule, invaded her kingdom with a powerful force of picked warriors. We had foreseen this, and sent auxiliary battalions to support her. The engagement that followed had no positive results at first but ended more favourably."

Venutius was driven out of the Brigantian territory, whereupon Cartimandua married his armour-bearer. Then, in 69–70 A.D., when the death of Nero was followed by civil war and the legions' loyalty divided, Venutius seized his opportunity, re-invaded Brigantia and took it. Cartimandua was rescued with difficulty by the Roman auxiliaries and then disappeared from the scene. Thus when Vespasian, former commander of the Second Augustan Legion, became Emperor in A.D. 69

[1] " Roman Britain," by I. A. Richmond (Penguin Books).

the province of Britain was by no means secure. Not only were the Silures and the Ordovices of Wales unconquered, but the Brigantian kingdom was now hostile to Rome, and barred the way to the north.

Now Vespasian knew Britain well, and his first act was to appoint as Governor Petilius Cerialis. This was the same Cerialis who was in command of the Ninth Legion in A.D. 61 when he marched them down from Lincoln in a vain attempt to save Camulodunum from Boudicca. At Lincoln he had, of course, been in direct contact with the troublesome Brigantes. Now, eight years later, he came back to the island where he had been an Army Commander, this time as Governor of Britain. He brought with him another Legion, the Second Adiutrix, to replace the Fourteenth " Gemina ".

The land of the Parisi, on the Humber estuary, which lay wedged between Brigantia and the then Roman Frontier, provided a bridgehead, across which the Romans began to advance slowly northward. " The steps of Cerialis," says Richmond, " can be traced, first at Brough, on the north bank of the Humber . . . then at Malton, a second important Parisian centre, from which all parts of the Vale of York can rapidly be reached, and finally at York."

Thus the Ninth Legion came to York, and built their fortress to dominate the Yorkshire plain, just as Caerleon controlled the plain of Glamorgan. And, as at Caerleon, there was a good waterway to the sea. From York, also, Petilius Cerialis was in touch with the Twentieth Legion at Chester, and this also could be brought into action against the Brigantes who could now be attacked on both their eastern and western flanks.

The Legate of the Twentieth Legion at this time was a young man named Julius Agricola, destined also to become Governor of Britain and to carry the invasion deep into Scotland.

Between York and Carlisle archæologists have discovered three marching camps, each big enough to hold a legion and some cavalry. These may have been built by the army of Cerialis on his way to the Solway. And at Stanwick, in the extreme north of Yorkshire, Sir Mortimer Wheeler has excavated an enormous defensive enclosure, 800 acres in area, where the Brigantes made their last stand against the Romans.

The site which the Romans chose for their legionary fortress was not the Brigantian tribal capital, Isurium (modern Aldborough), but a place where there was an easy crossing of the marshy Vale of York, and a good waterway to the sea. The town they built, Eboracum, was first an advanced base of the Ninth Legion when they moved up from Lincoln, then the permanent headquarters of that Legion (which was later replaced by the Sixth) and finally the most important city in north Britain, where two Emperors died and one was crowned. Not even Londinium, though large and of greater commercial prominence, can rival York in political and military importance. To-day, like Gloucester and Lincoln, it is a great cathedral city and the capital of a county, but in Roman times it outrivalled them both.

As at Canterbury and Lincoln, it is the medieval and later buildings which dominate the scene, and it is best therefore, to see these first before even thinking of Eboracum. From the roof of the Minster you get a good idea of the outline of the old town, girdled by its great walls, which can be followed for a good part of their length; these and those of Chester are the finest town walls surviving in Britain, Eboracum also had a wall and parts of it lie under the medieval rampart. However, you can see an impressive stretch of the original Roman structure still standing in the gardens of the Yorkshire Philosophical Society, and at one corner of it the famous Multangular Tower, one of the finest Roman buildings in Britain.

York was one of the main supply-bases from which Agricola, when he became Governor of Britain in A.D. 78 consolidated the conquest of northern Britain and part of Scotland. The thirty years following Agricola's recall in A.D. 85 are obscure, but there was trouble in the north, culminating in a great upheaval in A.D. 117–118 when the northern tribesmen broke through the line of Agricola's forts in Scotland and the Brigantes rebelled again. To this troubled period dates one of the great unsolved mysteries of history—what happened to the Ninth Legion? They were stationed in York, and it seems certain that they would be involved in the fighting following the break through of the Caledonians. In A.D. 122 the Emperor Hadrian arrived in York with the Sixth Legion, and the Ninth disappeared for ever from the army lists. What happened to them? Historians are suspicious of drama, and the disappearance of the Ninth Legions *is* dramatic. However, as they cannot find an explanation, prosaic or otherwise, some of us prefer to believe that at some time, in some unfrequented spot on the borders of Scotland, or even in Scotland itself, a man will put his spade in the earth and come upon the skeletons of the legionaries who marched out of Eboracum 1,800 years ago and never returned.

Hadrian came to York and supervised the arrangements for building the great wall between the Tyne and the Solway which bears his name, though it was built by the then Governor of Britain, Platorius Nepos. Less than twenty years later Lollius Urbicus built another wall further north, linking the Clyde and the Forth; it is called the Antonine Wall after the Emperor Antonius Pius. But about A.D. 155 there was another widespread rising of the Brigantes which had to be repressed, and then, at the end of the century came the break-through of the northern tribesmen following the withdrawal of troops from Britain.

When Septimius Severus came to Britain after defeating Clodius Albinus he based himself on York when he began his campaign of re-conquest. The city rose from its ashes more magnificent than before, and within its walls the Emperor died, old and worn out by his campaigns but mentally active to the end. His last words are said to have been: "Is there anything else to attend to? Hand it here!" His ashes were taken to Rome, and there is a story that before his death he was shown the urn which was destined to contain them, and addressed it with the words: " You are about to contain a man for whom the world was too small."

Nearly a century later another Emperor died at York; Constantius, who was born in what we call Yugoslavia. Constantine, his son, was proclaimed Emperor in the city. During the reign of Constantine, Christianity became the official religion of the Roman Empire; a Bishop of York was present at the Council of Arles in A.D. 314.

But Constantine had to fight to establish his right to wear the purple, and when he set out on the campaign which was to make him the first Christian Emperor he started from York. Very probably he marched down the north road to Brough-on-Humber, crossed the river, went on through Lincoln, Great Casterton, Stamford, and on through Huntingdon and Godmanchester, to London, the Channel, and so to the Continent, where he won his victory. So when you travel along this familiar highway it is worth remembering that Christian Europe may have begun with the march of the legions along that historic road.

Apart from the Multangular Tower, part of the town wall, and such remains as have been excavated from time to time under modern York, there is little to see of Eboracum; that is, *in situ*; but some objects can be seen in the Museum of the Yorkshire Philosophical Society, which also owns the grounds in which the Multangular Tower stands.

Look out especially for the lock of auburn hair of a Roman lady whose coffin was found under the booking-office of York Station. Sticking in the hair are her jet hair pins. Many jet ornaments have been found in the ruins of Eboracum, pins, rings, cameos, hair-combs, besides scores of the usual bronze brooches.

Inevitably there is the piece of tile with the imprint of a dog's feet. No Romano-British dog could resist walking on a wet tile, and you will find similar examples in museums all over Britain. But among the less hackneyed objects are a child's whistle, children's feeding bottles, children's toys, and an exhibit labelled (I know not with what authority) "shells brought from the seaside by Roman children".

There is an interesting set of Roman surgical instruments, tiles with the stamp of the Ninth Legion, glassware, a pavement from the temple of Serapis, an Egyptian god who was worshipped among many others, in York. Silvanus, for instance, the woodland god, had an altar, which is shown in the Museum, with a dedication by an officer of the Ninth Legion.

Some of the many tombstones found in Roman York have touching inscriptions, which bring us near to the people, humble and great, who lived through and were affected by, events which now seem infinitely remote. One of them reads: "*Julia Fortunata, a Sardinian, Faithful Wife of Verecundus Diogenes, Governor of York.*" Most of these *memento mori* are austere and formal, in the true Roman manner. But there is one which breaks through the barrier. There is a child's small coffin inscribed with the words: "*To the Gods, the Shades: For Simplicia Forentina, a Most Innocent Being, Who Lived Ten Months. Her Father, Felicius Simplex, of the Sixth Legion, Dedicated This.*"

Personally, that tells me more about the citizens of Eboracum than all the chronicles of Cartimandua, Petilius Cerialis, Hadrian and Constantine put together.

CHAPTER SEVENTEEN

FROM YORK TO THE WALL

THERE are many other Roman sites in Yorkshire besides Eboracum. For instance, between Whitby and York, on Wheeldale Moor, you can see one of the best preserved pieces of Roman road in Britain. Most unusually, it was a paved road, and the large stone flags can still be seen for a considerable distance. From Whitby it is a short drive to Scarborough, where there is a Roman signal-tower on Castle Hill, built towards the end of the fourth century as part of the defences against raiders. It may have stood originally to a height of 100 feet.

Remains of other towers have been found at Filey, Ravenscar, Goldsborough and Huntcliff. When archæologists dug at Huntcliff many years ago they found dramatic evidence of the fight which must have taken place near the tower near the end of the Roman occupation, when sea-raiders were harrying the coast and the defensive system was breaking down. At the bottom of a well beside the tower lay the tumbled skeletons of men—probably its last defenders. And a dog's skeleton.

There are, of course, many forts, some of which have been excavated; at Ilkley, for example, behind the Wheatsheaf Hotel, inscribed bricks were found bearing the name of the 2nd Cohort of the Lingones from France. There were other forts at Stamford Bridge near York, at Tadcaster, Castleford, and Doncaster, though these have now disappeared. So has the fort which used to exist at Templeborough, near Rotherham, though objects found there and at other sites can be seen in the Museum at Clifton Park, Rotherham.

However, holiday visitors to Yorkshire are unlikely to linger in such places as Rotherham and Doncaster; they are more likely to climb on to the high moors, and explore the dales. Though they will find few physical remains they will be nearer to the spirit and atmosphere of Roman Britain than on many more important sites which have been completely transformed by industrial development. On the high, windy moors, and in the gentle river valleys, the old nature-gods of the Britons still linger. The Romans accepted these local deities and sometimes built shrines to them. At Chester-le-Street, where the Cong Burn joins the River Wear, there was an altar to Condatis, god of the watersmeet. The River Ribble was a god—Belisama. At Eller Beck, south of Bowes, in Yorkshire, 1,275 feet above sea-level, the local commandant, whose name was Caesius Frontinus, set up shrines to a stream-god named Vinotonus.

"The Temples," writes Richmond, "were simple structures, one round and the other rectangular, with stone walls and thatched roofs. Their ruins still half-buried the altars when they were first observed by a shepherd. If this could happen after seventeen centuries, how manifestly grim and true must have been the allusion of Gildas in the sixth century A.D. to the ruins of shrines everywhere, 'their walls, inside and out, bristling with weathered idols of savage mien'. His phrase reveals in startling fashion the effect of belief in a multiplicity of deities upon the landscape or the countryside when the power of heathendom was exalted."[1]

But perhaps the most romantic shrine of all was that found at Bollihope, high on the moors. It was put up by one Sabinianus, commandant of calvalry, "after catching a lovely boar which previous hunters had hunted in vain. . . ." When you drive or walk over this remote moorland country, where the curlews cry above the weathered rock, the shades of the Romans will still follow you; not grim-faced legionaries hunting down the Brigantes, but young officers stealing a few hours of leave from some lonely fort, galloping across the heather in pursuit of a "lovely boar".

From York I drove along A59 and picked up the Roman road again at Green Hammerton, where I turned

[1] "Roman Britain," by I. A. Richmond (Penguin Books).

north. The modern road (A167) follows the Roman thoroughfare to the crossing of the River Ure at Boroughbridge. Just south of this small market town lies the hamlet of Aldborough, which is generally believed to have been the site of the Brigantian capital of Isurium. It was excavated many years ago, and most of the fine mosaics recovered by early antiquaries have been destroyed or removed, but a few remain, and are worth seeing. The village itself is attractive, climbing the slope of a hill, with houses grouped around a village green, and overlooking the wide valley of the Ouse. The best pavements, I am told, are (1) in a house opposite the church called the Old Manor, though special permission must be obtained from the owners, (2) in the garden at the back of the "Aldborough Arms," (3) in a cottage garden a few yards away from the inn. In this same garden you can also see remains of a large building which may have been the Basilica. There is also a small but interesting Museum.

From Boroughbridge to four miles beyond Catterick, the Roman road lies under the modern Great North Road, which precisely follows its undeviating line, until, beyond Scotch Corner A1 swings away to the right, and the Roman road, still following the northerly course, becomes B6275 (a "good class secondary road") and carries you on for ten straight miles, until joined by A68, two miles south of West Auckland.[1] Here I followed A68 through Witton-le-Wear to Tow Law, where I turned right along B6301 and picked up the Roman road again at Lanchester.[2] From here you can follow it, with a few deviations, straight to Corbridge and Hadrian's Wall.

Beyond Lanchester the country became more interesting, a country of austere, flat-fronted greystone villages, thin, brownish grass and trees permanently bent by the prevailing wind. The wind sang in the telegraph poles

[1] At Piercebridge where A67 crosses the Roman road, there are remains of a Roman Station and an interesting little Museum.

[2] Northern readers have since pointed out to me an alternative route, through Bishop Auckland and Binchester where the Vinovia fort is reputed to be the finest in County Durham.

which strode over the bare horizon. I crossed the river Browney and drove north-westward along A691. It was a harsh, forbidding but exciting landscape. Away to my left lay the Consett steelworks. The wide, grey sky seemed nearer, and the boom of the engine emphasised the loneliness. Kipling's words crept back into my mind. " The hard road goes on and on, and the wind sings in your helmet-plume, past altars to legions and generals forgotten, and broken statues of gods and heroes, and thousands of graves where the mountain foxes and hares peep at you. Red hot in summer, freezing in winter, is that big purple heather country of broken stone."

From Leadgate the road goes straight to Ebchester, a small town of dun-coloured houses where the Roman highway crosses the main Newcastle Road. You plunge down a steep hill into a green valley, then cross the main road, wiggle right-left, and then take a narrow road which crosses the Derwent.

From Ebchester the lane is delightful, winding through low hills, or past woods and farms. Turn left at the signpost marked Riding Mill. After about one mile you enter the main road, and sweep down to Riding Mill, a pleasant village beside the river. Here the stone houses are cleaner, and there are more trees. You pass through the village, the road following the river past a plantation of conifers on the left. Soon you are at Corbridge, a clean little stone-built village with a comfortable inn—" The Angel "—a few shops, a small square and a church. The main road from Newcastle to Carlisle goes through it, but one wonders how many motorists know (or care) that near this little town stood Corstopitum, the supply base for the eastern end of Hadrian's Wall, which is only five miles away.

A preliminary visit to Corstopitum whets one's appetite for the Wall. It is one of the best excavated forts in the north of England, standing in open fields in lovely country, and beside it is one of the most fascinating small museums on any Roman site in Britain. You reach it along a lane which leaves Corbridge at the Church. After half a mile you see a signpost on the left directing you to the site, which is on a plateau overlooking stone-fenced fields, with low hills rising to the south.

There were four stages in the development of Corstopitum (1) a cavalry fort built by Agricola in A.D. 79, (2) a larger fort built in A.D. 86 accommodating units of 500 cavalry and 1,000 infantry. This was abandoned when additional garrisons were provided on Hadrian's Wall round about A.D. 120. (3) A fort built by Lollius Urbicus—Governor of Britain under Antonius Pius—who built the Antonine Wall between the Forth and the Clyde in the years following A.D. 139. It was built by engineers of the Second Legion. (4) A reconstruction built by Alferius Senecio, *circa* A.D. 203.

All these stages have been traced by the archæologists who have excavated the site; and to-day you can see quite clearly the outline of the fort, with its Headquarters House and other administrative buildings, a large part of the military compounds with their barracks and granaries, a series of temples, a great store-house, and the houses occupied by the artisans, leather-workers, potters, smiths, etc., who provided what might be called the Army Ordnance services for the garrisons on the Wall.

In describing the many Roman sites and museums I visited during my tour, I have tried to bear in mind that few readers will be able to visit them all, and it would be pointless to make comparisons; to tell the Greenshire reader that his local museum is not as good as that of Brownshire, 200 miles away. It is the local museum which he is most likely to visit, and therefore, I have tried to describe each museum as fully and fairly as space permits, even when this involves some repetition. But the Corstopitum Museum tempts me to break my rule, because in my view this is one of the most fascinating collections of Roman antiquities in the British Isles.

Not that it is large or impressively housed—it is a

modest-sized wooden hut on the site of the fort—but the objects all illustrate one subject, the life of a Roman military camp, and they gain enormously in interest by being seen a few yards from where they were found. A few minutes after seeing the remains of the workshops you are looking at the weapons and tools which were made in them. A random list of objects reads like an inventory of military stores:

Entrenching tool	Scale armour
Spear butts	Horse accoutrements
Spear heads	Sling bullets
Helmet fittings	Handcuffs.
Arrow heads	

Readers who are themselves hand-craftsmen will find it difficult to leave the cases displaying workmen's tools. There is no more representative collection in Britain, and some of the tools might well have been made yesterday.

Among the builders' and carpenters' implements are wood-chisels, a spoon-bit (exactly like its modern counterpart) holdfasts, plumb-bobs, pulley-blocks, slaters' hammers and masons' chisels. Nearby are the tools of the blacksmith, including crucibles, drills, drifts, files, cold chisels, punches, and—yes—a *soldering iron*. These are well-made practical tools which any modern craftsman would be pleased to own and use; but their owners lived nearly 2,000 years ago.

Women visitors to Corbridge will be interested in the exhibits of household pottery of all kinds, cups, flagons, beakers, bowls, cooking pots, and such things as a child's tea-set and an infant's feeding bottle. There are also the familiar spindles and spindle whorls with which the soldiers' wives and daughters busied themselves, while their husbands perhaps lounged in the baths over a game of dice or draughts. There is a well-preserved set of draughtsmen on view, with two sets of pieces, one red and one buff-colour.

But the dominant atmosphere of Corstopitum is military. Here, in the Museum, is a *Phalera*, a military decoration worn by a Roman officer; nearby is a legionary's mess equipment; his mess tin, camp-kettle, etc. There are the official seal of the Sixth Legion, the Twentieth Legion, and of a cavalry regiment, the *Ala Sabiniana* (which was stationed at Chesters, one of the forts on the Wall).

Outside, the practical layout of the streets, the rows of barracks, the officers' houses, the workshops and the great store-house (an acre in extent) all speak of a life of order, service and discipline. So do the inscriptions in fine Roman lettering, picked out in red as they were originally, proudly recording the names of the legions which built and re-built Corstopitum. The size of these inscribed tablets conveys some idea of the splendour of the buildings they once adorned; and even in translation, the words have the ring of ceremonial trumpets.

FOR THE EMPERORS AND CÆSARS MARCUS AURELIUS ANTONIUS AUGUSTUS, TRIBUNE FOR THE SEVENTEENTH TIME, CONSUL FOR THE THIRD TIME, AND LUCIUS AURELIUS VERUS AUGUSTUS, CONQUEROR OF ARMENIA, TRIBUNE FOR THE THIRD TIME.

A DETACHMENT OF THE XXTH LEGION "VALERIA VICTRIX" MADE (THIS BUILDING) UNDER THE CARE OF SEXTUS CALPURNIA AGRICOLA, PRÆTORIAN LEGATE OF THE EMPERORS.

There is an alert, almost exciting quality about Corstopitum which defies description. Perhaps it is due partly to the fact that only a few miles away the Wall begins, for centuries the northern frontier of the empire. Whatever it is, there is no doubt that here, if nowhere else, one feels almost in the presence of the Roman Army.

When I was at Corstopitum some years ago, a party of visitors was going round the site. One of them kept up a running fire of little donnish jokes interspersed by giggles from his companions. As his fluting treble voice floated across the old walls, I longed for some rough legionary of the Twentieth "Valeria Victrix" to come up behind and prod his backside with a spear, amid coarse soldierly laughter.

* * * * *

From Corbridge you continue north along A68, past the church and up the hill. It is a steep climb, out of the lush valley of the Tyne, past Beaufont Castle, and on to the high tableland. As you continue to climb past stone walls, sparse grass and clumps of twisted oaks, the air becomes distinctly cooler. Just beyond the " Errington Arms " you come to cross-roads, where you should turn left along the road signposted Chollerford. A mile beyond these cross-roads the road climbs on top of a wide embankment. You are now driving on the foundations of Hadrian's Wall, for this is the bank on which it stood. About a mile further west the road dips and there is a side-road going off to the south. Here you can see clearly (*a*) the outer ditch on the north side of the modern road, (*b*) a flat space where the wall stood, and (*c*) three distinct embankments parallel with the road on its south side.

It will help us to understand the significance of Hadrian's Wall, and to imagine its original appearance in the second century, if we consider first the steps which led to its construction. In the previous chapter I described how Petilius Cerialis, governor of Britain between A.D. 71 and 74, moved the Ninth Legion from Lincoln to York, where he was in touch with the Twentieth Valera Victrix at Chester, and how from these two bases the Romans began the conquest of Northern Britain. During the governorship of Cerialis the Legate (or Commander-in-chief) of the Twentieth Legion was a young man named Cnaeus Julius Agricola. Petilius Cerialis was followed by Julius Frontinus, the man who finally subdued the Silures of South Wales (see Chapter Nine) and when his term of office ended Agricola was appointed Governor. Here you can see in action the system of promotion which I outlined in the section on the Roman Army (Chapter Ten). Vespasian, Commander of the Second Augusta during the first stages of the invasion, later became Emperor, and appointed as Governor Petilius Cerialis, who had commanded the Ninth Legion when Suetonius was Governor. During Cerialis' governorship Agricola is Commander of the Twentieth. Then he goes back to

Rome to resume the civilian part of his career, and a few years later returns to Britain, this time as Governor.

Agricola's reputation stands deservedly high, both as a soldier and administrator, but had the unfair advantage of an historian in the family. His son-in-law, Tacitus, wrote Agricola's biography. Other Governors may have been equally able, but, lacking a biographer, have left us only the bare records of their careers.

He arrived in the midsummer of A.D. 78 and began by rounding off Frontinus' conquest of Wales by defeating the Ordovices of the north, and accepting the final surrender of Mona (Anglesey). He may have built Segontium, in Caernarvonshire, or if not, re-occupied it. Then, after introducing reforms in the administration which ensured more just treatment of the natives, he prepared to move into North Britain. He based his operations on the legionary fortress of Deva (Chester). Most of his campaigning took place west of the Pennines, though his work is recognisable also in County Durham and between the Tyne and the Solway.[1] Eventually he established a line of forts between the Forth and the Clyde to resist any move by the tribesmen of Scotland, and then pushed up into what is now Perthshire, where he fought the decisive battle of Mons Graupius, and his steps can be traced deep in Aberdeenshire. When he was recalled in A.D. 85 (after a longer governorship than was usual) the Romans had reached the most northerly limits of their conquest.

With the penetration, though not the conquest of Scotland, the period of Roman frontier expansion came to an end. It had coincided with the reigns of the "Flavian Emperors", Vespasian, Titus and Domitius—so called because they belonged to the Flavian family—but after the death of Domitius in A.D. 96 there was a change. The Flavian policy had been to increase the Auxiliary army but with no increase in the legions, which "were the carefully balanced pieces on the chess-board

[1] The Stanegate, the Roman road between Corbridge and Carlisle is probably his.

of the Empire and their number was not even slightly increased without the weightiest reasons." The result was that when trouble threatened on any frontier, the only way to deal with it was to transfer legions for other frontiers. This is what happened in Britain, for the Second Adiutrix Legion, which Petilius Cerialis had brought to Lincoln in A.D. 71 and which was subsequently based on Chester, was removed to Dacia, the Romans relying on the frontier forts of Britain to keep the enemy at bay.

This encouraged the northern tribes to attack, and they made several incursions, notably in about A.D. 100 when many of Agricola's forts in Scotland were evacuated.

More trouble occurred after the death of Trajan in A.D. 117. Then, in 121–122, Hadrian, perhaps the greatest of the Emperors, came to Britain. He stayed only a few months, and his visit was only one of the many journeys which he made to the frontiers of the Empire, strengthening and consolidating its defences. But he rapidly got to grips with the problem and found a practical solution, which was immediately translated into action. Platorius Nepos, the new Governor, was given the task of building a scientifically planned frontier system from the Tyne to the Solway roughly along the line of Agricola's Stanegate, but this system was *much more than a mere wall.*

Now we will return to the place where we halted, on B6318 (the road between Heddon and New Brunton) about two miles west of the point where A68 (Corbridge to Jedburgh) crosses it. If you could have stood here in, say, about A.D. 130, this is what you would have seen.

To the south (left of the modern road, looking west) would be the *vallum*, a flat-bottomed ditch 30 feet wide and 7 feet deep, with embankments on each side made from the upcast from the ditch, each embankment being 20 feet wide and 6 feet high, but separated from the ditch by a flat section, or " berm ", about 25 feet wide. The whole system—embankment, berm, ditch and further embankment, would have been between 100 and 150 feet across. Next, on the site of the modern road, would be a great stone-built wall, 10 feet wide and between 16 and 18 feet high, with a parapet walk on the top sufficient for two soldiers to walk abreast. Next, to the north, was the ditch in front of the Wall, V-shaped, over 30 feet wide and separated from the wall itself by a 20-foot berm. And a little to the south of this system of vallum, wall and ditch was the Military Way, a road running parallel with the wall and linking up the forts and mile-castles along its seventy-mile length.

There were seventeen of these forts, each housing a garrison, and covering the main lines of approach; between them were smaller forts or "mile-castles" placed at every Roman mile, each with its gateway or sally-port through which the defenders could emerge and then encircle the attackers, driving them against the wall as hunters corral their prey.

This complete defensive system—vallum, outer ditch and wall with adjoining forts, was not planned as such from the outset. At first the idea seems to have been to use Agricola's existing forts along the line of the Stanegate—the road between Corbridge and Carlisle—such forts as Corbridge itself, Chesterholm and new forts on the same line. The Wall itself would only have mile-castles to house the frontier guards, who, says Mr. Eric Birley, "at the first appearance of open enemies . . . would be able to call up detachments of troops from the nearest fort if need be; and meanwhile the troops would be able to continue their normal military training." [1]

Part of the duties of these frontier guards or policemen included what we would call customs and passport control. At each mile-castle there was a gate wide enough for wheeled traffic, through which the local inhabitants could pass on legitimate business. The Wall was, in fact, more than a military defence. It was also a Customs barrier. The old-fashioned conception of Hadrian's Wall as a mere defensive rampart, with Romans behind it and

Eric Birley, "Housesteads' Roman Fort" (Ministry of Works Official Guide).

wild Britons in front, is a half-truth. There would be Britons on both sides, and they could pass through the Wall, but only under Roman supervision and control.

But soon this plan was modified, and it was decided to move the troops up to the Wall itself, and to house them in new forts built at intervals along its length. The system was completed by the great vallum with its accompanying embankments, on the south side, forming a long narrow band of cleared and controlled territory crossing Britain at its narrowest point.

Walkers can easily spend a fortnight tramping the Wall and exploring the forts along and behind it; given good weather I can imagine no pleasanter way of spending a holiday in Britain because for the most part, Hadrian's monument clings to the high ridges from which one looks across a romantic landscape of moorland and valley. Motorists are also fortunate, for from Heddon-on-Wall to Thirwall Castle (B6318) the modern road runs very close to the Roman rampart, so that older or lazier mortals like myself can combine motoring with a little judicious walking, thus getting the best of both worlds.

Owing to limitations of space, however, I must be content with describing one section of the Wall, and two of the forts which I know best, and only briefly mention the others.

One of the most fascinating sites on the Wall is the fort of Cilurnum (Chesters) which is within a few minutes drive of the place where we halted. Continue westward along B6318 through Low Brunton, where you cross the Tyne and the main road from Hexham to Chollerton (A6709). Just beyond the bridge take the left turn, keeping to B6318, being careful not to miss the turning (as I did and found, after many miles, that I was on the Pictish side of the frontier).

About three-quarters of a mile from the road junction look out on the left for an ornamental gateway leading to a beautiful private park called Chesters which used to belong to a Mr. John Clayton, who excavated the site many years ago. The estate is still privately owned, but the remains of the fort and the excellent little museum founded by Mr. Clayton, are now supervised by the Ministry of Works.

There is no lovelier site in Northumberland. The grey walls of Cilurnum rise out of smooth turf which slopes gently down to the river, beyond which a hill rises; away to the left lies the bridge at Low Brunton, and beyond, to the west, you can make out the triple ramparts of an Iron Age Fort on Warden Hill. Probably the Romans had to storm it when they came this way, as they did Maiden Castle in Dorset.

Cilurnum was quite a small fort, but its layout follows that of larger establishments such as we saw at Caerleon. There is the headquarters' building near the centre, the house of the Commandant, the granaries, stabling and barrack blocks for a cohort of cavalry. The foundations of these can be clearly seen, also the principal gateways with the grooves made by the chariot wheels. Another curious survival, which I have not seen elsewhere in Britain (although there are many at Pompeii and other Italian sites), is a large phallus carved out of a stone let into a pavement near the south-western barrack blocks. In Pompeii such signs point the way to the brothel, but I doubt if such facilities were provided within the narrow confines of a Northumbrian fortress, though they probably existed outside. Most likely it was a symbol of good fortune.

One of the most interesting remains of Cilurnum is the strong-room in the Headquarters Building. Here you walk down a flight of stone steps and pass into a vaulted chamber in which the troops' pay was kept. There is a story that when John Clayton excavated it he found the entrance closed by an oak door studded with iron. But there was no treasure inside—only a few odd coins which had rolled into chinks in the floor.

Outside the walls, near the river, are the remains of the baths, with the arched recesses in which the bathers hung their clothes. You may see the furnaces, the massage and oiling rooms and remains of the plunge baths. The walls stand almost to their original height in places. Even one of the windows is preserved, and fragments of glass from it were found during the digging. Here it is not difficult to imagine the cavalrymen of the Second Ala of Asturians (who were stationed here for a time) walking down the slope from the fort to the river, laughing and chatting at the end of a hard day's duty, while their grooms fed and stabled the horses. To-day, there is peace where once was the clatter of hooves and shouted words of command. The North Tyne chatters between its smooth boulders, a tractor sounds across the valley, and tourists wander across the lawns, taking photographs.

Yet even when this was the Roman frontier Cilurnum must have its times of tranquillity and beauty. The rural deities were worshipped; the water-goddess Coventina (whose well was discovered near Carrowborough, not far away) and Atys sitting cross-legged, playing a pipe. You can see their altars in the Chesters Museum near the fort. In 1876 Clayton found, under large stones covering Coventina's well, coins, jewels, brooches, jars and cups—offerings to the goddess of the waters. There are many fine altars in the museum, with such dedications as: "*To Jove, Best and Greatest of the Immortal Gods*", and "*To Jove, Best and Greatest, and the Genius* (*of the Camp*) *and to the Guardian Gods* ".

Besides objects found at Cilurnum itself there are many found at other sites along the Wall; for example the stones put up by " centuries " of the legions on the portions of the Wall which they had built. "*Centuria of Kalpurnianus*", "*Centuria of Nasidius Balbus* 1st *Cohort* ", and "*To the Emperor* (*Titus*) *Hadrianus Antonius Pius, the Father of his Country, by a Detachment of the XXth Legion.*"

The emblem of the Twentieth " Valeria Victrix " Legion was the Boar, just as that of the Second Augusta was first the Capricorn and then the Winged Horse. You can see the Boar inscribed on a stone set up in the Museum for the Twentieth Legion, like others, assisted in the building of the Wall. Most of the objects displayed are redolent of a military establishment—axe-heads, chains, horseshoes, arrow-heads, iron tools and weapons. But perhaps the most interesting relic of all is a copy of a bronze diploma or discharge certificate which was issued to an auxiliary soldier on completing his twenty-five years' service.

It is one of a number of such documents which have been found on Roman sites throughout the Empire, inscribed on bronze, testifying that the holders had completed their military service and had become Roman citizens, and why. With such a diploma a retired veteran could settle down, buy a small farm with his gratuity and become a substantial citizen. Many retired Roman soldiers must have settled in Britain, where their descendants are still living to-day.

From Chesters it is a short run to perhaps the finest and certainly the best preserved fort on Hadrian's Wall, that at Housesteads. To reach this you must return to Low Brunton and turn westward along B6318 for about nine miles. All the way you are on or near the Wall, and there is no more inspiring drive in all England. From time to time the grey bulk of the ancient rampart rises from the dun-coloured fields like a submarine surfacing. Then for a time it keeps company with the modern road until you see the triple line of ditches and vallum away to the left and above the road, marching on across the undulating fields to where a jagged cliff rears up to the west. When I last drove along that road the sun was at its zenith. So the legionaries felt it burning their battle harness as they sweated along the Military Way behind the Wall.

At last you see, away on the northern skyline, the buildings of Housesteads Farm. Take the field path across the fells; it is a long tramp, especially under a hot sun, and you may find yourself wondering, as I did, how much a Roman infantryman's kit weighed. All around stretches the wild, dun-coloured landscape, scored by stone walls and dotted with lonely grey farms. Outcrops of weather-beaten rock thrust out of the turf. The curlews cry, and from far off comes the subdued roar of traffic on the Carlisle to Newcastle Road. Even this dies away and, as you near the fort, there is only the sigh of the wind in the tussocky grass and the distant bleating of sheep.

No visitor with a real interest in Roman Britain would visit Housesteads without buying the authoritative but inexpensive little guide to the site at the Curator's hut. To try to summarise it in a few paragraphs would be an impertinence, particularly as it is written by Mr. Eric Birley, of Durham University, who is one of the leading authorities on the Roman Army. He lived for years in a house adjoining one of the forts, and has carried out important excavations there.

However, here are a few impressive features of the fortress. First, the *principia* or headquarters building at the junction of the two main roads through the camp, the *via prætoria* and the *via principalis*. You may see the *tribunal*, a stone platform, on which the commanding officer of the garrison took his seat on ceremonial occasions. There is the unit's chapel where the standards were kept, and the cross-hall, where in Birley's words: " . . . the commander of the battalion issued his orders, dealt with defaulters, and heard requests for leave, complaints and the like; here, too, the company commanders (centurions) may have had their meeting-place, while the non-commissioned officers probably had similar meeting-places (for the clubs of men holding the same or similar ranks were a distinctive feature of the Roman military system)."

In the most northerly room of this great block, which in its prime was the Adjutant's office, the excavators found relics dating from the end of the occupation, revealing very vividly the changed situation when Rome's dominion was ending and the barbarians were pressing down on the frontier. On the floor of the room where, in more peaceful days, the company adjutant had presided over his clerks lay hundreds of arrow heads, in stages of manufacture " showing that, in the closing days of the occupation no attempt was made, in the face of grave emergency, to continue book-keeping."

Notice also the massive gateways, especially that on the south, with the grooves in the pavement made by chariot and cart-wheels, and the more imposing north gate which heads through the Wall itself into the wild country beyond. Originally there was an inclined roadway leading down from the gate but this was removed by Bruce when he excavated the gate in 1853, in order to reveal the massive foundations. Standing in " enemy territory " below the ruins of this gate, one can imagine it as it once stood, 16 feet high, with some boastful inscription in huge carved letters above. One would hear the clink of armour and the distant note of a trumpet, the whinnying of horses and the tramp of armed men. There would be foreign soldiers speaking Latin with outlandish accents; a cohort of Tungrians was stationed at Housesteads in the third century; they were originally raised in the district of Tongres in Belgium. Another time a cavalry unit from Friesland (North Holland) was stationed here.

To the south, beyond the walls of the fort, lie the remains of the civil settlement, which in the peaceful period of the occupation came close to the walls, and was not defended. In one of the houses in this area excavators found evidence of a murder committed in the fourth century. Below the clay floor lay the bodies of a middle-aged man and a woman; both had been done to death; the man still had the broken end of a sword in his ribs. As burial within a town was forbidden by Roman law, and as this clay floor could be dated to the fourth century of the Roman occupation, there can be no doubt that the murderer hid the bodies of his victims, where they remained undetected for some sixteen centuries.

I ended my visit to Housesteads with a long walk along the most splendid section of the wall, a mile long, which runs along the top of the cliff above the Knag Burn, to the west of the fort, and then dips and climbs over the fells, past a well-preserved mile-castle with its gate, and so over the horizon. Although this section has been restored both in Roman times and since, the facing stones are Roman, and here you walk in the very footsteps of those auxiliary troops who patrolled the northernmost limit of the Roman Empire.

There were seventeen forts along the wall, including those at Pons Aelius (Newcastle-on-Tyne) and Stanwix (Carlisle). Housesteads is the finest, but there are others almost equally impressive at Carrowburgh—east of Housesteads—the site where a fine Mithraic temple was discovered, and still further east at Halton, Rudchester and Benwell. West of Housesteads lay Carvoran, Birdoswald and Castlesteads—all of which are marked on the map and should be visited—and other forts exist south of the wall, as at Chesterholm (not far from Housesteads) and at Bewcastle to the north, linked to the Wall by a Roman road.

Although the Wall proper began near Newcastle and ended at Burgh-on-sands, the west flank in Cumberland was protected by a chain of small forts and signal towers, and there were outpost forts at Birrens and Netherby, beside Bewcastle.

Hadrian's Wall and its forts is undoubtedly the most stirring monument to Roman might in the British Isles; I would put it even higher than that. To me it is as exciting as any Roman building in the world, ranking equally with Baalbeck and Palmyra in Syria, and the Pont du Gard in Provence. Of course, it cannot be compared with them in beauty or monumental splendour, but it has a grandeur of another kind. Here, as Dr. Nash-Williams said, " you can see what the Romans were capable of when they were really up against it." The grey, rain-beaten bulwark, undulating for mile after mile over the Northumbrian fells, is as dramatic as the wilder country through which it runs—as untrammelled and as austere as it was when the legions knew it.

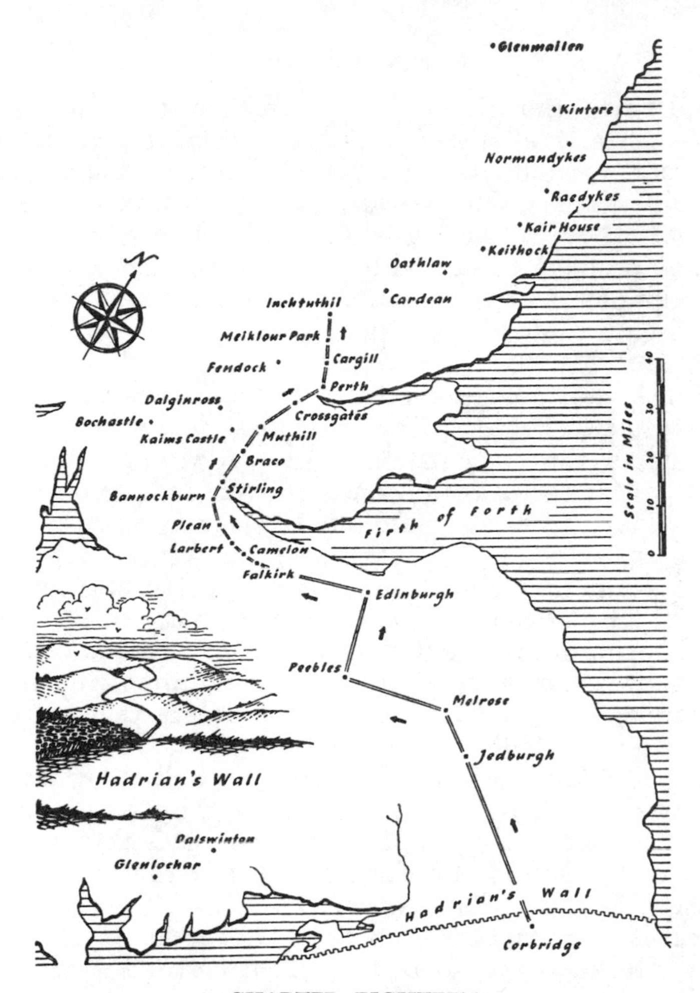

CHAPTER EIGHTEEN

WITH AGRICOLA INTO SCOTLAND

WRITING about Roman Scotland presents a difficulty. There are many interesting Roman sites north of the Border and with few exceptions they lie in remote and beautiful country—in itself a sufficient reward for the visitor. In England, Roman remains are often attractively sited. In Scotland, as in Wales, they are almost invariably so. In this respect the Scottish seeker after Roman antiquities has the advantage over the

Englishman, though not over the Welshman. But, as in Wales, nearly all the relics of the Roman invasion of Scotland are military; a legionary base, auxiliary forts, signal stations, military roads, and a great wall stretching between the Firth of Forth and the Firth of Clyde.

The problem presented to the writer is that a detailed description of each of these sites would soon become wearisome through repetition, since to the layman one Roman fort is very like another.

I make no apology, therefore, for concentrating on the two features of Roman Scotland which make the greatest appeal to the imagination; first, Agricola's invasion route as far as Inchtuthil on the Tay; and, second, the Antonine Wall built by Lollius Urbicus in A.D. 142.

In any case, people are more interesting than the monuments they build, and in this respect also Scotland has an advantage; for most of her Roman remains bear the imprint of the one Roman Governor of Britain whom we know as a human being. Julius Frontinus, Suetonius Paulinus, Petilius Cerialus are little more than names. But Agricola still lives in the pages of Tacitus; we know the kind of man he was, as well as what he achieved. It is Agricola of whom we think as we travel into Perthshire along the road he took; it is through the eyes of his son-in-law that we see the rugged eastern coast of Scotland, its lochs and rivers and mountains, as Agricola may have recalled them to Tacitus in his later life. He first came to Britain in his early twenties as a military tribune—rather like a staff captain—and served in the army of Suetonius Paulinus—the Governor who destroyed the Druid stronghold in Anglesey and quelled the revolt of Boudicca.

This was during the gravest period of the Roman invasion. " Neither before nor since," wrote Tacitus, " has Britain ever been in a more uneasy and dangerous state. . . . We had to fight for life before we could think of victory." Suetonius picked out Agricola and tried him out on his staff. " He got to know his province and be known by the army. He learned from the experts and chose the best models to follow. He never sought a service for self-advertisement, never shirked one through cowardice. He was always energetic; careless never."

Returning to Rome after his service in Britain, he married Domitia Decidiana, " child of an illustrious house. . . . They lived in rare accord, maintained by mutual affection and unselfishness; but in such a partnership the good wife deserves more than half the praise. . . ."

Then followed the usual steps in the Senatorial career; *quæstor* (a junior financial officer) in Asia under Salvius Titianus, then back to Rome as Tribune of the Plebs, followed by a period as *Prætor* or Justice. When Vespasian made his bid for the Empire, Agricola joined his party, and was given command of the Twentieth Legion, then at Chester. So he returned to Britain, and, under the Governor Petilius Cerialis began operations against the Brigantes, as described in an earlier chapter. Thus he gained experience of the northern part of Britain which he was ultimately to conquer.

But he had still to mount another step in his official career. After his service as Commander of the Twentieth Legion he was appointed to command the province of Aquitania, in what is now south-western France. This was not a military appointment but a high civil post, which he filled admirably.

After three years he was recalled from Aquitania and shortly afterwards made Consul, during which period Tacitus informs us that " he betrothed to me, in my early manhood, his daughter, a girl of rare promise, and after its close he gave her to me in marriage. Immediately afterwards he received the command of Britain, coupled with the priestly office of ' pontifex '."

One of his first acts was to march into North Wales and subdue the troublesome Ordovices. Although it was midsummer, when campaigning would normally be over, Agricola " marched his men into the hills, himself in the van, to lend his own courage to the rest by sharing their peril. Thus he cut to pieces the whole fighting force of the nation." He followed this up by an audacious attack on the still unsubdued Isle of Anglesey, although there was no fleet at hand to transport the army across the Menai Straits. But Agricola, like other great generals, exploited the advantage of surprise.

"Agricola picked out the best of his auxiliaries, who had experience of fords and had been trained at home to swim with horses under control beside them, and made them discard their whole equipment. Then he launched them on a surprise attack, and the enemy, who had been thinking in terms of fleet, ships and naval war, completely lost their heads. What could embarrass or defeat a foe who attacked like that? They sued for peace and surrendered the island."

The new Governor had shown his military genius. Next he displayed those qualities of mercy, incorruptibility and justice which he had shown in Aquitania.

"Beginning with himself and his staff, he enforced discipline in his own household first—a task often as difficult as the government of a province. He made no use of freedmen and slaves for official business. He would not be influenced by personal feelings, recommendations or petitions in choosing his centurions and men. He preferred to appoint to official positions men he could trust not to transgress, rather than punish the transgressor. He eased the levy on corn and tribute by distributing the burden fairly, and cancelled those charges, contrived by profiteers, which were more bitterly resented than the tax itself."

By initiating and enforcing such reforms, Agricola was preparing for the time when, the conquest completed, Britain would become a peaceful and stable province of the Roman Empire.

But the conquest was far from complete, and, after establishing forts along the Stanegate, in Northumbria, as previously described, he began his advance into Scotland in A.D. 80. His armies seem to have taken two routes; from the east via Corbridge, Chew Green, Cappuck, Newstead on the Tweed, and so to Inveresk on the Forth. Thence he probably went via Camelon (near Falkirk) and northwards through Ardoch to Inchtuthil on the Tay. The western route was from Carlisle, Birrens, Milton, and to the Clyde Valley, from whence the road turned towards Inveresk and so joined the eastern route. Tacitus, while describing Agricola's campaigns, annoyingly fails to mention place-names, so that we can only deduce the approximate line of the Roman Governor's advance from archæological evidence.

At the above-mentioned sites archæologists have found the remains of forts, and temporary marching-camps in which were found pottery of a distinctive type which is known to have been fashionable in the Flavian period, i.e. in the last part of the first century. Some of these sites later became permanent forts of the Antonine period (A.D. 138–161), but the presence of Flavian-style pottery indicates that they were occupied in Agricolan times. I mention this because one has to be very careful in making definite statements about the line of Agricola's progress into Scotland. However, Tacitus explicitly states that in A.D. 80, the third year of campaigning, " he opened up new nations, for the territory of tribes as far as the estuary named *Tanaus* was ravaged ". Some scholars have thought that the historian meant the Tyne, but nowadays the general opinion is that the Tay is indicated.

" Our army was seriously buffeted by furious storms," he goes on, " but the enemy were now too terrified to molest it. There was even time to spare for the establishment of forts. It was observed by experts that no general had ever shown a better eye for ground than Agricola. No fort of his was ever stormed, ever capitulated or was ever abandoned." (i.e. while Agricola was in control). There can be no reasonable doubt that the forts in which Agricolan pottery have been found were among those which he built.

Visitors to Scotland can, of course, take either the easterly or westerly route. I took the easterly one, from Corbridge, along A68 (a Roman road later called Dere

Street by the Saxons) and along the valley of the Rede to Jedburgh, St. Boswell's, Melrose (with its lovely Abbey associated with Scott's " Lay of the Last Minstrel "), and so to Galashiels, there I turned west along A71 through the Tweed valley, to Peebles, and then north again along A703 to Edinburgh. A mile from Melrose, on the Tweed, is the site of the Roman fort of Trimontium. Although there are now no visible remains there it is well worth a visit, if only because this was for a long period one of the most important Roman fortresses north of the Border.

The Romans called it Trimontium from the great hills which dominate it—landmarks for many miles. One of them is Eildon Hill, on which, says Scottish legend, Thomas the Rhymer spent a year and a day in the arms of the Queen of the Fairies—and thought it was only one night. Nearby is Abbotsford, Scott's birthplace, and the whole of this rich Lowland country, from which he drew much of his inspiration, abounds in legends older than Trimontium itself.

Standing on high ground south of the Tweed, it was in its time the most powerful fort in the Lowlands, a large enclosure of some fifty acres—as big as Caerleon—surrounded by thick walls pierced by four great gates. The excavations, which took place years ago under the supervision of Mr. Curle, yielded more objects than any Roman site in Scotland, though naturally nearly all were military; helmets of iron and brass, pioneers' axes and picks, cavalry harness, bridles and bits, smiths' tools and so on, all of which can be seen displayed in the National Museum of Antiquities at Edinburgh. The first fort was built by Agricola, but was greatly rebuilt and extended in the following century, and remained in occupation until the Romans withdrew from Scotland.

There is little to be seen now save a few mounds, but the site, magnificently backed by the three hills which gave Trimontium its name, should be visited for its scenic splendour alone.

From Peebles along A703 to Edinburgh, and a night-stop. Next day off again along A8 and A9 to Camelon, a few miles beyond Falkirk. From here one can trace the length of the Roman Antonine Wall (A.D. 142) to beyond Glasgow, and some readers may prefer to make this trip first; if so they will find details in the next chapter. However, in order to keep as far as possible within my chronological framework, I shall describe first the road into Perthshire, approximately along the line followed by Agricola in A.D. 80. This can only be approximate, because the exact line of his advance is not known; but the presence of Agricolan forts along this route leaves no doubt that he came this way.

As scholars differ in their interpretation of Roman sites in Scotland, I have adopted as guide Miss Anne Robertson, Dalrymple Lecturer in Archæology and Under-keeper of the Hunterian Museum in Glasgow. Miss Robertson, a charming and erudite lady, is one of the distinguished band of women archæologists who have done much to reveal Roman Britain. At the same time, while I have tried to stick to her facts, she is in no way responsible for my opinions.

There seems to have been a gate through the Antonine Wall at Camelon, which is itself a Latin-sounding name, unlike the unmistakably Scottish Falkirk which adjoins it.

"The single Agricolan road running northward from the Forth to the Tay," writes Miss Robertson, "was flanked to the west by forts which blocked the entrances to mountain passes. Three of these flanking forts have been identified with certainty, one at Fendoch, at the mouth of the Sma' Glen, the second at Dealginross, at the entrance to Glen Artney, and the third at Bochastle, near Callander, blocking the Pass of Leny."[1]

I did not have the opportunity of visiting these sites, as they lie some distance from the modern road to the Tay. But they are marked on the Ordnance Survey map of Roman Britain, and it should not be difficult to locate them, although little can be seen above ground,

[1] Anne S. Robertson, "Guide to the Hunterian Museum. University of Glasgow."

unless one is lucky enough to go there when new excavations are in progress, as they may be.

From Camelon, where the iron-works loom above the grimed, grey streets, I turned north along the Stirling road, and crossing the river Cart, came to Larbert, where was also a Roman fort (marked on the Ordnance Survey map). Beyond the mine-dumps and pit-heads of Plean is a range of hills, where a Roman signal station stood on Carron Hill. These signal-stations, of which there are several examples in Scotland, were built to enable the frontier troops to keep in touch with each other, and to pass information quickly to base. Being built of timber, none have survived, but we know what they were like from the sculptured scenes on Trajan's Column in Rome. (There is a facsimile reproduction of this column in the Victoria and Albert Museum.)

Trajan's Column depicts scenes from the Emperor's Dacian War, and we can learn from it a great deal concerning how the Roman Army looked, moved and fought. There are scenes of Roman troops on the march, crossing rivers, building forts, and signalling from high towers. High in the wall of the tower is a window through which a soldier projects a pole—rather like a barber's pole. At night signalling was presumably done by torches. Using this method, signallers could pass information over long distances, probably in little more time than it takes us to get a long distance telephone call.

The modern road follows the valley floor, but the Roman road was probably nearer the high ground to the west, but along this narrow strip between the mountains and the sea have passed many armies. You will pass Bannockburn, for instance, where Robert the Bruce set up his standard before the battle. Turn off along a lane to the left just before reaching Stirling and you come to a railed-off stone by the roadside, with a hole in which the Bruce set up his standard before the fight. Away to the north Stirling Castle rises proudly on its crag. Agricola probably forded the river a little to the west of the town at Kildean, where Roman remains have been found.

From Stirling I took the road to Braco. Just beyond this village, to the right of the road to Muthill, there is a stone wall beyond which lies the most impressive Roman fort in Scotland. Though fenced in with wire, a stile has been conveniently left near the road, so it is clear that visitors are not unwelcome, although the fort is on private land.

Though probably begun by Agricola, Ardoch (its Roman name is not known) was extended and re-used by later Roman invaders and must have been occupied for long periods before its final abandonment. It is impressive, but not in the way that Caerleon and Housesteads are. Here are no stone walls; not a scrap of masonry remains above ground; but the concentric rows of huge grass-covered embankments which surround it are evidence enough that here the Romans were really " up against it ".

While unmistakably Roman in its rectilinear plan, the defences are reminiscent of an Iron Age hill-fort. Here evidently the invaders took the utmost precautions against attack, and (though there is absolutely no evidence for it) I like to think that here took place the battle so vividly described by Tacitus when the Ninth Legion had to fight for its life when the Caledonians almost broke into their encampment.

Whatever else you take with you on your tour of Roman Scotland, do not omit a copy of Tacitus. Sitting on the high embankments of Ardoch, where to-day the trees' rustle and the lowing of cattle are the only sounds, it is startling to read this passage:

" As soon as the enemy got to know of this move " (Agricola's decision to advance with his army to avoid encirclement) " they suddenly changed their plans and massed for a night attack on the Ninth Legion. That seemed to them the weakest point. Striking panic into the sleeping camp, they cut down the sentries and broke in. The fight was raging inside the camp when Agricola was warned by his scouts of the enemy's march. He followed close on their tracks, ordered the speediest of his cavalry and infantry to skirmish up to their rear, and finally made the whole army join in the battle-cry. Dawn was now breaking and the gleam of the standards could be clearly seen. The Britons were dismayed at being caught between two fires, while the men of the Ninth took heart again; now that their lives were safe they could fight for honour. They even effected a sally, and a grim struggle ensued in the narrow passage to the gates. At last the enemy broke under the rival efforts of two armies—the one striving to make it plain that they had brought relief, the other that they could have done without it. Had not marshes and woods covered the enemy's retreat, that victory would have ended the war."

Is there a more vivid battle-piece in all literature? But Tacitus does not seem to have thought much of the Ninth Legion. I wonder if this was a prejudice passed on by his father-in-law? Agricola, it will be remembered, had been commander of the Twentieth once. "The Ninth?" one can almost hear the old general saying, "—never were any damned good."

From Ardoch you travel to Muthill, then right at the church, then immediately dive down a little lane to the left, between two houses. After about half a mile you cross a level-crossing, after which the lane goes on through quiet, low-lying pastoral country, with views of the distant Lurgan Hills. There are a number of Roman forts in the area, such as Strageath, near Muthill, Dealginross, near Comrie, and, some miles to the east beyond the Tay crossing is Grassy Walls. On the Gask Ridge nine signal stations have been identified, but the best preserved example is near Muthill itself, and is clearly marked on the Ordnance Survey Map. This is Kaims Castle, a mound near the road with a flagpole which makes the station easy to identify. But the routes are narrow and devious, and to those wishing to explore these remains I recommend an Ordnance Survey Map and a lot of patience.

The old road goes on through Muir o' Fauld and Crossgates, past tall, cylindrical haystacks with conical tops like pepper-pots—typical of this part of the Scottish Lowlands. At last it joins the busy Perth road. Beyond Perth take the Blairgowrie road (A93) through Old Scone, and then follow the line of the Tay. Wooded slopes overlook the broad river; you pass the high grey walls of Scone Park where there are more Roman remains, then continue near Gallow Hill and Cargill until you cross the lovely bridge of Isla. Beyond here you skirt Meiklour Park with its famous beech hedge, and cross the rich water-meadows of the Tay, a lovely but lonely land with few houses. Yet, hidden away behind woods near the river, buried beneath the turf of a disused golf course lie the ruins of the only legionary headquarters in Scotland, in Roman times as important a military base as Caerleon, Chester and Lincoln.

It was probably from here, in A.D. 83, that Agricola advanced northward into the Highlands, until his way was barred by the Caledonian Army massed on the slopes of Mons Graupius. This famous battlefield, in which Agricola inflicted a heavy defeat on the north Britons, has so far eluded discovery. Archæologists have identified a series of temporary camps dotted along the eastern coastal districts, but so far have not established whether they are of Agricolan date, or were built by one of the later Roman invaders.

To find Inchtuthil one needs a 1-inch Ordnance Survey map and much patience. It lies tucked away behind a farm in a clump of woodland, approached by a narrow lane which leaves the main road on the left about midway between Meiklour Park and Capath. An inquiry at one of the cottages is usually necessary before you can find Inchtuthil. When at last you walk across the turf, with a precipitous slope on one side you will see only a wide plateau bordered by woods and distinguished only by a few humps. Not far away the Tay sweeps round in a wide bend, protecting one side of the ancient embankment, which once housed 6,000 men. Agricola's favourite legion, the Twentieth, was stationed here for a time before it was moved to Chester.

The late Sir Ian Richmond excavated at Inchtuthil for several years, and the site continues to yield valuable information, but each year the excavation pits are filled in again, in order to interfere as little as possible with agriculture.

The very fact that, relatively, so little is known about this mysterious frontier region of Roman Britain must add a special zest to archæology in Scotland. Tacitus has provided the actors and given them parts. It is the archæologists' task to find settings for the play. Whenever one turns to the pages of the Roman historian one longs to know where this or that action took place.

What were the harbours used by the Roman fleet? And where were the camps where the soldiers and marines "would mess and make merry together? They would boast, as soldiers will, of their several exploits and adventures, and match the perilous depths of woods and mountains against the hazards of storms and tides, the victories on land against the conquest of the ocean."

It is not difficult to imagine the fear that even well disciplined soldiers must have felt in this wild, mountainous land with its fierce inhabitants. There were moments of doubt and uncertainty, as Tacitus tells us when "cowards in the council . . . pleaded for a 'strategic retreat' behind the Forth, claiming that 'evacuation is preferable to expulsion'." He also tells us an extraordinary and horrible story concerning a cohort of the Usipi—a German tribe—who had been transferred to Britain and "had attached to them a centurion and soldiers, to teach them discipline. . . . These they now murdered. They boarded three warships, constraining the pilots to do their will. Two of these incurred suspicion and were put to death; the third did as he was told.

"As their story was still unknown, they sailed along the coasts like a ship in a fairy-tale. But the time came when they had to put into land to get water and other necessities. This brought them to blows with the Britons, who defended their property. Often successful, they were occasionally repulsed. They were finally reduced to such straits of famine that they first ate the weakest of their number, and then victims drawn by lot. In this fashion they sailed right round Britain, then lost their ships by bad seamanship, were taken for pirates and were cut off by the Seubi and then by the Frisii. Some of them were sold as slaves and passed from hand to hand till they reached our bank of the Rhine, where they gained notoriety by a circumstantial account of their great adventures."

Perhaps some day archæologists will at last locate the battlefield of Mons Graupius, where Agricola defeated the Caledonians in a pitched battle, killing ten thousand. Tacitus puts into the mouth of Calgacus, their chieftain, a battle oration of Shakespearean nobility.

" We, the choice flowers of Britain, were treasured in her most secret places. Out of sight of subject shores, we kept even our eyes free from the defilement of tyranny. We, the last men on earth, the last of the free, have been shielded till to-day by the very remoteness and the seclusion for which we are famed. . . . But to-day the boundary of Britain is exposed; beyond us lies no nation, nothing but waves and rocks and the Romans, more deadly than they. . . ."

This speech contains that famous, bitter taunt which Calgacus flung against a system which brought peace, order and civilisation at the price of freedom.

" They create a desolation, and call it peace."

That was the other side of the Imperial medal, which Tacitus, himself a Roman, saw clearly.

CHAPTER NINETEEN

THE ANTONINE WALL

INCHTUTHIL is not the most northerly Roman fort by any means. Small fortifications have been traced as far north as Glenmalen, within twenty miles of the north coast of Aberdeenshire. Who built them we do not yet know, but it may well have been Agricola. He also operated in south-west Scotland. Tacitus tells us that, in the year before he fought the battle of Mons Graupius he " began with a sea passage, and in a series of successful actions subdued nations hitherto unknown. The whole side of Britain that faces Ireland was lined with his forces. Ireland, lying between Britain and Spain, and easily accessible also from the Gallic sea, might, with great general advantage, bind in closer union that powerful section of the Empire. . . . I have often heard Agricola say that Ireland could be reduced and held by a single legion and a few auxiliaries."

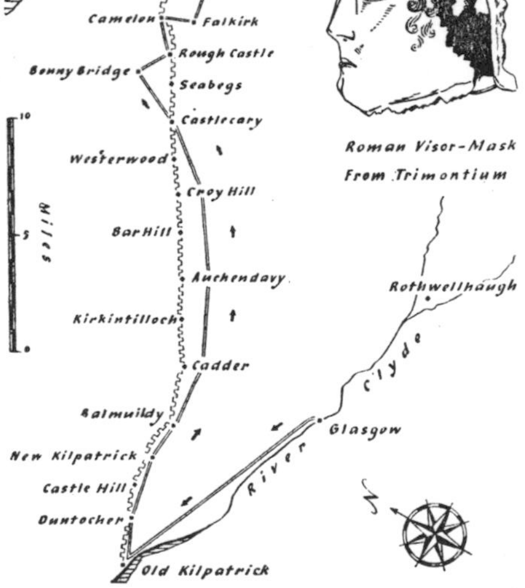

Roman Visor-Mask From Trimontium

Agricola, however, never attempted the conquest of Ireland, though he established forts in Dumfriesshire and Kirkcudbrightshire. Until recently not much was known about the Roman occupation of south-west

Scotland, but aerial reconnaisance has enabled Dr. St. Joseph to identify several sites, and at least two of these, Glenlochar and Dalswinton, have since been proved to be of Agricolan origin.

Much more work remains to be done in south-western Scotland, and it is more than likely that by the time these words are in print fresh discoveries will have been made. Aerial photography has placed a new and powerful tool in the hands of archæologists and many sites, hitherto undetected on the ground, are beginning to give up their secrets.

Agricola was recalled in A.D. 84—the year after his victory in Caledonia. Tacitus, who was naturally prejudiced, ascribed this to the Emperor Domitian's jealousy. The popular enthusiasm for Agricola was immense. "There was nothing Domitian need fear so much as to have the name of a subject exalted above that of his prince." So the great general returned to Rome, and died not long afterwards. The conquest of Scotland was left incomplete and the Romans never succeeded in subduing the rest of the country; indeed, a time came when they had to withdraw to Hadrian's Wall, which for centuries remained the northern frontier of Britain.

Before that happened, however, an attempt was made to hold a more northerly line, across the Forth-Clyde isthmus. Agricola had already established a chain of forts here, and in A.D. 142, twenty years after Hadrian's Wall was begun, the Romans built a second wall, this time of turf, with a very deep protective ditch in front, but no *vallum* behind. It was not a mere imitation of Hadrian's rampart, but an improvement upon it. It was only thirty-seven miles long, against Hadrian's seventy, there were no mile-castles, and the forts were placed much closer together, not more than a couple of miles apart, so that the defending troops could be concentrated more swiftly. Some of Agricola's forts were incorporated in the defences, supplemented by new ones. All except one—that at Bar Hill—were erected against the wall itself, which was built on a stone foundation, with drainage culverts beneath it where it lay on a slope.

Several explanations have been offered for the building of this second wall. Haverfield thought that it was done to provide another barrier outside the still occupied Hadrian's Wall, thus increasing the difficulty of a barbarian invasion. Collingwood suggested that the purpose was to hem in the subject tribes between the two walls and prevent them breaking out. But archæologists such as Professor Richmond, who have conducted more recent excavations along Hadrian's Wall, have shown that when the Antonine rampart was built (it is so called because it was built in the reign of Antonius Pius) the doors of the mile-castle gateways along Hadrian's Wall were dismantled, allowing free passage through. The Wall itself ceased to be patrolled and only its forts were held. Parts of the great *vallum* behind it were filled in to allow unimpeded passage across it, and to the south some of the forts among the Brigantes were abandoned or dismantled. All this strongly suggests that at this stage the Romans thought that in Richmond's words " a new age of peace had begun ". They were wrong, however, and a time came when the Antonine Wall had to be abandoned and Hadrian's Wall again became the frontier.

Stretches of the Antonine Wall still remain, and though they lack the lonely magnificence of Hadrian's monument, they have a different type of appeal. Unlike the Northumbrian Wall, which runs mainly through unfrequented country, parts of the Antonine rampart now keep company with factories, golf-courses, suburban gardens and other evidences of Scotland's more recent history. Oddly enough, these do not detract from its fascination; in some ways they increase it.

The Wall is easily accessible from either Glasgow or Edinburgh and can be traced for most of its length. I made the journey from the Glasgow end after a long talk with Miss Anne Robertson of the Hunterian Museum, who told me what to look for.

From Glasgow city I followed A81 through the northern suburbs, then turned on to A810, and with the help of the Ordnance Survey ¼-inch map (No. 2) found my way along by-roads to Balmuildy. Here stood one of the forts on the Antonine Wall; the old rampart is not very distinct, but can just be discerned here and there as a slight ridge in the turf. The faint mounds which mark the camp are in a field north of a marsh and near a small wood. From them you can look northward across a shallow valley to the Campsey Fells, which join the Kilsyth Hills further eastward.

From Balmuildy I wandered along circuitous lanes, up and down gentle hills, to New Kilpatrick, where a large cemetery stands on a hillside. Near its centre is an impressive section of the foundations of the Antonine Wall, a broad grey scar between the rows of graves. It is about 15 feet wide and consists of a base of smallish stones with larger boulders laid above them, with drainage channels at intervals. The whole thirty-seven mile length of the Wall was built on a similar foundation, above which rose the turf bank with a ditch on its northern side. The stones appear to be river boulders.

Beyond the cemetery wall lies the New Kilpatrick golf-course where the turf ramparts still stand to a fair height—higher than the wall of the cemetery. Members of this Club should be grateful to Lollius Urbicus for providing them with a ready-made plateau green from which to play their shots.

Sir George Macdonald, in his book on Roman Scotland, makes an interesting point concerning this western end of the wall. Like Hadrian's Wall, it was built by detachments of legionaries who were in the habit of erecting " distance slabs " at various points to mark the sections of the defences which each had built. (You can see examples of these " Centurial Stones " in the Hunterian Museum in Glasgow and in the National Museum of Antiquities in Edinburgh.) Sir George states that the sections near the western end are shorter than those further east, and offers an interesting theory to account for this. This section is overlooked by the Campsey Fells and the Kilsyth Hills, which may have been in enemy hands when the rampart was being built. Perhaps, for this reason, the working parties had to be closer together in order to protect each other against sudden attack.

Another fragment of the Wall is visible at Duntocher, further west, and the rampart ended at Old Kilpatrick, on the east bank of the Firth of Clyde. Still further westward the Romans built outlying forts to protect the seaward flank of the wall, and remains of these forts have been found at Bishopton and Larg Moor. Of these, however, little if anything remains above ground, and to the lay visitor the most impressive sections of the Antonine Wall lie east of New Kilpatrick.

The next fort east of Balmuildy was at Cadder, but this has now been destroyed by gravel digging, and nothing remains to be seen, apart from objects displayed in the Hunterian Museum. After Cadder came Kirkintilloch (nothing visible), Auchendavy and Bar Hill—where there is a very fine fragment of the rampart—then Croy Hill, Westerwood and Castle Cary. The road which will take you nearest these sites is A803, but there is little to be seen until you reach Castle Cary. Here on the right of the road, between it and the railway, are some mounds, and a few stone foundations of a small auxiliary fort which was once manned by men from Italy and Austria. An altar found on the site bears the inscription:

" *To the god Mercury, soldiers of the Sixth Legion, the Victorious, Faithful and Loyal, citizens of Italy and Noricum* (Austria) (dedicated) *this shrine and image; and have performed their vows willingly, gladly and deservedly*."

About a mile east of the Castle Cary fort the road is squeezed between the Forth-Clyde canal on the left and, on the right, a high bank some 300 feet long, and crowned by trees. This is the Antonine Wall. A gate on the right of the road near this spot admits to a lane running behind the Wall, which is high and well preserved, though not so impressive as the section near Camelon, much further east. But it is worth stopping and taking a stroll along the crest, where miners from the nearby pits sit smoking their pipes in the evening, and children play in the great ditch.

Just beyond this point the road crosses a narrow bridge over a stream. I noticed large stones in the stream-bed, similar to those in the cemetery at New Kilpatrick. Could these be remains of the foundations of the Wall?

Next comes the small manufacturing town of Bonnybridge, with its clanging foundries overlooking narrow streets of workers' houses. I drove under the railway bridge and just beyond it turned left along a small road of trim villas, each with its well-kept garden. I stopped the car, passed through a small gate and climbed a grassy bank beside the railway cutting. You cannot mistake the spot, which is marked by a tall electric power pylon. If you stand beneath this and look eastward, with your back to the railway you will see a magnificent stretch of the Wall, with its deep ditch, running across the fields. This violent juxtaposition of the ancient and modern gives an extraordinary fascination to the Antonine Wall. Life has not left it. Men have hacked it about, built factories and houses on it, driven railways through it; but still much remains; and it is still the Antonine rampart, though golfers drive off from its crest and the Electricity Board has stuck pylons on the top.

A few miles further east and you are in open country again and the Wall shows itself in yet another aspect. The section near the fort of Rough Castle, particularly in the Tentfield Plantation, is as impressive as Hadrian's Wall. Here are no factories or villas, not even cultivated fields, but only bracken-choked woods, through which run the great ramparts of earth, untouched since the legionaries built it nearly twenty centuries ago.

Having struggled up the steep slope and arrived panting at the top, you will sympathise with the British tribesmen who had to storm it. Even if they reached the crest in the face of enemy fire, they had still to cross a broad flat space beyond which was a further defensive breastwork providing protection for the defenders. One wonders, too, how many impressed tribesmen were needed to shift the thousands of tons of earth to make the ditch and the embankment.

At Rough Castle archæologists found an inscribed tablet set up by the Sixth Cohort of the Nervii who "erected the *Principia* (Headquarters building) in honour of the Emperor Cæsar Titus Aelius Hadrianus Antonius Pius, Father of his country".

There is another section of the Wall which has survived almost unchanged through the centuries, and, like the section near Rough Castle, still commands respect as a military obstacle. It is at Camelon, near Falkirk, which I mentioned in the last chapter as the starting point for the journey into Perthshire. This stretch is even finer than the section in the Tentfield Plantation. The turf rampart is still some 30 feet high, the sides steep and straight, the ditch a true V.

From the top of the rampart you look down on the steelworks opposite, and the grey houses and smoking chimneys of industrial Camelon. Some may regret the proximity of a factory to a Roman monument, but to me there is no fundamental disharmony. Both are the work of engineers, and though Nature has clothed the Wall with grass and trees, nothing can conceal its grim, functional line. If it can still impress us, at a distance of eighteen centuries, what must have been its impact on the Britons, who saw the naked bank and fresh-cut trench, like a raw weal slashed across the face of their land?

From Camelon I drove to Falkirk. On the left of the main road into the town is Dollar Park with its grey stone mansion standing in lawns. This building houses an average collection of Roman antiquities found near Falkirk. Macdonald has an interesting story of a nearby house which was continually subsiding and threatening to collapse. On one occasion the main staircase gave way. Investigation proved that the house had been built on top of the filled-in ditch of the Antonine Wall.

Next comes Linlithgow with its splendid castle, the birthplace of Mary, Queen of Scots. Here, inevitably, one is drawn away from Roman to medieval Scottish history. It was in St. Margaret's Kirk nearby that James IV had a vision warning him not to go to Flodden, and atop the Castle is " Margaret's Bower " where the Scottish Queen, wife of James IV, waited for news of that fatal battle.

The rest of the journey through West Lothian to Edinburgh does not pass near any notable Roman sites, though the country is pleasant enough, slightly undulating with thick belts of woodland and many gracious eighteenth-century houses standing among ancient trees. There were other Roman forts east of Camelon; at Mumrills, Inveravon, Kinneil and Carriden, near the coast. Unfortunately I did not have time to visit these, although I am informed that there is little to see; but in any case it is essential to visit the National Museum of Antiquities in Edinburgh, which, with the Hunterian Museum in Glasgow, houses the great bulk of Roman antiquities found on the Antonine Wall and at other Scottish sites. The Roman objects are well displayed in a well-lit hall accompanied by maps, diagrams and models.

One of the most absorbing exhibits is the collection from Newstead (Trimontium), the large military base mentioned in the preceding chapter. The collection of Roman ironwork is one of the finest in Britain; there is a turf-cutter, a pruning hook, an ox-goad, a rake, a pioneer's axe, smiths' tongs, hammers, picks and nails—all solid, well-made, practical tools which could be used to-day.

The " dig " at Newstead, carried out by Dr. James Curle, was one of the most fruitful of any Roman site in Europe, though, of course, nearly all the objects are connected with the Roman Army. There is a splendid parade helmet of iron with a visor, and another of brass ornamented with a figure of Victory, bronze cooking pots, spear and javelin heads, and other equipment used by the Army in the field. An unusual exhibit consisted of fragments of leather tents. Amid the chain-mail, harness-mountings and other warlike panoply, it is interesting to see also a few objects belonging to womenfolk; there is a woman's openwork leather boot, and light shoes for children.

Look out also for the fragment of a colossal statue of bronze found at Mislington, near Hawick, more than a century ago. It was probably looted in a raid on some Roman town south of Hadrian's Wall in the latter days of the occupation and finally abandoned in the hills. Why, we shall never know. But the most dramatic, as well as the richest find of this kind was made on the ancient hill-top town of Traprain Law, about twenty miles east of Edinburgh. This was a pirate's hoard of more than 160 pieces of magnificent Roman silver-ware found in a hole in the ground, just where it had been placed by some sea-raider in the fifth century. The "Traprain Treasure" is world-famous, rivalled only by the Mildenhall plate found in Suffolk, and now in the care of the British Museum.

Roman antiquities soon become boring, unless they happen to be beautiful (which they rarely are) or open a window on to the life of the people who used them. The Traprain Treasure satisfies both these requirements. Mutilated as it is, the richly engraved flagons, dishes and spoons are still splendid, evoking a picture of rich banquets in some elegant household of a man of rank. But the circumstances and situation of their finding tell a grimmer story; of those last days when the hand of Rome had loosened its grip on the island province. Then pirates from Gaul, from Ireland, Germany and Scandinavia were plundering the rich, once-peaceful cities, breaking up bronze statues for the sake of the metal, ransacking the unprotected villas and carrying the loot back to their ships.

During one such raid, in the fifth century, a party of

raiders found the rich silver plate of some wealthy man; he may have been a British chief or a high Roman official. Where was his home? In York perhaps, or some fortress settlement south of Hadrian's Wall. They broke up the plate in order to share it out among themselves, but for some reason they could not take their loot with them, and hurriedly buried it on a hill-top. Or, perhaps, did one of their number, unwilling to share the plunder, hide it and then escape from his companions, intending to return later? Whoever he was, he must have been a clever and resourceful crook, because when the archæologists examined the broken fragments, some of which had been bent and rolled up together, they found a heavy lump of pewter inside and concealed by an outer wrapping of silver. It is believed that the raiders were Gaulish pirates.

There are also a number of inscriptions left by the three Legions which helped to build the Antonine Wall, the Second Augusta, the Sixth " Adjutrix " and the Twentieth " Valeria Victrix ". However, all the " Centurial Stones " or distance-slabs, except one, are in the Hunterian Museum, Glasgow, which I also visited.

It would be unfair to make comparisons and I found both collections equally interesting, for whereas Edinburgh can boast the Newstead finds and the Traprain Treasure, the Hunterian has a far more complete collection of objects illustrating life on the Antonine Wall, and especially some excellent scale models of some of the forts, which repay careful study. After visiting the actual sites, and examining the model reconstructions, the objects found there take on a special interest.

From Bar Hill, for example, there is a well-made chariot wheel and a Roman soldier's leather shoe with hob-nails in the soles (" real square-bashers " my companion remarked), and the staves of a wooden barrel with the name of its owner (or maker) " Januarius ". The same site yielded ballistæ balls fired from Roman catapults, glassware, bronze brooches, a whetstone, and the usual stock of conduits, terra-cotta pipes with flanges, and so on. There is a copper pot, probably used as a camp kettle, and an " Olla " or cooking-pot, still caked with soot.

From Cadder came a remarkable entrenching tool, exactly like those used in the 1914–18 War, and from Loudoun Hill a beautiful bronze lamp complete with its hanging chain, and some sling-bullets of baked clay. From Old Kilpatrick (the westernmost fort on the Wall) there is a distance slab of the Twentieth Legion, with a reclining figure of the goddess Victory holding a wreath, and another set up by the Sixth near Duntocher, with winged Victories, Mars and Virtus (Valour). This inscription contains the phrase *opus valli*—" the work of the vallum, or rampart "—which, says Miss Robertson, " gives us the name by which the Antonine Wall was known, at least officially, by the men who built it."

Though the legionaries built the Wall and some of its forts, the duty of garrisoning it fell to the auxiliaries. These troops have also left many memorial stones; the First Cohort of Tungrians (Lower Rhine) at Castlecary; the First Cohort of Hamii (Syrian archers) at Bar Hill; the Fourth Cohort of Gauls at Castlehill, the Sixth Cohort of Nervii (Lower Rhine) from Rough Castle, and several others. Castlecary was also garrisoned for a time by Vardulli from Spain.

In Scotland, as in England and Wales, there is a new stir of movement in Roman archæology. As new sites are discovered and excavated so the pattern of knowledge changes; a new fact overthrows an old theory, or perhaps confirms it. For instance, archæologists were puzzled for a long time by the fact that the Antonine Wall could apparently be easily outflanked at its western end. But in 1949 the discovery of the fort at Whitemoss, Bishopton, on the south side of the Clyde Estuary, showed that the Romans were ready to prevent enemy landings to the south of the western end of the Wall, and more recently still, a structure has been identified at Lurg Moor, above Greenock, which has every appearance of being a Roman fortlet. " The possibility now suggests itself," Miss

Robertson writes, " that there may have been a series of forts and fortlets along the Renfrewshire coast."

There are, of course, a number of other Roman military sites in Scotland which I have not had the opportunity of visiting, but which readers should certainly see. Miss Robertson recommended particularly the fort at Castledykes, near Lanark, on a road leading up to the Wall. Dr. Stewart Henderson, Keeper of the Hunterian Museum, mentioned to me a section of a Roman wall which can be seen at Cleaven Dykes, north of Inchtuthil. It was excavated by Professor Richmond, who did some of his most notable work in Scotland.

The knowledge, training and experience of such scholars as Richmond, Birley, Robertson and others, provide the only means by which these mute monuments can speak to us. Some of the more spectacular sites, such as the Antonine Wall, make an obvious appeal to the imagination, but, as with music and painting, even a little knowledge greatly increases one's enjoyment. This is especially true of Roman sites in Scotland and northern England (*a*) because many present little to the eye and need skilled interpretation, and (*b*) because, for various reasons—expense, the requirements of agriculture—excavated sites are usually filled in again after the archæologists have examined them.

Much information is readily available, in excavation reports published by local societies, in newspaper articles and radio and television broadcasts. Personal contact with archæologists is even more rewarding. A friend of mine told me of an excursion he once made with Professor Richmond to one of the forts lying north of Hadrian's Wall. To the uninstructed eye it conveyed very little, but, said my friend, " Richmond took me to one of the gates and pointed to a ' gun-platform ' beside it, made with puddled clay to make it springy so as to take the recoil of the *ballista*. Then he walked across the heather and showed me, some distance away, a huge stone missile which had been thrown by the *ballista*, and which was two and a half times larger than any of those recorded by the Roman historian Polybius.

" Then he explained how, towards the end of the occupation of the fort, the North Britons had attacked it, and in order to resist such attacks the Romans had built a recessed gateway, so constructed that they could enfilade an enemy trying to get in. But the enemy had eventually succeeded and the Professor told me he had discovered, between the bastions, remains of the burned brushwood with which the Britons had burned down the gate and so forced an entry."

I cannot resist quoting one more illustration of the archæologist as interpreter. Again this particular scholar happened to be Richmond. Some years ago he was excavating at Woden Law, near Selkirk. To the layman it presented the usual appearance of such remains—a series of grass-covered banks and ditches. Richmond noted that some of the ditches had been made by the Romans, and to a superficial glance this would seem to indicate that the fort had been invested and attacked by them, just as Maiden Castle was reduced by Vespasian. But closer investigation convinced the archæologist that when the Roman trenches were dug the Iron Age camp had ceased to be occupied. Why, then, the Roman siege-works ? The answer seems to be that the Roman soldiers, perhaps from their base at Newstead (Trimontium) had been made to dig them as part of their military training. To keep them in good fettle during periods of inactivity, their commander sent them to make an imaginary attack on a deserted British hill-fort.

Modern servicemen, parading at the crack of dawn for battle practice in the hills, may like to know that nearly two thousand years ago other soldiers must have greeted the day with the words, " Another —— exercise! "

CHAPTER TWENTY

WEST OF THE PENNINES

THE time had come for me to return to London. As I had travelled north on the eastern side of the Pennines, I decided to return by the western route, through Carlisle, Kendal, Wigan and Preston. A little to the north of Carlisle lies Stanwix, another fort on Hadrian's Wall, of which little was known until recently. In 1940, when the local authorities were draining air-raid shelters, they found the double ditch which defended the western side of the fort. From this point Richmond was able to trace the south-west angle, south wall and east wall of the fort, and thus to measure its area, which was very large, some 700 by 580 feet, *bigger than any other fort on the Wall.* He also found objects which linked the fort with a cavalry regiment, such as " an elegant late-Imperial cheek-piece from a trooper's parade helmet ".

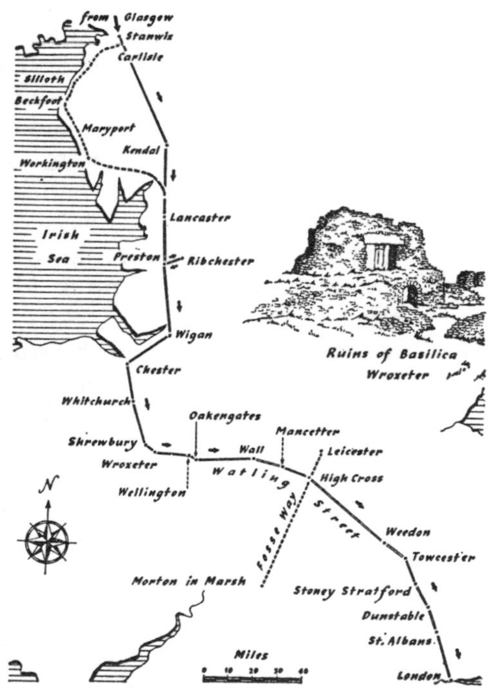

" It is clear," he wrote in 1950, " that this . . . exploration had incidentally solved the oldest topographical crux on the Wall, namely the whereabouts of Petriana, the headquarters of the *ala Petriana milliaria torquata civium Romanorum*, the senior regiment of the

Wall garrison. The extra size of the unit no doubt explains the provision of a granary in the prætentura, in addition to those which are yet to be found flanking the headquarters building." [1]

I was unable to trace these remains in 1955. No doubt they have been re-covered, but there is a good little Museum in Tullie House which contains many objects connected with Hadrian's Wall and other sites. By a most fortunate chance, this Museum stands on a Roman site, and the foundations of Roman buildings can be seen in the Museum gardens.

Most visitors going south from Carlisle will obviously prefer the Penrith—Windermere—Kendal route which, though lacking Roman remains, runs through the Lake District. But readers who live near this area, or who have plenty of time, might like to follow B5307 west of Carlisle, through Kirkbride and Abbey Town to the coast at Silloth. From this little coastal resort they can follow B5300 southward along the shore of the Solway Firth as far as Maryport and Workington. This area has recently yielded fresh evidence of Roman thoroughness in defensive planning, and, even more interestingly, evidence of its cast-iron inflexibility.

In the last chapter I mentioned the flanking defences of the Antonine Wall at Bishopton and Lurg Moor. Similar fortifications existed along the Cumberland coast to prevent the outflanking of Hadrian's Wall. Three large forts are known, at Beckfoot, just south of Silloth; at Maryport and at Moresby, north of Whitehaven. It was also realised that there were linking defences—tiny structures able to hold four men each, very like the "mile-castles" which were built along the Wall at a distance of 540 yards. Mr. Joseph Robinson found four of these in 1880, he called them "signal towers". [2]

R. G. Collingwood, when he surveyed the whole Cumberland coast in the 'twenties, suggested that there

[1] "Hadrian's Wall, 1939–1949," by I. A. Richmond. *Journal of Roman Studies*, XL (1950).

[2] For this information I am partly indebted to Mr. Brian Blake, who published a report on the Solway defences in *The Manchester Guardian*, April 23rd, 1955.

would have been a complete system of these " signal-towers " situated on high ground suitable for watching over and signalling along the entire coastal strip. However, he now appears to have been partly wrong. In 1944 Miss K. S. Hodson and Mr. F. G. Simpson made excavations at Cardunock, between Bowness and Moricambe, and disclosed a series of fortlets and " signal-towers " corresponding precisely to those on the Wall itself. "The important fact," writes Mr. Brian Blake, "was that the fortlets were a Roman mile, 1,620 yards apart, and that between each pair were two signal-towers, equally spaced, i.e., every 540 yards. On the Wall, this figure of 540 yards has achieved an almost ritual significance."

Then, in the autumn of 1954, Mr. R. L. Bellhouse, a Cumberland archæologist, decided to investigate the stretch of coast south of Moricambe. He happened to be reading Collingwood's thirty-year-old report when he was spending a day with his family on one of the Solway beaches. It occurred to him that Collingwood might have been wrong in assuming that the Romans would have placed their towers on any suitably high ground. If, instead, they had simply stuck to the regulation 540 yard intervals (as on the Wall) and he could find the foundations of one such building under the sand-dunes, the chances were that he could locate the rest by measuring out 540 yards and then probing the dunes with a metal rod.

" . . . was it just luck that he found a stony structure about a thousand yards south of Beckfoot fort. It was certainly not luck that caused him to mark out on a map intervals of 540 yards, using Beckfoot Fort as a temporary zero. At six times 540 yards south of Beckfoot was some surface evidence of sandstone working and at four times 540 to the north of Beckfoot the probe again proved itself.

" Helped by volunteers Mr. Bellhouse dug these three sites during October 1954, and each one has revealed a signal-tower. In one case the walls had been robbed to the foundations, but in the other two were low walls of solid, neat, three-feet-wide masonry."[1]

Coins and occupational debris found in the towers gave a date between A.D. 125–140. The excavators found hearths, remains of meals, spear-heads, pottery, and "a fragment of a large vessel scrawled upon in Spain before it was fired in the kiln with three cursive notes:

> "Unsalted
> "7½ pints
> "ESURI" (probably a place in Lusitania).

From these and other excavations it now seems certain that this system of defensive towers and fortlets extended right down the Solway coast, although the Wall itself does not. Another camp of the typical rectangular plan with rounded corners, was found at Burrow Walls near Workington. But there are probably still over twenty more mile fortlets and about fifty signal towers still to be discovered.

The regular spacing of the towers at 540-yard intervals —one-third of a Roman mile—is significant. Collingwood thought that the Romans would have chosen the sites to suit the lie of the land, irrespective of spacing, but Collingwood may not have been familiar with a certain type of Army mentality which still exists. Some Roman military manual had laid down that towers should be erected 540 yards apart: and so they were. "Orders is orders."

An amusing example of this kind of obtuseness can be seen on the Wall itself. near Housesteads fort. Mile-castle No. 37, west of Housesteads, originally had a large gateway wide enough to take wheeled traffic, and closed by double doors. But the slope to the north is so steep that it would never have been possible for carts to negotiate it. Seventy years after the gateway was built it was reduced to a 4-foot-wide passage, which was all that was required in the first place. But, as Mr. Birley says, "the blueprint called for a mile-castle of standard type, and it was

[1] "The Solway Defences," by Brian Blake. *Manchester Guardian*, April 23rd, 1955.

not until the time of Severus that common sense prevailed and the gateway was adapted to the realities of the situation."

* * * * *

Driving south through Kendal and on to Preston I reflected on the kind of life which was lived by the Brigantes, the British inhabitants of these northern fells and hills. True, it was a military area and there were hardly any large planned cities comparable to Bath, Cirencester or St. Albans. Yet, outside the forts the life of the farming communities must have gone on. How did the subjugated British tribesmen live? Some of them, tradespeople and craftsmen, eventually settled in the *vicæ* or villages which grew up outside the fort, as at Housesteads.

" Most of the buildings associated with them are long narrow shops or taverns with an open front shut with sliding doors and a large back room for goods and services " (Richmond). Settlements such as these have been identified at Old Penrith, where a military road centre supplied the traffic routes to a market.

The majority, however, continued to farm, and probably their only contact with the Romans would be through the local tax-collectors. In the north, according to Professor Richmond, the tribesmen were cattle-raisers more than agriculturists, at least until the Romans began to encourage crop-raising in certain areas. Decorated objects of the pre-Roman and Roman period frequently show horses or cattle, and cauldrons, for seething meat, were manufactured in this area. " These facts," he suggests, " imply a Homeric type of society . . . in which wealth is reckoned not in broad acres but in heads of cattle. . . . Many of the upland natives' farms of Cumberland and Westmorland plainly continued to reflect these conditions."

The Roman Army must have consumed enormous quantities of hides; their jerkins and breeches, their shoes, shield coverings and tents were all of leather, made, no doubt, from the hides collected by the Roman tax-gatherers in lieu of corn. Carcasses were also needed in great quantity, for lard, with corn and wine, was one of the staple diets of the Roman Army.

So if we are to obtain a picture of life in Northern Britain during the Roman occupation we should think not only of the forts and military stations, but of the settlements which grew up alongside them, and also of the numerous farming settlements in the hills, some of which practised agriculture. When the Romans stopped the Brigantes indulging their pastime of cattle-raiding there was an increase of population.

" There came a time when the main settlements swarmed and minor farms grew up not far away, so that all the available land in the neighbourhood was pastured to the full. This is particularly evident in such a valley as that of the Fyvennet, south of Penrith, and other areas tell the same story." [1]

I visited this valley but, as I expected, there was nothing which could be identified from the ground. No doubt, aerial photography tells a different story. Scores of British farming settlements have been discovered in this way, and others, which used to be marked " villages " on maps of Roman Britain, are now known to be Celtic farming communities. British market-centres have also been found, sometimes in association with religious shrines, as at Gosbecks Farm, near Colchester, and Wood Eaton, north east of Oxford. Here the Romans could allow fairs and other tribal gatherings to be held, since the holiness of the shrine would prevent any disturbance.

Describing Roman Lancashire presents a problem, since most of the important sites are now covered by industrial towns, and hardly anything remains save objects in Museums. If, therefore, I treat the county briefly I hope that Lancastrians will forgive me, since this book is intended to help readers to *see* Roman Britain; and apart from Museum objects there is little Roman to be seen in Manchester, Preston and

[1] " Roman Britain," by I. A. Richmond (Penguin Books).

Wigan—though they were all important Roman settlements.

At Lancaster, which boasts one of the best preserved medieval castles in Britain, there was a Roman fortress, and the Museum will repay a long visit. At Wigan there was another fortress, identified with the Roman Coccium, though no trace of it has yet been discovered. An inscribed altar, however, was found on the site many years ago. Wigan and Lancaster stood on the Roman road which ran from Chester to Carlisle. The other two principal Roman centres of Lancashire, Manchester and Ribchester, stood on the road which came up from the south and passed through the Midlands, via Buxton, and so also to Carlisle.

Mr. J. A. Petch, of Manchester University, has recently carried out excavations on the site of the Roman fort lying under Deansgate, and has gathered some useful information, though without making spectacular discoveries. This was not the first time that excavations had been made; the main lines of the fortress, which was of the usual " playing-card " plan, were established many years ago, and a fragment of the outer wall can still be seen under a railway arch near Knot Mill station, at the bottom end of Deansgate. Mr. Petch's recent work has enabled students to follow the wall for about 100 feet, though at the time of writing the North Gate has not yet been located. Quantities of pottery, iron, bronze and lead were found, and these are exhibited at the Museum of Manchester University.

The Roman name for the city was Mancunium, or possibly Manucium. The fort, which occupied a commanding position on a spur of rock overlooking the confluence of the Irwell and Medlock may have been on the site of an earlier British settlement. Weapons of pre-Roman date and a dug-out canoe were found on the site of Chetham Hospital, and the origin of the name may be *Maen*, a British word meaning a rocky place. The Queen's Park Museum contains some interesting Roman and earlier antiquities found on the site. There is a broken altar dedicated by an officer of the Ræti—Swiss troops—and a tile bearing the stamp of the Twentieth Legion. There were Dutchmen, too, in Roman Manchester. A cohort of Friesians recorded that they built 24 feet of its wall, and a tile stamped with the letters CIII BR may possibly stand for the Third Cohort of Bracarians, who came from Portugal.

The most interesting Roman site I visited in Lancashire was at Ribchester, near Preston. On my journey south from Kendal I followed the main A6 road through Lancaster and Garstang until I reached the northern outskirts of Preston. Here I turned left along a narrow road leading to Longridge, a dull manufacturing town-cum-village, where blackened mills and green meadows are startlingly juxtaposed.

Beyond Longridge I turned right along another lane to Ribchester, another small manufacturing town, smaller than Longridge but as grim. Mills, Methodist Halls, Working Men's Clubs stand beside the narrow streets of austere houses, which rise abruptly from the pavements. Then suddenly I came on to the bank of the Ribble, near the fourteenth-century church, and immediately the atmosphere changed. At a bend of the river two workmen were fishing, and in an allotment nearby two old gentlemen in shirt-sleeves leaned over a stone wall smoking their pipes. There was a distant noise of children playing in the school ground, but no other sound save the rustle of trees and bird song.

For weeks I seemed to have been living with the Legions and when I came to the site of the fort—ancient Bremetennacum—it had more reality for me than the nearby mills. Again, there were the solid, knubbly walls of stone with the familiar red tile courses. Again the little Museum with its array of inscribed stones and unlovely, practical objects, pieces of leather from a military coat, pottery and glass, tools and weapons, and the inevitable badly-sculptured figure of a cavalryman riding down a fallen enemy. Again the motley collection of nationalities; Asturians from Spain, Sarmatæ from Hungary. One of the

Sarmatæ left a touching inscription to his wife, son and mother-in-law. Though the original inscription has been lost, a copy remains. It has been translated:

> " By this earth is covered she who was once Aelia Matrona, who lived 28 years, 2 months, and 8 days, and her son Marcus Julius Maximus, who lived 6 years, 3 months and 20 days, and her mother Campania Dubitana, who lived 50 years. Julius Maximus of the Sarmatian cavalry, attached to the staff of the Governor, has placed this as the memorial of a husband to an incomparable wife, of a father to a dutiful son, and in memory of a most devoted mother-in-law."[1]

The finest treasure from Ribchester is now in the British Museum. It is a magnificent bronze helmet covered with figures of warriors in relief, and with a thin mask of metal attached to it. For visitors to the Roman collection at the Museum, this helmet is a " must ".

The fort was a small one, covering about six acres, and was of the usual " playing card " plan. The south-eastern corner has disappeared altogether, washed away by the river which has changed its course since Roman times, but by peeping over the hedge to the north of the church you can see the overgrown foundations of one of the buildings, probably a granary, and excavations have revealed the north gate and what may have been the armoury, now covered by the parish hall. These remains have now been re-covered. The church itself is said to have been built over the ruins of the temple of Minerva and the Prætorium, or headquarters building, lies under the churchyard.

Ribchester was first excavated many years ago. More recently Mr. J. V. H. Eames and a party of students from Liverpool University carried out a modest dig in the area. They found the stumps of two substantial squared timber posts, bedded in the natural gravel and inclined at an angle. They may have formed part of the substructure of a signal tower. The excavators also discovered the remains of a clay rampart. These remains strongly suggest that there was some kind of semi-permanent timber fort at Ribchester long before the stone

[1] Arthur Weigall, " Wanderings in Roman Britain." Thornton Butterworth.

buildings were erected; probably a simple fort was built here during the early years of Agricola's campaign against the Brigantes.

In the field to the west of the church the archæologists made a trial trench which disclosed remains of the camp ditch, and, says the report, " it is very likely that the whole of this area is crossed by a system of parallel ditches, of which this excavation revealed only the innermost ". This is much more interesting and significant than would appear at first sight, because we know that multiple ditches of this type are typical of the Antonine period (A.D. 138–161). This was the time of the Brigantian revolt, and the additional defences, if they exist (and only further excavation can confirm this) suggest that the fort was reoccupied and refortified during those troubled times. Here is another example of archæology coming to the aid of history.

From Ribchester I plunged into the industrial belt, through Preston and Wigan. It was a dreary drive but unavoidable; traffic jams and choking diesel fumes for a time obliterated all thoughts of Roman Britain. And then, just outside Warrington, I turned right on to A56, by-passed most of the town, and turned my wheels towards Chester. After a while the country improved, and so did the road. There was less grime on the hedges, and providentially the sun came out. I hurried on through Frodsham and Helsby, and so came at last to the proud city on the Dee which the Romans called Deva; the base from which Suetonius launched his attack on Anglesey; the place where the young Agricola got his training as a staff officer and where he later commanded his favourite legion—the Twentieth Valeria Victrix whose emblem was the boar. I was at Chester.

CHAPTER TWENTY-ONE

BACK TO THE WATLING STREET

THERE is no city in England like Chester. There is no city in the world more proud of its past, or one which carries its great age with more dignity, charm and grace. Of all English cathedral cities I know of none—not even Lincoln—to which the atmosphere of the Middle Ages clings with such tenacity. And yet Chester is a lively, bustling place. Still a garrison town, as it was in Roman times, the streets are thronged with military traffic, and soldiers in battle dress move in the shadow of medieval walls which once knew the tramp of men-at-arms; and before them Roman sentries guarded walls which followed the same line.

At first, inevitably, Rome has to give way to the Middle Ages. One must first visit the medieval " Rows " with their fine half-timbered facades ; a double tier of shops, one at ground level and the other on the first floor, with a second footway or gallery above the lower one. The Romans may have been indirectly responsible for this distinctive architectural feature of Chester. It has been suggested that there were so many massive Roman ruins along the streets (which follow the Roman plan) that the earliest medieval inhabitants had to build their shops at street level in front of the ruins and at a higher level above them. " This arrangement would naturally evolve into the present tiered frontage and the constant reconstruction of individual buildings would gradually result in the replacement of the ruins by cellars and in the enclosure of the first-floor footway, as a matter of convenience by overhanging the second storeys. . . ."[1]

Then you must see Eastgate Street, which is Roman (an altar dedicated to " the genius of the century " was found under Messrs. Dutton's Sigarro Stores) ; Water-

[1] Chester Official Guide. (Chester Corporation).

gate Street with its " God's Providence House " and sixteenth-century Leche House ; Bridge Street, where there is a Roman hypocaust under Messrs. Dentons Ltd., and part of a Roman pavement in the basement of Messrs. Francis' shop in the Arcade. Such remains, however, are pitifully small compared with Chester's treasures of medieval architecture, of which the most glorious are the Cathedral and the City Wall.

Chester is the only city in England which still possesses its walls complete. They extend for two miles and there is no better way of understanding Roman Deva than by making the entire circuit of the raised rampart walk, which offers magnificent views of the city, the river and the surrounding country. Those on the north and east sides are built on Roman foundations; and from Morgan's Mount to Newgate they still contain substantial portions of the original Roman work. Here you are walking almost in the footsteps of the Twentieth Legion.

The great Eastgate stands on the site of its Roman predecessor and material from the Roman structure was incorporated in it. On the right near the steps leading down to Frodsham Street you will see the lower courses of the Roman Wall. There is more Roman work near the Northgate, including a cornice moulding almost at the height of the present parapet. Still following the rampart you will come to a stretch overlooking the " Roodee " where the Roman harbour stood; part of their quay is still visible below the walls, and can be seen from the racecourse below.

Near the Wolf Gate the south-east angle of the Roman fortress abuts on to the medieval walls; on a small lawn near the gateway you can see one of its angle-towers, dating from the first century, and a little further along, in a garden beside the ramparts, are columns and other pieces of Roman masonry which have been re-erected after removal from another site. The Roman amphitheatre, the largest yet discovered in Britain, lay to the east of the Northgate. The northern part has been purchased and will eventually be excavated and preserved.

The legionary fortress of Deva was begun under the governorship of Julius Frontinus, conqueror of the Silures. Agricola, who had served in this area under Suetonius, used Deva as a base for his operations against the tribesmen of North Wales (the occasion when he crossed the Menai without a fleet—his cavalrymen swimming beside their horses). Later it controlled North Wales as Caerleon controlled the southern part of the peninsula. The fortress was garrisoned at one time by the Second Adiutrix, but when this was removed to Europe in the late 'eighties, Agricola's trusty Twentieth was brought down from Inchtuthil and based on Chester, where it remained for centuries.

I saw many relics of this famous unit in the Grosvenor Museum in Grosvenor Street, an unattractive red-brick building which houses one of the finest and best-displayed Roman collections in England. The enthusiastic and knowledgeable Curator, Mr. Thompson, and his predecessor, Mr. Graham Webster, have made the utmost of their opportunities; when I was there the Curator had arranged a fascinating display designed to illustrate the organisation of the Roman Army. No child entering this room could fail to be attracted by the life-size wax figure of a Roman soldier in full uniform, with his shoulder and breast-guards, woollen kilt and articulated bronze strips protecting his thighs. He carries the slender *pilum* or javelin with its long tapering steel head; his short broad-sword or *gladius*, his shield and dagger, and he wears segmented body armour, a helmet with cheek-pieces, and a neck guard, leather breeches and boots.

Another case was devoted to a display showing the system of payment in the Roman Army, and there is a very comprehensive collection of the usual military equipment: axe-heads, spear-heads, bronze harness equipment, besides such feminine *trivia* as hairpins and thimbles.

Another room is full of inscribed stones, perhaps the most striking collection of Roman monuments in England. A Greek doctor, Hermogenes, dedicated an altar to " the gods that are strong to save "; a tombstone of a camp prefect of the Twentieth Legion states that he was born in Syria; others came from Emerita in Spain, Arles in France, Samosota on the Euphrates, and from Italy and the Rhine. One soldier, " who was honourably discharged from military service " as his inscription states, lived on in Britain and died at the age of eighty; and a clerk of the Twentieth erected a tombstone to his " most chaste and pure wife " Cocceia Irene.

These and other names kept recurring to my mind as I made a second circuit of the walls in the calm evening. For 300 years men of this famous Legion, with their wives and families, lived and died at Chester, and looked out from these walls across the sands of Dee, or away to the distant mountains of Wales. It must have been a fine city then; and it still is.

* * * * *

My tour of Roman Britain began with a journey along the Watling Street from London to Canterbury. It ended with a journey from Chester to London along the same Roman road, which ran from the coast of Kent to the coast of Wales. The Watling Street is perhaps the most historic highway in Britain. It follows the line of the advance of the Twentieth and Fourteenth Legions, the third prong of the attack which took the Second Augusta into the West and the Ninth to the North. It heard the hoof-beats of Suetonius' cavalry hurrying southward to meet the challenge of Boudicca; to-day it hears, day and night, the roar of lorries grinding north to Holyhead.

From Chester I drove southward along A41 through Whitchurch, then along A49 to Shrewsbury, where a by-pass took me on to A5, the main London-Holyhead road. A few miles eastward, between Shrewsbury and Wellington, a by-road leads off to the right, signposted Wroxeter, near which lie the excavated remains of Uriconium, a Romano-British city which kept watch over the Welsh Marches. There is no grander Roman site in Britain. The ruins lie in open fields, with the solitary Wreken Hill thrusting up out of the plain to the east, and the forested crest of Wenlock Edge away to the west. A little distance away the Severn winds its way to the sea. No modern buildings clutter up the site. A mighty fragment of the basilica dominates the scene, and at its feet lie paved streets, and the foundations of houses, shops and baths. Much more remains under the soil, waiting to be excavated.

Uriconium has stirred generations of visitors. The poet Housman saw the " forest fleece " of Wenlock Edge heaving under an autumn gale, and wrote:

> " 'Twould blow like this through holt and hanger
> When Uricon the city stood:
> 'Tis the old wind in the old anger,
> But then it threshed another wood."

I saw it on just such a gusty autumn day, and the same melancholy caught hold of me, as it has so many pilgrims to Uriconium. For some reason one thinks not of the time when the Fourteenth and Twentieth Legions set up their camp here, not of the city in its peaceful prime, but of the sunset days when the splendour was dying, and the chill wind was blowing in from the North, filling the sails of the raiding ships which brought the destroyers.

Many years ago, when Uriconium was being excavated, archæologists found a grim relic of the city's fall. Under the hypocaust of the baths lay the skeleton of an old man, and in its arms was a bag containing 132 coins. Evidently he had crawled into this hiding place when the raiders broke into the city and had died there.

Uriconium must have been a great city in its heyday; occupied first by the Fourteenth and Twentieth Legions, it was extended and improved in the time of Domitian (A.D. 81–96) and reached its glory in the time of Hadrian when the builders decided on a completely new lay-out. " The half-finished baths were demolished, and their place was taken by a Forum and Basilica, the construction of which is dated to the year A.D. 130 by a magnificent inscription to the Emperor Hadrian."

These and other facts will be found in the little pamphlet " Wroxeter, Roman City " written by Miss Kathleen

M. Kenyon for the Ministry of Works, and available on the site. Here I shall only point to a few features which impressed me. First, of course, there is the great wall of the Basilica, which for hundreds of years was the only visible sign of the city, sticking out of the fields, worn and weathered by nearly 2,000 winters.

There are also the public baths, with the hypocausts, and an exercise hall adjoining them. West of the lane which runs through the site are the columns which supported the colonnaded portico of the Forum. Over its entrance stood the magnificent inscription recording the erection of the building in A.D. 130 under Hadrian.

A well-arranged Museum on the site includes some of the inscriptions and objects found at Uriconium, and there are others in the Shrewsbury Museum. One inscription mentions Tiberius Claudius, a horseman of the Sixth Thracian Cohort, from the coast of the Black Sea, who died aged fifty-six; another commemorates a standard bearer of the Fourteenth Legion, who died aged thirty-eight after eighteen years' service, and there is the tombstone of a lady named Placida, who died at the age of fifty years " after thirty years of married life ". But the finest inscription of all is that which stood above the Forum; the lettering has a nobility which brings readily to mind the magnificence of the building which it once crowned.

As at Caerleon, Uriconium and its glories have entered into Welsh legend. A Welsh poet named Llywarc Hen wrote a poem about the last days of " The White City in the Valley ", home of Kyndylan, probably the last of its rulers. It is probably Uriconium. He tells of the city standing in silent desolation "without fire, without light, without song ".

It was this impression which remained in my mind as I climbed into the driving seat and headed south along the Watling Street. The Wrekin stood out like a black cone against the fading sky and the wind buffeted my little car,

> " The gale it plies the saplings double,
> It blows so hard, 'twill soon be gone,
> Today the Roman and his trouble
> Are ashes under Uricon. . . ."

Whether it was caused by the melancholy associations of Uriconium, or the fact that I was nearing the end of my journey, I do not know; but this mood of finality followed me for mile after mile along the Watling Street, through Wellington and Oakengates, and over bleak Cannock Chase where rain slashed against the windscreen and the engine's note slammed back from the grim walls of mining villages.

In the kindly south it was easy to imagine the beginning of the occupation; Chedworth in the Cotswolds had spoken of the long tranquil years of peace, Hadrian's Wall of the organised and disciplined defenders of that peace. But now I could think only of retreat, collapse, disintegration, a period as inchoate and formless as the industrial limbo through which I was driving.

At the village of Wall, just south of Lichfield, I parked the car under some trees, out of the way of the thundering lorries, and went in search of Letocetum, a Roman posting-station on the Watling Street, at the point where it was crossed by the Icknield Street. I found it behind a group of cottages in a field below the smoke-blackened church; at least I found the fragment which is on view. Here is a group of well-preserved public baths, with their hypocausts, furnace-chamber, cement-lined plunge baths, and palæstra or exercise-ground. This little Staffordshire village can boast one of the finest specimens of Roman baths in the British Isles, well-tended by the National Trust. The Curator told me that archæologists from as far afield as Italy have come to study them. But they are only a small portion of the Roman settlement, the rest of which still lies under the fields. The cemetery was found some years ago to the west of the village, and there are a number of funerary urns in the museum, containing charred bones and ashes. There is also a tradition that the church stands on the site of a Roman temple.

Rest stations such as Letocetum—and others have been found along the line of the Watling Street—sometimes had a military purpose. For instance, it has been suggested that Letocetum had to keep watch over the Celts of Cannock Chase and South Staffordshire, and this may account for the barricade which was found on Pipe Hill nearby.

Recently, West Midland archæologists such as Mr. Graham Webster and Mr. Adrian Oswald, of Birmingham have excavated other Roman sites in this area, which was once described by a leading antiquarian as " archæologically, a barren waste ". Much needs to be learned about the progress of the Roman advance through the Midlands in the early years of the invasion, when, as we know, the Fourteenth and Twentieth Legions came this way. No legionary fortress corresponding to Lincoln or Gloucester has yet been found to indicate more precisely their course and progress. Yet it is very probable that that there was a legionary base marking the interim pacification of the area. Wroxeter (Uriconium) has been suggested, but so far there is insufficient evidence to confirm this.

Again, there are a number of fine Iron Age hill-fortresses in the Midlands, corresponding to Maiden Castle in Dorset, where Sir Mortimer Wheeler found conclusive evidence of its having been stormed and taken by the Romans. Surely similar battles must have taken place in the Midlands? If such hill-forts as Bredon, in Worcestershire, Wychbury Hill near Stourbridge, and British Camp, Malvern, were subjected to the same intensive investigation some interesting evidence might be found. But excavating a large hill-fort is a lengthy and costly process.

Some military remains have been found, but these are all small marching-camps or temporary forts. One such camp has been identified at Metchly, near the Queen Elizabeth Hospital on the outskirts of Birmingham. Another was found at Ashwood Heath, near Kingswinford, and at Dodderhill near Droitwich, and at Stretton Mill near Gailey.

" These camps," says Mr. T. F. Wright, in his article,

" The Roman Midlands ", " were established in the late 40's or early 50's A.D. They continued in occupation until the end of the century. At Metchley, a smaller camp was built inside the larger one during the 70's. The one at Stretton Mill is less than a mile from the possibly legionary camp at Kinvaston. Their function was to guard the area lest trouble should break out among the British tribes. Intelligent field work might discover others of their kind by tracing out the blanks in our knowledge of the roads connecting them."[1]

One such road, the Icknield Street, can be traced for considerable lengths. I remember as a boy being shown a section of the *agger* running across Sutton Park, near Birmingham, and I have often travelled along the delightfully unfrequented stretch which starts near Beoley, not far from Redditch in Worcestershire, and travels in an almost straight line through Alcester,[2] Bidford-on-Avon and the Shakespeare country, to Weston-sub-Edge and so over the Cotswolds, where the line is more difficult to trace. This, incidentally, is the Roman road which crossed the Watling Street at Wall, and part of its course can still be traced across the fields to the south of the village.

From Wall I continued south-eastward along the Watling Street as far as the hamlet of High Cross, in Staffordshire. You must watch for it carefully, or you may miss it, as there is nothing to be seen save a few houses, in the garden of one of which is a battered eighteenth-century monument. Walk to the point where a narrow lane leads off to the right down a slight slope. You are now on the site of the Roman Vennonæ, where the Watling Street crosses that other great Roman road, the Fosse Way, which for a time was the northern frontier of Britain.

Standing at this spot, near the end of my tour, I thought of the long, exhilarating stretch of the Fosse which I had

[1] *Birmingham Post*, February 15th, 1955.

[2] I am informed that at Alcester, in Worcestershire, there is an almost perfect Roman pavement in the back-garden of a house in the High Street, but, as the owner naturally wants to use his garden, it has been covered up again. One wonders if something can be done about preserving it, either *in situ* or elsewhere.

followed through Somerset, more than 150 miles south, and that other stretch which streams over the Lincolnshire wolds to Lincoln. Here it was a mere rutted track between the sodden fields; yet it was the same road. I have also followed it northward—though not on this journey—to Leicester, another important Roman city which they called Ratæ. From the Watling Street you turn on to A46 a mile west of High Cross, and, after a detour, pick up the original Roman line near Sapcot, from which it takes you straight into Leicester.

The only Roman remains visible in this busy manufacturing city is the so-called Jewry Wall, which was probably part of the basilica or town hall; there is also a good collection of Roman antiquities in the Leicester Museum. The full name of Roman Leicester was Ratæ Coritanorum, after the Coritani tribe who inhabited the district. In the time of Hadrian a fine suite of public baths was built, with a public hall attached. It also had an aqueduct which didn't work. Professor Richmond tells us that—

> " By one of those mischances which are so vividly described by Pliny in the province of Bithynia, the line for the aqueduct feeding the establishment was miscalculated, and the water seems thereafter to have been supplied from the adjacent river to a hand-filled cistern; work for muncipal labour, but hardly consonant with the best standards of the day. It will suggest that the baths were by no means in continual use, and may serve to qualify a rosy view of universally extended social amenities frequently enjoyed." [1]

It is amusing to know that even the efficient Romans sometimes made mistakes.

South of High Cross the Fosse Way can be traced on for many straight miles, through Stretton under Fosse, Brinklow (where the main A4114 crosses it) and so via narrow lanes to Princethorpe. The stretch between Princethorpe and Halford, which I have travelled scores of times, passes through some of the loveliest of Warwickshire—which is saying a lot.

When I last explored it the fields were white with

[1] " Roman Britain," by I. A. Richmond (Penguin Books)

dandelion puffs. The narrow road gently dipped and rose, with thick hedges and ancient oaks on either side—the last survivors of the Forest of Arden. Solid Warwickshire farmhouses stood aloofly in their flat fields, but the road passed through few villages, and weekday travellers can usually have it practically to themselves. At one point it skirts a low hill on which stands Chesterton Windmill, designed, it is said, by Inigo Jones. Here the Fosse becomes a gated road, and week-end visitors picnic on the grassy slopes. Finally, at Halford, it becomes the main road from Stratford to Moreton-in-the-Marsh. Here there is a solid seventeenth-century coaching inn, " The Bell ", a favourite halt for Birmingham fishermen and cyclists. Beyond the inn the old road wiggles across a stream by a narrow bridge and continues its course over the Cotswolds. You will see no Roman remains on this route, apart from the road itself, but you will have a tranquil journey.

I would like to have made it from High Cross; the lane was very tempting, but I had not the time and in any case the weather was uninviting. I joined the procession of heavy transport vehicles and hurried south to London, through Weedon and Towcester (Roman Lactodurum), and so to Stony Stratford, Bletchley, and Dunstable, and beyond. It was a relief, after the forts and camps of the North and Midlands, to feel that I had left the Roman frontier behind and was back in the soft core of Roman Britain, the civilised area with its gracious towns, country villas, and broad, well-made roads with their comfortable posting stations. The trumpets sounded fainter, the tramp of armed men died away, and I was approaching the gates of Roman Verulamium, which we call St. Albans.

Verulamium was an important tribal centre, the capital of the Catavellauni—before Claudius came. It was burned and sacked during the Boudiccan revolt of A.D. 61. Rebuilt, it prospered, and eventually grew into a great walled city of some 200 acres, with a forum more monumental in plan than any in Britain, a small theatre and a market hall. In the residential quarter there were fine houses for the tribal aristocracy.

"They are comfortable dwellings", writes Richmond, "in many cases half-timbered and mostly a single storey in height, sprawling alongside or round a roomy garden. They are emphatically the country dwelling brought to town, and there is no sense of overcrowding or of the tight-lined planning that goes with urban development. Those who planned the town were determined that the gentry should have room. The shopkeepers, whose long narrow buildings justled one another on the main streets, belonged to a different class, whose policy was minimum capital expenditure combined with maximum profit. . . ."[1]

At the top of the hill, just where A5 takes a sharp turn to the left towards the traffic-lights, I escaped with relief down a narrow road bordered by charming seventeenth- and eighteenth-century houses standing behind walls of mellowed brick and flint. I parked near the "Fighting Cocks" Inn and crossed a wooden bridge over the little River Ver which runs at the foot of the valley. Opposite rose a grassy slope graced with trees, and straight ahead I could see near the footpath a long stretch of the Roman wall of Verulamium, standing to a height of about 9 feet, with the familiar projecting bastions at regular intervals. Their total circuit was originally about two miles. They were defensive, of course, but Verulamium was not a military station; the city was essentially a place of residence and a commercial centre.

Large sections of Verulamium have been excavated from time to time, notably by Sir Mortimer and the late Mrs. Tessa Wheeler in the 'thirties, but most of the ruins have been buried again. A diagram of the Roman city, available in the museum, shows that it was of roughly oval plan. The Watling Street entered it via the north-west gate, and left via the south-east gate. The forum stood to the south of St. Michael's Church, near the museum, with the theatre a little to the west, fronting on

[1] "Roman Britain," by I. A. Richmond (Penguin Books).

the Watling Street. The streets were laid out in the usual "gridiron" pattern, and excavations in the south-eastern sector of the city have revealed shops, villas and a temple. There was another larger temple immediately to the south-west of the theatre.

More recently, some excavations have been carried out at Verulamium, both by the Curator, Mr. John Lunn, and by Mr. Sheppard Frere, of the London Institute of Archæology, with voluntary helpers. One of these excavations was in a long, narrow area which is shortly to be occupied by a modern main road. Trenches revealed a row of houses facing a Roman street which ran further to the north. There were three large town houses, of the bungalow type, with tesselated floors and internal walls of clay and timber, but the outer walls were of course flintwork and brick. One of these internal walls had fallen flat, and still preserved large sections of decorated plaster of rather poor quality; there were no painted figures but only simple yellow, red and blue panels—the Roman equivalent of cheap wallpaper. Then Mr. Frere cut a trench through the later Roman fortifications and found an entirely new fortification which has not yet been explained. Underneath one of the Roman houses the archæologists came upon an earlier ditch, a very deep military obstacle, which had been filled in the late second century when the Roman houses had been built on the site.

It remained only to see the Museum, which I must admit to finding far more absorbing than the ruins of Verulamium itself. It is a fairly long, low-ceilinged room, lit from above, and in the center is a large-scale model of the Roman city. Around this central space are grouped the cases containing the very many interesting and often lovely things which have been found at Verulamium.

The artistic standard of many of the objects found at Verulamium is much higher than that of most of those I saw on my tour—an indication of the wealth and sophistication of the city. The tesselated pavements are as elegant as those at Cirencester, the glassware and pottery of the finest.

Among the oddities I remarked a bronze tube, which may have been a tap-nozzle, much like a modern example, and some very interesting tradesmen's tools, each displayed in separate cases according to the trade. Nearly all these things are humble, everyday objects connected with civilian life—a relief after the monotonous succession of spears, helmets, arrow-heads which naturally predominate in the northern collections.

In a case labelled " Butcher " there were skewers, flesh-hooks, knives and choppers, very like those used in butcher's shops to-day. In another case marked " Carpenter " were awls, a small axe, scrapers, iron nails, chisels and so on. The cutler had his bone-handled knives of various sorts, the shopkeeper his bronze balances, and the locksmith his padlocks, bar-bolts and catch-springs. Then there was the more delicate art of the bronze-worker. A thing which caught my eye was a drop-handle for a box or chest of drawers, almost exactly like the ornamented handles one sees on Victorian furniture. There were workmanlike farm implements which reminded one that Roman Britain was essentially an agricultural country; sickles (and whetstones for sharpening them), spades, shears, two-pronged forks, and linchpins and harness ornaments for the horses which drew the plough.

Of course that Roman dog had visited Verulamium—the one who wandered around Britain looking for wet tiles to walk on. But the Verulamium tile-maker was annoyed, and flung a small flint pebble at the dog, which retreated rapidly, leaving the imprint of its fleeing foot and the pebble embedded just behind it.

There were three main types of dog in Roman Britain—an Irish wolfhound, a kind of bulldog, and a retriever-like animal. They were much in demand on the Continent for hunting.

Fine fragments of architraves and fluted marble columns, probably from Carrara, in Italy, hint at the magnificence of the city, but the glory of the Verulamium Museum is its collection of Roman pavements. One of these is quite the most beautiful I have seen. It is in the form of a huge scallop shell, a vast semicircle with radiating flutings like a fan, or, as my fancy saw it, the rays of the setting sun. Again my thoughts returned to the sunset of Roman civilisation in Britain. Twelve generations were born, lived out their lives and died in the four centuries during which our island was a Roman province. There were occasional revolts and disturbances. Several times the barbarians broke through the Wall and came south to plunder, only to be driven back again. But on the whole they were peaceful years in which trade and commerce could flourish, and art and culture find time to develop. As Sir Winston Churchill has written in his " History of the English-speaking Peoples ", " For nearly 300 years Britain, reconciled to the Roman system, enjoyed in many respects the happiest, most comfortable, and most enlightened times its inhabitants have had." [1] Then it all ended, not suddenly and dramatically, but by a slow process of disintegration. Romano-British civilisation perished like the outer branch of a tree, the root of which was Rome. When the root began to decay, the branch withered and eventually died.

I left the Museum and walked down a lane until I saw, in gold letters the words, " The Roman Theatre ". It stands a few yards to the left of a drive leading to Gorhambury Park, which once belonged to Sir Francis Bacon. The Theatre has been completely excavated, and from the top of its smoothly clipped turf banks I looked down on the orchestra (or pit as we would call it to-day), the stage with its " curtain-slot ", and adjoining dressing-rooms for the actors, and the entrances on three sides. The central portion could be, and probably was, also used for gladiatorial sports, but nevertheless this was a true theatre.

To the north lay the gentle grass slopes of Gorhambury

[1] Sir Winston Churchill, " History of the English-speaking Peoples." Cassell & Company, 1956.

Park, shadowed by cedars, not yet encroached upon by villadom. To the south, above the red roofs of the town rose the heavy grey bulk of St. Alban's Cathedral—built partly from stone and tiles taken from the Roman city. Beyond that, only twenty miles away lay the end of my long journey; Londinium, in its time the greatest Roman city in Britain.

CHAPTER TWENTY-TWO

ROMAN LONDON

It may be wondered why, in a book on Roman Britain, its greatest city has been left to the last. The reason is that I have tried to relate a journey through Roman Britain to the main stages of invasion and occupation. When the Romans landed in Kent in A.D. 43, London did not exist. Colchester (Camulodunum) was the nearest approach to a capital. Later York became the military capital of the north; it had a *Palatium*, where Emperors would have stayed during their visits and Governors resided for at least part of the year.

But, although it did not, at first, have the status of Colchester, London soon became the natural centre for British trade and administration once the Roman engineers had selected it.

" Nature here contained the tidal Thames within hard gravel banks and made possible the construction of a bridge, where land traffic and sea traffic for the whole island met. The roads radiated from the bridge head, the sea lanes converged upon it from the Rhine, the Gallic coastal ports and the North Sea, or by the Channel route from Bordeaux, Spain, and the Mediterranean." [1]

Fifty years after the Romans landed, supremacy had passed from Camulodunum to London, which then had a garrison like any other provincial city.

" Within a generation the financial administration was using Londinium as its headquarters; while in the fourth century it was not only the seat of the provincial treasury but the residence of the civil governor who presided over the four divisions into which the province was then broken."

London grew steadily until it became the largest and

[1] " Roman Britain," by I. A. Richmond (Penguin Books).

richest city in Britain, covering more than 300 acres, larger than most Roman cities north of the Alps. It suffered several vicissitudes and changes of fortune. Burned to the ground by Boudicca in A.D. 61, it rose again, only to be burned down a second time during the reign of Hadrian. Again it was rebuilt, more splendid than ever, girdled by its great walls, and enclosing an extensive Forum, a huge basilica, temples to Mithras and other gods, and private buildings ranging from villas for the wealthy merchants to small shops and workmen's dwellings. Roman ships moored at its quays, bringing in fine Italian marble and other stone to adorn its monuments, and exotic imports to grace the home of its richer citizens—Italian statuary, fine Rhenish glassware, figured Samian bowls from Gaul, multi-coloured, pillared-moulded bowls and jars from Alexandria, table services of silver plate, olive oil from Spain, wines from Gaul and the Rhine.

Considering that the city of London has been continuously occupied for nearly 2,000 years, and the site built and rebuilt upon from century to century, it is surprising that any of the Roman city remains at all. But it does; though it has to be looked for. Although I have lived in London for fourteen years I had no idea, until recently, of how much of Londinium can still be seen; and as for Roman antiquities, more objects have been found in the city of London than on any other Roman site in the British Isles.

I suggest that the best way to see Roman London is in three stages. First, the City Walls, which survive in several places; second, the pavements and other remains which lie buried under offices and shops; third, the Roman collections in the London Museum, the Guildhall Museum and the British Museum. However, before beginning your tour, it is worth doing what I recommended at Canterbury; climb to a high point, such as the top of the Great Fire Monument in Bread Street, and look down on the city.

Begin by looking towards the Tower of London, which

marks the south-eastern corner of the Roman city. From this point the wall ran north-west to Aldgate, then turned west-north-west to Bishopgate. Here it turned west and continued towards St. Giles, Cripplegate, where it changed direction at a right angle. Just before Gresham Street it altered course again, west-south-west as far as Newgate. Thence it ran south to Ludgate until it reached the Thames. The distance thus covered by this landward side of the wall is about two miles, and the area enclosed is roughly 330 acres.

If you could have looked down on Londinium in, say, the fourth century A.D. you would have seen that it was divided roughly in half by the River Walbrook which came in from the north and flowed into the Thames near what is now Cannon Street Station. Entering from the west through Ludgate, you would pass under a massive arch built in the western wall, with a large entrance in the centre for wheeled traffic and smaller arches on each side for pedestrians. Once inside you would begin to climb a hill, then you would cross the Walbrook by a bridge and climb another hill by a road leading to the heart of the city. Near the centre was a wide open space, the Forum or market place, overshadowed by a long colonnaded building of about the same length as St. Paul's; the basilica or town hall. It stood where Gracechurch Street is to-day.

The streets would be laid out in a rectilinear plan, but at present we can trace only fragments of them. We do know, however, that there were streets of shops, like those discovered in other Romano-British cities, with open fronts and rooms at the back. There were also spacious villas near the Walbrook, and, along the Thames bank, the wharves, warehouses, commercial offices, and the dwellings of tradesmen and artisans. Outside the walls lay the cemeteries with their elaborately-carved and inscribed tombstones, and from the turreted gateways spaced along the walls, roads radiated like the spokes of a wheel—the same roads along some of which we have travelled during our tour of Britain. You would see the

Watling Street coming in from the south-east, crossing the Thames by a bridge, and then leaving the city again on the north-west. Due north you would see the Ermine Street crossing the hills on its way to Lincoln. North-eastward a fourth road led away to Colchester, the earlier capital, and on the south-western side two roads left the city, one going south-west to Chichester, the other following the Thames Valley for part of the way to Silchester. Farm-carts, troops of soldiers, mounted messengers would pass and re-pass. Smoke would be rising from the furnaces of the public baths; there would be hum of life; carts and chariots rattling along the streets, the distant shouts of stevedores and sailors unloading ships at the wharves, the ring of smiths' anvils, and the staccato yelp of saws from the artisans' quarter. . . . The picture fades; and there is the tight huddle of banks and commercial offices, the new glass and concrete skyscraper blocks, and the red buses crawling past St. Paul's. . . .

I began my exploration of the Roman city wall in a bombed area just south of Fore Street and north of London Wall, within sight of St. Giles' Church, Cripplegate. Owing to the destruction of this part of London, more of the Roman Wall is visible now than any time during the last few hundred years, and it is hoped that some sections will be preserved permanently. Here, between the gaunt skeletons of bombed-out offices, lies a section of the wall which was uncovered by the Corporation of the City of London as part of its contribution to the Festival of Britain. It is a curious patchwork of various styles of masonry, topped with brickwork. The lower part is Roman, the middle (of stone) is medieval, and the brickwork represents the last restoration of the wall during the Mayoralty of Ralph Jocelyn in 1476. Near this point you will notice what appears to be a crack running down the centre of the Roman foundation. Mr. Norman Cook, Keeper of the Guildhall Museum, pointed out to me that it is not really a crack in the masonry, but marks the place where the wall of the

Roman fort (the existence of which was not suspected until quite recently) met the city wall. The fort was built first, and when the city wall was erected its builders aligned it to that of the fort, but as the fort wall was thinner than the new wall, the former had to be thickened —hence the apparent crack. In 1956 Professor Grimes excavated the massive walls of this fort.

Further west, near St. Giles' Church (where Milton was buried) is the famous Cripplegate bastion, which marks the north-west corner of Londinium. It is one of the strongest of all the bastions, and the biggest, but all that can be seen above ground is medieval, though resting on Roman foundations. I turned southward and clambered across mounds of debris, on which grass and weeds are growing, and followed the line of the western stretch of the Roman Wall, where are other bastions which were once hidden under nineteenth-century offices, but now open, temporarily, to the sky. They reminded me very much of those at Caerwent.

Mr. Cook, who has made a close study of the wall, remarked to me that some of London's modern buildings, such as the Telephone Exchange which lies south of this point, owe their alignment to the presence of the Roman Wall beneath them. " You will notice," he said, " that the wall of the Telephone Exchange is bent at a most extraordinary angle. The reason is that the line of the existing Roman Wall dictated the shape of the property when that big building was put up. And as it happened that, at that particular point, the city wall leaves the old fort wall at an angle, the modern building had to follow suit."

This fascinating example of the past governing the present will probably bewilder Americans and irritate their British admirers who would like to turn London into another Chicago. It is, however, a point which perverse traditionalists like myself find thoroughly satisfying.

Next I went with Mr. Cook to the General Post Office at St. Martin-le-Grand, a huge building full of clerks and sorters, with a large yard from which the red mail vans hurry out on their journeys. An official led us into the basement, and there, perfectly preserved and well lit, was a magnificent section of the ancient wall and one of the bastions, which has been carefully preserved since the Post Office was built in 1909. Anyone who visits the Post Office in working hours and asks to see the wall will be shown it, for Her Majesty's Post Office is rightly proud of its relic of Roman London.

The longest and highest surviving stretch of London's Roman wall was until recently incorporated in one of the oldest bonded warehouses in the city, near Cooper's Row on Tower Hill. But it is now fully exposed to view.

Outside the warehouse, near Coopers' Row, is another stretch, recently revealed by the bombing of London. On it is a reproduction of a monumental inscription[1] found nearby, and put up in memory of one of the Roman benefactors of Britain, Julius Classicianus, Procurator (Financial Officer) of Britain after the revolt of Boudicca. The translated inscription reads:

"In memory of Gaius Julius Alpinus Classiciani of the Fabian tribe, son of Gaius; Procurator of the Province of Britain. This monument was set up by his sorrowing wife, Julia Pacata, daughter of Julius Indus."

[1] The original can be seen in the British Museum.

During the revolt of Boudicca, the then Procurator, Decianus Catus, whose injustice may have been partly responsible for the revolt, fled to Gaul (see Chapter Fourteen). The new Procurator, Julius Classicianus is mentioned sneeringly by Tacitus.

" Nations, too, so high-spirited inclined the more slowly to peace, because Julius Classicianus, who had been sent as successor to Catus, let private animosities interfere with public interest, and had spread an idea that they ought to wait for a new governor, who, having neither the anger of an enemy nor the pride of a conqueror, would deal with those who had surrendered." [1]

Some scholars believe that Tacitus, wishing to glorify Suetonius, was unfair to the new Financial Officer, who had the difficult task of overcoming the hatred of the defeated Britons.

Until the inscription to Classicianus was discovered nothing was known about this official, apart from the reference in Tacitus. But those few formal Latin words, which to most of us would be just another piece of a memorial inscription, revealed one vital fact—that Classicianus was the son of a Gaul. He may have remembered, when his own country was conquered, that the Romans had been clement, had delegated authority to the tribal chieftains and encouraged them to become Roman citizens. He himself had risen to fairly high rank within the Roman system, and, in opposing Suetonius he may well have been trying, gently, to teach the new generation of Romans their own colonising business. He seems to have been successful, for Suetonius, who was probably better at fighting than thinking, was withdrawn, and a new, more lenient governor appointed in his place.

One wonders if Julia Pacata, who, as the mere wife of a Roman official, did not rate a mention by Tacitus, may herself had some influence in this matter? Incidentally, her father, Julius Indus, recruited the *Ala Indiana*, a cavalry regiment which was stationed for a time at Cirencester.

[1] Tacitus.

Of the many Roman pavements discovered under London the best have been removed to the Museums, though a few still remain in their original position. When the blitzed offices of a firm of chartered accountants in Ironmonger Lane was being rebuilt after the war one such pavement was found, and has been preserved in the basement and can usually be seen on application. The building is a few yards down Ironmonger Lane on the right, going from Gresham Street. To reach it one has to descend a number of stairs, which lead from the modern street-level to the Roman level. It is not the most brilliant of pavements, and cannot be compared with those from Leadenhall Street, now in the British Museum. But this one is *in situ*, and although it is now in a basement surrounded by filing cabinets and office equipment, it was not a Roman cellar-floor but a living-room floor. The stairs lead us down through the accumulated debris of nearly twenty centuries, modern, Victorian, Georgian, Carolean, Elizabethan, medieval, Saxon; and so at last to the Roman pavement at the bottom.

There is another Roman pavement in the basement of the Coal Exchange in Billingsgate, with remains of the conduit which conducted warm air into the walls of the room. This also can be seen on application to the Exchange.

The famous temple of Mithras discovered at Bucklersbury in 1954 has now been re-erected outside the new office-block which stands on its former site. The discovery of this temple, the existence of which had long been suspected, attracted thousands of visitors, to the astonishment of the archæologists. Mithras, god of the Sun, was the soldiers' deity, in whose worship were embodied the military virtues of courage, constancy and endurance. The legionaries found him in Persia, on the eastern frontier of the Empire, and brought him to Britain, where he was worshipped in many places, even as far north as Hadrian's Wall among the heather and the crags of Northumberland.

Cottrell.

Hadrian's Wall

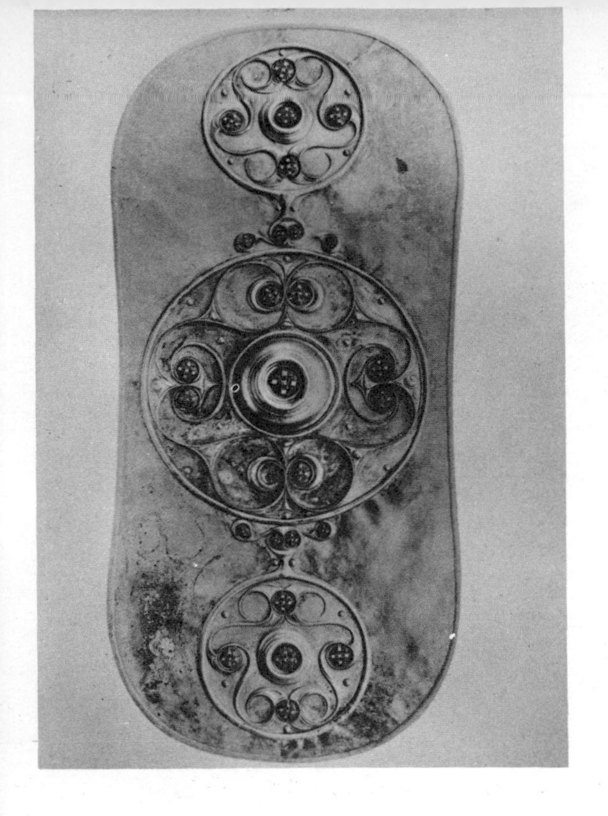

British bronze shield found
Battersea. (Late first centu
B.C. or early first century A.D.)

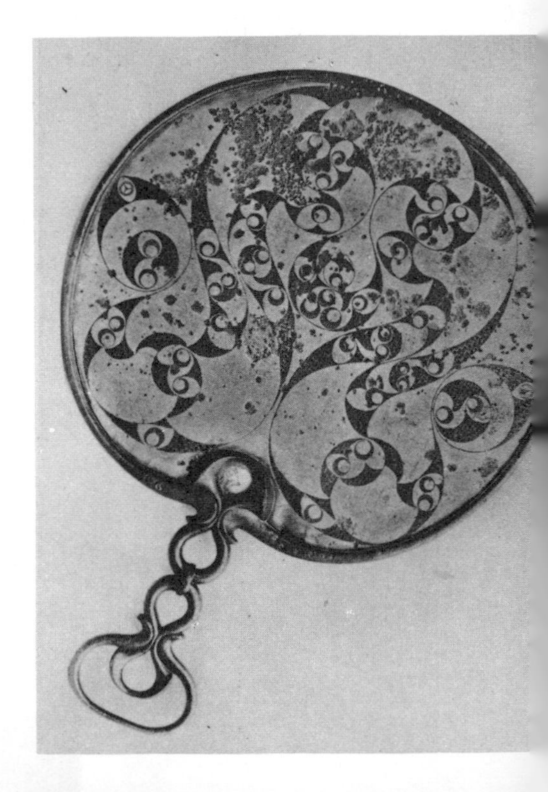

British decorated bronze mirror of the first century A.D.

Walmer Beach, near where Cæsar is believed to have landed.

Interior of the Roman Lighthouse, Dover.

The multiple embankments of the great fort at Ardoch, Perthshire.

Model of the auxiliary fort at Cadder, built alongside the Antonine Wall.

A well-preserved section of the Antonine Wall and Ditch at Camelon, near Falkirk.

The turf rampart and ditch of the Antonine Wall passing under an electricity pylon at Bonnybridge.

Bronze figure of Venus from Colchester.

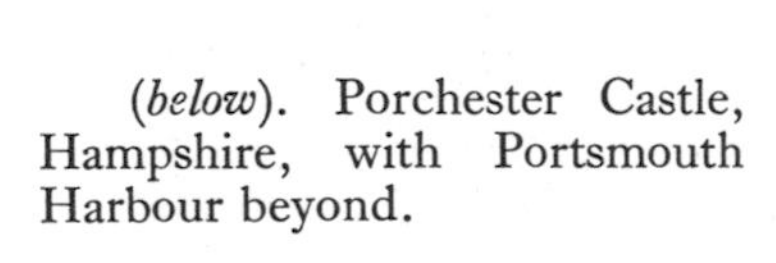

(*below*). Porchester Castle, Hampshire, with Portsmouth Harbour beyond.

The Emperor Hadrian (bronze head found in the Thames).

The Ackling Dyke, near Salisbury, Wilts.

Head of Mithras, as found in the Temple of Mithras, Walbrook.

Part of the Roman City Wall of London, near the Tower.

One of the principal streets of Chester, built on Roman foundations. The famous "Rows" (see *right*) may owe their origin to the presence of substantial Roman remains which had to be built over.

General view of Uriconium showing the remains of the great Basilica or Town Hall in background, baths and other buildings in foreground.

Uriconium. Part of the colonnade of the Forum, the rest of which is still buried.

Roman mosaic pavement in the form of a scallop shell. (From St. Albans.)

A roof-tile from St. Albans with paw marks of a dog, and the pebble thrown at it.

Model of the South-east gate of Verulamium (St. Albans).

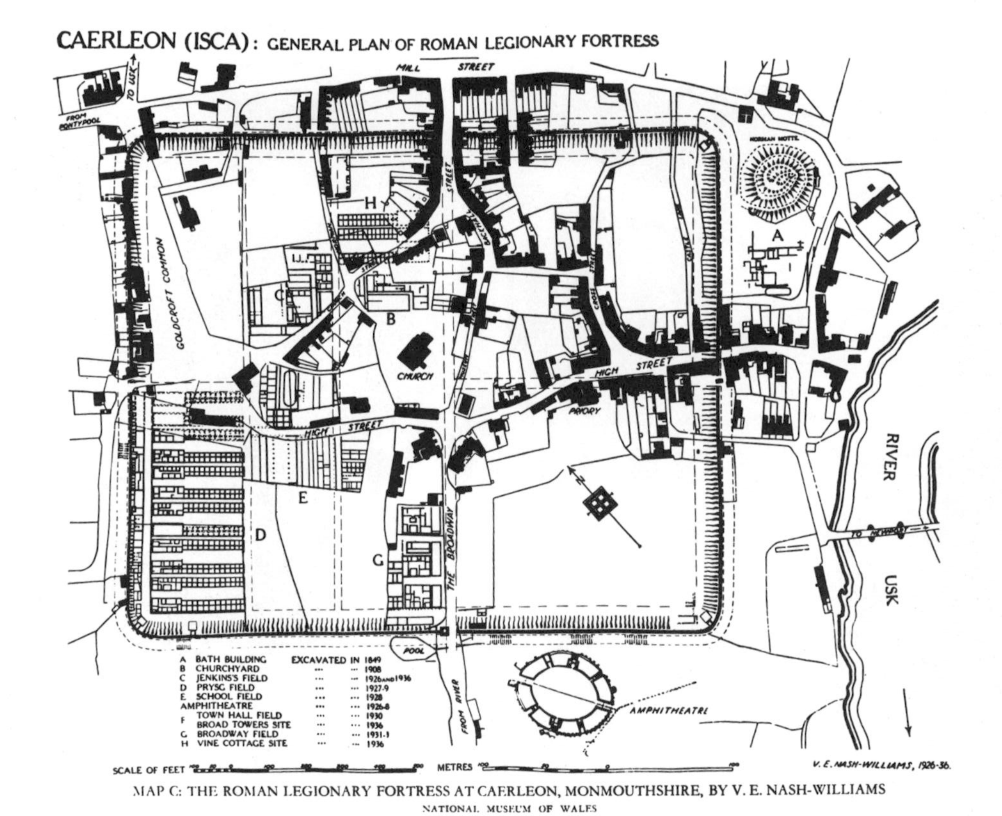

MAP C: THE ROMAN LEGIONARY FORTRESS AT CAERLEON, MONMOUTHSHIRE, BY V. E. NASH-WILLIAMS

NATIONAL MUSEUM OF WALES

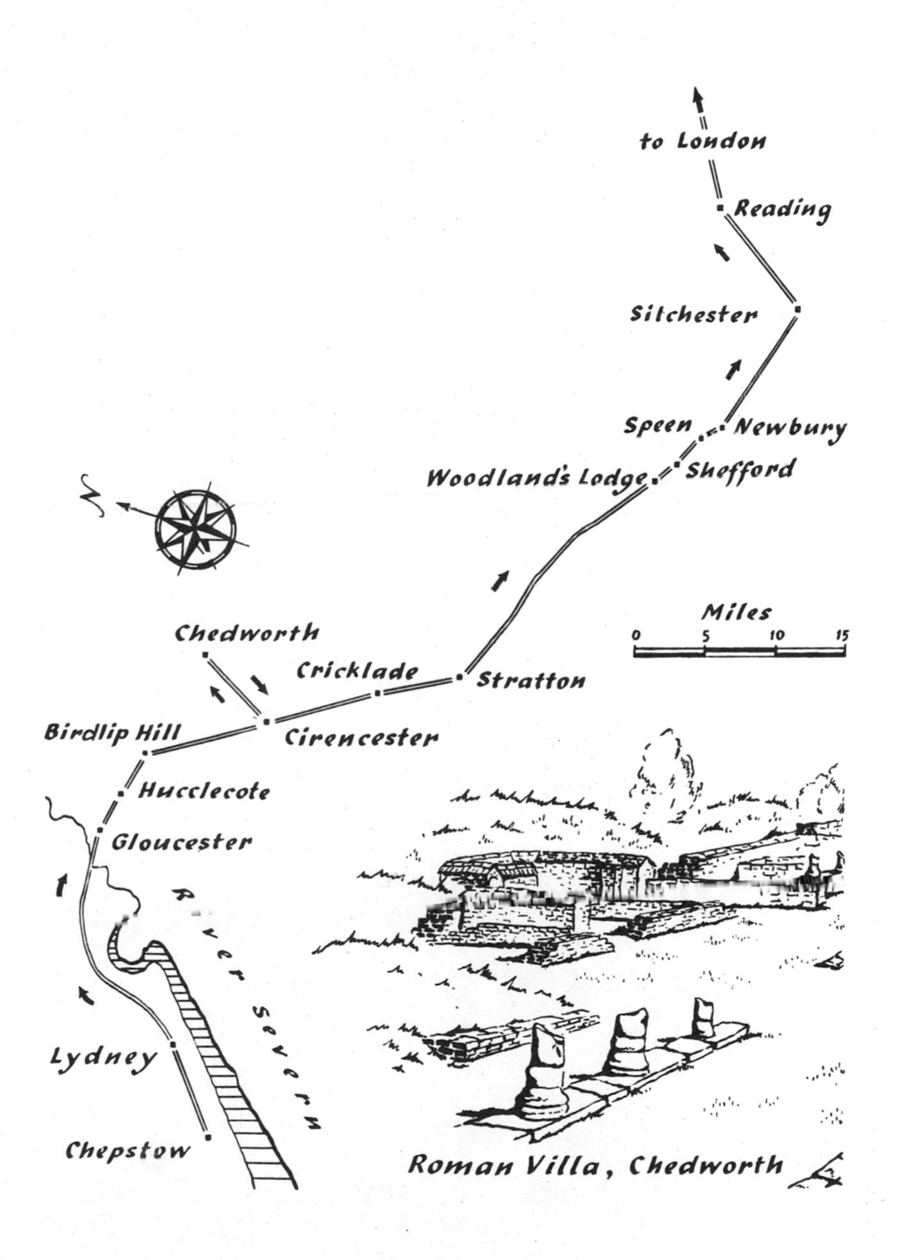

Roman Villa, Chedworth

Malaivs Ins.

Blatobvlgivm

HIVERNIA

Monavia Ins.

Mona Ins.

Canovivm

Alabvm

Oceanvs

Atlanticvs

Isca Dvmnoniorvm

Mare Germanicvm
Hadrian's Wall
Vindomora
Ebvracvm
Abvs Fl.
Lindvm
Branodvnvm
Gariannonvm
Ratae
Venonae
Venta
Camvlodvnvm
Corinivm
Londinivm
Calleva
Dvrovernvm
Dvbris
Portvs Advrni
Vectis Ins.
J R A C

Electrum (gold and silver alloy) *torc*. First century B.C.

Silver dish, part of the " Mildenhall Treasure," found at Mildenhall, Suffolk. Fourth century A.D.

The Ermine Street, just south of Lincoln. Here the Roman highway, built on its high bank, has become a drove-road.

Bronze figure of Hercules, found in a fort on Hadrian's Wall.

From the British Museum. Richly decorated Roman parade helmet, with reliefs of fighting warriors, found at Ribchester, Lancashire.

Richborough Castle, Kent. Part of the defensive wall.

Glass flagon from Baysford, Kent.

The twentieth meets the third century. TV aerials leaning against the Roman city wall, Colchester.

Samian vase with hunting scene in relief.

The Fosse Way, near Charlton, Somerset.

A contrast. The Fosse Way between Newark and Lincoln.

Maiden Castle, Dorset. View from the crest of the ramparts.

Maiden Castle, Dorset. Ditch between the ramparts on the north side.

The Severn at Aust.

Roman city wall at Caerwent, Monmouthshire.

Caerwent. A bastion of the city wall.

19. The Great Bath, Bath.

Head of the Gorgon from the Temple of Minerva, Bath.

British burial mounds at Priddy, Somerset.

The Roman Villa, Chedworth.

Wall among the heather and the crags of Northumberland.

> " Mithras, God of Midnight, here where the great bull dies
> Look on thy children in darkness; oh take our sacrifice!
> Many roads Thou hast fashioned; all of them lead to the Light,
> Mithras, also a soldier, teach us to die aright! "

Rudyard Kipling, who wrote those lines, probably came nearer to the spirit of Imperial Rome than most of us are likely to get.

Londinium, though it had a fortress, was not primarily a military centre, and the bulk of the objects found within its walls speak of civilian life, and especially of trade and commerce. The few letters and documents which have been found often contain phrases like this:

> " Rufus, son of Callisunus, greeting to Epillicus and all his fellows. I believe you know I am very well. If you have made the list please send (it). Do you look after everything carefully. *See that you turn that slave-girl into cash* (my italics)."

And this one:

> ". . . which money by the terms likewise of the claim shall be paid to me by Crescens or by the person concerned. . . ."

Tradesmens' stamps sometimes turn up. Near London Bridge was found a tablet of steatite or soapstone, 2 inches square and $\frac{3}{8}$ of an inch thick, for impressing on cakes of ointment of different varieties. It bore these words:

> " Caius Silvius Tetricus's scented ointment for granulations "
> " Caius Silvius Tetricus's salve applied with a swab, for an attack of inflamation (or onset of blepharitis) "
> " Caius Silvius Tetricus's salve for diseases and sores of the eyes."

Many Roman officers seem to have retired to London at the end of their military service, and died there.

> " To the Divine Shades; Flavus Agricola, soldier of the Sixth Legion, ' Victorious '; lived 42 years and 10 days; Albina Faustina had this made for her matchless husband."

> " To the Divine Shades; Julius Valens, soldier of the Twentieth " Valeria Victrix " Legion; aged 40; here he lies; set up by his heir, Flavius Atticus."

> " Aulus Aldidius Olussa of the Pompontine tribe; set up by his heir in accordance with his will; aged 70; born in Athens; he lies here."

The very terseness and simplicity of these inscriptions makes then the more moving:

"To the Divine Shades and in memory of Tulla Numidia, a most devoted woman. . . ."

and—most touching of all—

"Good Dexios, son of Ditimos, farewell . . ."

These inscriptions, with other remains, which can be seen in the London, Guildhall, and British Museums, are our main source of information about Roman London. The remains number so many thousands, and more are discovered each year, that it is impossible in this brief chapter to name more than a few. Relics of the early years following the invasion are few, but they exist. At Walbrook in 1949–50 when foundations were being dug for a new block of offices, the excavators found sixteen Roman cooking pots and two jugs which had been crushed, apparently by a large *amphora* which had been thrown into the pit. On the old ground level were found plates of red glazed ware and other pots, none of them later than about A.D. 60—seventeen years after the Romans landed. The interesting point about these remains is that they bore the marks of fire; almost certainly that which destroyed Roman London when Boudicca sacked it in the year A.D. 61.

Other finds, prosaic in themselves, draw us nearer to the citizens of the Roman city than pavements, fortifications, and the foundations of buildings. At Walbrook was found a double-handed glass bowl, remarkably like a modern glass cooking-dish. In Coleman Street were pins, needles, buckles, tweezers, and a comb. My own favourite story of Roman London was told to me by Norman Cook. When building contractors' bulldozers were preparing the Walbrook site for the foundations of a modern office block, Cook was asked to keep an eye open for Roman antiquities. He noticed one of the workmen using an unusually shaped iron shackle-hook on his bulldozer. It proved to be Roman. The workman had found it in the earth, and used it to replace a broken shackle-hook on his machine. . . .

Recently a disused Roman well yielded, among other things, a wooden ladle, a long ladder, and, most extraordinary of all, part of a Roman " Bikini " costume of leather. At the Piazza Armerina, in Sicily, are mosaics showing young girls wearing just such a costume; a narrow band across the loins and another barely covering the breasts. Unromantic scholars, however, have suggested that the London example was not worn by an athlete or a dancing-girl, but some female drudge who had to work almost naked in the muddy water of the Thames or the Walbrook.

Some of the objects I have mentioned were found many years ago; others, such as the " Bikini " came to light within the last few years. The best place to see the most recent finds—and, no doubt, there will be more discoveries—is the Guildhall Museum at present housed in the Royal Exchange.

From Bucklersbury you will see a set of workmens' tools, including a neat folding foot-rule, and leather and metal-working tools belonging to tradesmen who lived along the river bank. Notice also a set of brass balances with a horizontal arm along which a weight was moved—just like a set of baby-scales in a modern chemist's shop.

You will also see the objects found in the Roman well on the site of the Bank of England and South America, including the bottom half of the " Bikini " (prosaically labelled " leather trunks ") a wooden ladle and an 18-foot ladder. Other recent finds in the Walbrook area include an agate seal from a signet-ring with a tiny intaglio of a chariot, and a brass finger-ring with the single word *Amica* (sweetheart or lover).

Then, of course, there are the famous sculptured heads found on the site of the temple of Mithras, so often photographed and described. They were discovered under a floor of the early fourth century and have been identified, provisionally, as the heads of Mithras, of Serapis, the

Egyptian corn-god, and of Minerva. Even more striking is a massive marble hand, more than twice life-size, which must have belonged to a great statue, probably of the god himself. There is little doubt that these marble sculptures, of foreign provenance, were reverently buried by worshippers of pagan gods, probably to save them from destruction at the hands of the fanatical Christians.

Unlike Romano-British sculpture, there is nothing crude and provincial about these fine heads. Their delicate and sensuous modelling calls for Mediterranean sunshine. They look lost and slightly pathetic in our grey, joyless, northern light.

London speaks with many voices. There is modern London, with its nervous, concentrated life, its streets bursting with traffic for which they were never designed; there is Victorian London, solid, prosperous, somewhat Philistine, speaking with the voices of Trollope, Dickens and Thackeray; eighteenth-century London, where Johnson thundered, Reynolds painted and Handel composed; there is the London of Pepys, the London of Gower and Chaucer; and deep, deep down, hidden from view for the most part, Roman London. Most of the time Londoners are unaware of it, this city which lasted for 400 years, which, near the beginning, saw Boudicca's wild horsemen hurling burning brands into its timber houses, and, near the end, was threatened by a combined force of Gauls, Scots and Saxons until the forces of the Roman general Theodosius entered and saved it. That was in A.D. 368, more than three centuries after the Iceni sacked the city—as long a stretch of time as separates us from Oliver Cromwell.

It is all so very, very long ago, and may seem unimportant at a time when the hand which flung the blazing brand could, if it lived to-day, press a button which would utterly destroy a city more than a hundred times the size of Roman London. Yet when the contractors' bulldozers lay bare a grey wall even the least imaginative of us can be stirred, and hear, very faintly, the voice of the earliest London of all.

My last visit was to the British Museum, in which is

assembled some of the finest treasures of Roman Britain. As I wandered from gallery to gallery, looking at the labels under the exhibits, I recognised many names which reminded me of places I had visited on my journey. Here, for instance, was the famous Ribchester Helmet, from that grass-grown fort beside the Ribble, in Lancashire. How amused its original owner would have been if he could have known, as he rode on to the parade-ground in his glittering casque, that eighteen centuries later it would rest in a glass case for people like myself to stare at! From another case came the gleam of silver; here were the embossed dishes, plates, flagons and spoons which once graced the table of some great official, and then lay hidden under the Suffolk fens at Mildenhall until the plough revealed them. From Hadrian's Wall came a gilt-bronze figure of Hercules; from Cheapside, London, another vigorous bronze of an archer.

There were the mosaic pavements; Bacchus riding on a panther, from Leadenhall Street, London; Oceanus, with dolphins and sea-monsters, from Withington, in the Cotswolds; a chariot-race, from Horkstow, in Lincolnshire. Gold bracelets from Llandovery, in the mountains of Carmarthenshire, a gold pendant set with pearls, from Kent; writing tablets and pens, from London; scale-armour from Chester, and a heavy-limbed Venus from Colchester.

Each of these things, labelled and static in their Museum cases, evoked a memory; of white clouds drifting over the Downs at Bignor, of the lonely majesty of the Wall, of Chedworth beside the softly-gliding Colne, of Colchester's mighty Balkerne Gate, of the gulls crying above the flint walls of Porchester Castle, of the mist rising over the fields of Silchester, and the taut grey ribbon of the Fosse Way endlessly unwinding across the green hills of Somerset.

When I left the Museum and climbed into my car I glanced at the speedometer. It told me I had journeyed 3,558 miles within this little island, as far as from London to the Caspian Sea; and all in search of Roman Britain.

I would willingly travel them all again.

CHRONOLOGICAL TABLE

B.C.	
55–54	Expeditions of Julius Caesar to Britain.
A.D.	
43	Claudian invasion with four legions under Aulus Plautius.
	Defeat of Caratacus and capture of Camulodunum.
	Campaigns in the west (Legio II Augusta under Vespasian), in the midlands (XX Valeria Victrix and XIV Gemina) and in the east (IX Hispana).
47	Ostorius Scapula, governor, draws a frontier from the Trent to the Severn.
49–50	Foundation of Colonia Victricensis at Camulodunum.
	Mendip lead mines already in Roman hands.
	Legionary fortresses at Glevum and Lindum.
	Invasion of South Wales.
51	Caratacus, finally defeated in North Wales, flees to Cartimandua, queen of the Brigantes, and is surrendered to the Romans.
c. 55	Didius Gallus, governor, intervenes on the side of Cartimandua in Brigantian civil war.
61	Suetonius Paulinus, governor, attacks Anglesey.
	Icenian revolt under Boudicca suppressed after sack of Camulodunum, Londinium and Verulamium.
66	One legion (XIV Gemina) withdrawn from Britain.
68	Army in Britain refuses to join the governor, Trebellius Maximus, in revolt against Galba.
69	Romans fail to prevent the defection of the Brigantes.
71–74	Petilius Cerealis, governor, with a new legion (II Adiutrix) conquers the Brigantes.
	Legionary fortress at Eboracum.
74–78	Sextus Julius Frontinus, governor, subdues Wales and plants garrisons there.
	Legionary fortresses at Isca and Deva.
78	Cn. Julius Agricola, governor, completes the conquest of North Wales and Anglesey.
79	Consolidation of Brigantian conquest.
81	Agricola advances to the Forth–Clyde line.
83–84	Agricola advances north and defeats the Caledonians at the battle of Mons Graupius.
	Roman fleet circumnavigates Britain.
	Legionary fortress at Inchtuthil.
84–85	Agricola recalled by Domitian.
86	One legion (II Adiutrix) withdrawn from Britain.
c. 90	Legionary fortress at Inchtuthil evacuated.
90–96	Foundation of Lindum Colonia at Lincoln.

96–98	Foundation of Colonia Nervia Glevensis at Gloucester.
99–100	Legionary fortress at Isca and many auxiliary forts in Wales rebuilt in stone.
	Scottish forts evacuated.
c. 103	Legionary fortress at Deva rebuilt in stone.
107–108	Legionary fortress at Eboracum rebuilt in stone.
c. 117	Revolt in north Britain.
122	Hadrian visits Britain.
	Legio IX Hispana replaced by VI Victrix.
	Construction of Hadrian's Wall from Tyne to Solway begun by Aulus Platorius Nepos.
139–142	Q. Lollius Urbicus, governor under Antoninus Pius, advances into Scotland and builds the Antonine Wall across the Clyde–Forth isthmus.
155–158	Rebellion in north Britain suppressed by C. Julius Verus.
	Antonine Wall temporarily evacuated.
161–165	Forts rebuilt by Calpurnius Agricola.
180–184	Further revolt in north Britain subdued by Ulpius Marcellus.
	Antonine Wall broken.
193	On the assassination of Commodus, Pertinax (lately governor of Britain) is chosen emperor by the Praetorian Guard but quickly killed. Empire auctioned to Didius Julianus, who is defeated by Severus.
196–197	Clodius Albinus, governor, takes troops from Britain to fight for the throne and is defeated by Severus.
	Hadrian's Wall, the fortress at Eboracum and many forts overrun and destroyed by the Maetae.
197	Virius Lupus restores the situation and rebuilds many forts.
205–208	Rebuilding of Hadrian's Wall by Alfenus Senecio.
208	Severus, Geta and Caracalla arrive in Britain and prepare for northern campaigning.
209	Severus and Caracalla campaign in Scotland and receive the surrender of the Caledonians.
210	Revolt of the Maetae and second Scottish campaign.
211	Severus dies at York.
	Withdrawal to Hadrian's Wall and organisation of southern Scotland as a protectorate.
212	Caracalla extends Roman citizenship to all free provincials.
	Britain divided into two provinces.
259–274	Britain a part of the Gallic Empire of Postumus and his successors.
275–287	Saxon pirates in the Channel.
287	Carausius, commander of the British fleet, usurps the title of Emperor in Britain and northern Gaul and is temporarily recognised by Diocletian and Maximian.
293	Constantius as Caesar reconquers Carausius' continental possessions.

294 Carausius murdered by Allectus, who succeeds him.
296 Britain restored to the legitimate emperors by Constantius, who crosses the Channel and defeats and kills Allectus.
Barbarian inroads in the north.
Hadrian's Wall and legionary fortresses at Eboracum and Deva rebuilt.
Diocletian's reorganisation divides Britain into four provinces, separates the military from the civil administration and institutes new military offices.
306 Constantius, now emperor, with his son Constantine campaigns in Scotland.
Death of Constantius in Eboracum.
313 Edict of Milan grants toleration to the Christian Church.
314 Three British bishops attend the Council of Arles.
343 Constans visits Britain and pacifies the Scottish tribes.
360 Julian sends Lupicinus to repel raids of Picts and Scots.
364 Picts, Scots, Attacotti and Saxons raiding Britain.
367 Great invasion of Picts, Scots and Attacotti, aided by Saxon pirates and a simultaneous attack on Gaul by Franks.
367 Treachery in the Wall garrison. Nectaridus, Count of the Saxon Shore, killed and Fullofaudes, Duke of Britain, routed.
369 Count Theodosius, sent by Valentinian I, clears Britain of invaders and restores the Wall.
Signal stations built on Yorkshire coast.
383 Magnus Maximus, a military commander in Britain, revolts and conquers Gaul and Spain from Gratian.
Hadrian's Wall swamped by invaders and not rebuilt.
388 Maximus defeated at Aquileia by Theodosius.
395 Stilicho improves the defences of Britain.
406 Constantine III, a usurper, strips Britain of troops for his conquest of Gaul and Spain.
410 Honorius tells the civitates of Britain to arrange for their own safety.
c. 446 Last appeal of the British civitates to Aetius.

Reproduced from a " A map of Roman Britain," by courtesy of the Ordnance Survey Department.

SOME ROMAN PLACE-NAMES, WITH ENGLISH EQUIVALENTS

Roman name	English equivalent
Adurni, Portus	Portchester
Aelii Pons	Newcastle
Anderida	Pevensey
Aquae Sulis	Bath
Ariconium	Weston-under-Penyard
Atrebatum, Calleva	Silchester
Belgarum, Venta	Winchester
Branodunum	Brancaster
Camulodunum	Colchester
Clausentum	Bitterne
Corinium Dobunorum	Cirencester
Corstopitum	Corbridge
Dubris	Dover
Durnovaria	Dorchester, Dorset
Durobrivae	Castor, Northants
Durobrivae	Rochester, Kent
Durovernum Cantiacorum	Canterbury
Eboracum	York
Gariannonum	Burgh Castle
Gessoriacum	Boulogne
Glevum	Gloucester
Icenorum, Venta	Caistor by Norwich
Isca	Caerleon
Isca Dumnoniorum	Exeter
Isurium Brigantum	Aldborough
Lavatrae	Bowes
Lemanis	Lympne
Lindum	Lincoln
Londinium	London
Luguvallium	Carlisle
Othona	Bradwell
Pontes	Staines
Ratae Coritanorum	Leicester
Regnum	Chichester
Regulbium	Reculver
Rutupiae	Richborough
Segedunum	Wallsend
Silurum, Venta	Caerwent
Sorbiodunum	Old Sarum
Vectis Insula	Isle of Wight
Verterae	Brough
Eiroconium Cornoviorum	Wroxeter.

Reproduced by permission of the Publishers of "Britain Under the Romans," by S. E. Winbolt (Pelican Books).

SOME MUSEUMS WHICH EXHIBIT ROMAN-BRITISH SPECIMENS

Audley End Museum.
Aylesbury Museum.
Bangor University College, Welsh Museum.
Basingstoke Library and Museum.
Bath, Museum of Royal Lit. and Sc. Inst. Roman Baths Museum.
Brading, I.O.W., Roman Villa.
Brighton Public Library and Museum.
Bristol Museum.
Bury St. Edmunds, Moyses Hall.
Caerleon Museum.
Cambridge, Fitzwilliam Museum.
University Museum of Archæology.
Canterbury, Royal Museum.
Cardiff, National Museum of Wales.
Carlisle, Tullie House Museum.
Carmarthen, Antiq. Soc. Museum.
Carnarvon Museum.
Chedworth, Roman Villa.
Chelmsford Museum.
Chester, Grosvenor Museum.
Chesters, nr. Chollerford, Northumb.
Chingford, Epping Forest Museum.
Cirencester, Corinium Museum.
Colchester Museum, Castle Branch.
Corbridge Museum.
Devizes Museum.
Doncaster Museum.
Dorchester (Dorset) Museum.
Dover Museum.
Durham, Cathedral Library Museum.
Eastbourne Museum.
Edinburgh, National Museum of Antiquities.
Exeter Hist. Museum, Rougemont House.
Falkirk, Dollar Park Museum.
Folkestone Museum.
Gloucester Museum.
Guildford, Museum of Surrey Archæological Society.
Haslemere Museum.
Hereford Museum.
Housesteads Museum.
Hove Museum.
Huddersfield, Tolson Memorial Museum.
Hull, Mortimer Museum.
Ilkley Museum.
Ipswich Corporation Museum.
Kendal Museum.
Kettering Museum.
Lancaster Museum
Leeds City Museum.
Leicester City Museum.
Letchworth Museum.
Lewes, Sussex Arch. Soc. Museum.
Lincoln Museum.
Littlehampton Museum.
London, British Museum.
Cuming Museum.
Guildhall Museum.
London Museum, Lancaster House, St. James's.
Luton Museum.
Maidstone Museum.
Malton (Yorks) Museum.
Newark Museum.
Newcastle Museum.
Newbury Museum.
Newport (Mon.) Museum.
Northampton Central Museum.
Norwich Castle Museum.
Ospringe (Kent), Maison Dieu Museum.
Oxford, Ashmolean Museum.
Peterborough Museum.
Piercebridge Museum.
Reading Museum, Silchester Collection.

Ribchester Museum.
Richborough (Kent) Museum.
Ripon Museum.
Rochester, Eastgate House Museum.
Rotherham, Templeborough Collection.
Saffron Walden Museum.
St. Albans (Herts.) County Museum.
Salisbury Museum.
Scarborough Museum.
Sheffield, Weston Park Museum.
Shepton Mallet Museum.
Shrewsbury, Wroxeter Collection.
Southampton, Tudor House Museum.
Stockport Museum.
Sunderland Museum.
Taunton Castle Museum.
Thetford, Ancient House Museum.
Tunbridge Wells Museum, 6 Upper Grosvenor Road.
Warrington Museum.
Warwick, N.H.S. and Arch. Museum.
Wells Museum.
Whitby Museum.
Winchester Museum, The Square.
Worcester, Hastings Museum.
Worthing Museum.
Wrexham Museum, Holt R. Pottery Collection.
Wroxeter, Uriconium Museum.
Yeovil, Wyndham Museum.
York, Yorkshire Museum.

Reproduced by permission of the publishers of "Britain Under the Romans," by S. E. Winbolt (Pelican Books).

NEW DISCOVERIES

1. Roman Kent

Among the many recent discoveries in Roman Kent are the following:

Faversham

While excavating the site of a new football field for Faversham Grammar School, building contractors unearthed the remains of a very large Roman villa, larger even than that at Lullingstone. It measures some 120 feet by 60 feet and was apparently the home of an upper middle-class Roman family.

Swanscombe

While widening a road in 1964, workmen came upon a hoard of silver coins near the known Roman settlement at Springhead. There were 441 coins in all, including those of Constantius II, Julian, Jovian, Valentian I, Valens, Gratian, Valentian II, Theodosius I and Magnus Maximus.

Reculver (Regulbium)

An area east of the excavated area was opened up in 1960. Remains of the Headquarters Building were found, including part of the underground Strong Room (Sacellum) in which the soldiers' pay was kept (there are other examples, notably at Chesters in Northumberland). This one was three feet below the Roman ground level; there were also fragments of inscriptions, one of which could be translated: "For the Emperor . . . Fortunatus . . . built this shrine of the Headquarters with the cross-hall under Aulus Triarius Rufinus, consular governor." The period of his governorship was between 210 and 216 A.D.. "Fortunatus" was the "cognomen" of the then Commander of the fort.

During the following season further buildings were found, the larger of which was 85 feet long, with walls which had been decorated with painted plaster. By c.300 A.D. it had fallen into ruins, and the smaller building had been burned down after A.D. 270.

In 1964, during a three-week excavation by the Reculver Excavation Group, including 60 volunteers, another building was found on the edge of the *via principalis*. This turned out to be a bath-house, 40 feet by 22 feet with three apses, each of which had contained a semi-circular bath. It was probably reserved for the officers, since it was too small to have served the entire garrison of 500 auxiliaries, whose bath-house was probably outside the walls. Date, about 210 A.D.

Near Gravesend

On the marshes near Cliffe, Gravesend, two schoolmasters found remains of three distinct Roman settlements. Near the same village, Mr. Raymond Chaplin has found the reed floor of a Belgic farmstead and the chalk and gravel floor of a Roman building 40 yards long; its purpose has not yet been established.

Canterbury

More evidence of the Roman city of Durovernum continues to appear during building operations, and is being recorded. For instance, in 1960, behind the Dane John Mound, archaeologists examined the Roman defences at the south corner. A few feet west of the medieval angle-bastion lay the foundation-trench of a Roman angle-turret, horseshoe-shaped and apparently contemporary with the city wall. In the yard of Simon Langton School were found six Saxon huts of the fifth century, in the ruins of a Roman house.

In 1961, while trenching for gas-mains in Castle Street, workmen exposed the south-east side of the Roman Worth Gate, with a tile-floored recess lying between the front and rear piers, which were of large ragstone blocks. The defensive ditch beyond it was 9 feet deep. In the same year a hoard of 52 coins was found hidden in a small hypocaust at Butchery Lane, but much more exciting to the layman was the finding, in 1962, of treasure trove hidden outside the town wall in Westgate Gardens. Among this was a set of 9 exquisite silver spoons, including two with a swan's neck; there were also two ingots of silver, a gold finger-ring, and a *ligula* in the form of a twisted silver rod with a minute bowl at one end and a disk with prong at the other. This, together with one of the swan-necked spoons, was stamped with the CHI-RHO emblem, one of the earliest symbols of Christianity. Probably, like other hoards (such as the Mildenhall Treasure) this was hidden during the troubled period of the Saxon invasions.

Near Aylesford

Half a mile west of *Eccles*, at Rowe Place Farm, a large villa has been discovered, in which successive stages of building and rebuilding continued from shortly after the Conquest down to the third century. Besides an extensive bath-suite of the usual heated type with the *tepidaria*, *caldaria*, cold plunge baths, etc., there was also, most unusually, an indoor swimming pool, 44 feet long; in the late second century this fell into disuse. At the time of this writing, the excavations are not accessible to the general public.

Rochester

Archaeologists have long tried to establish the point at which the Roman invaders crossed the Medway, which has been presumed to have been just above Rochester, where there is firm ground down to the river's edge. (This is why the builders of the new Medway Motorway chose this spot for their bridge). Up to the time of this writing, no new evidence has come to light, either from the air or ground, and this is surprising, since one would have thought that remains of entrenchments would have shown up as crop-marks. The only archaeological trace which may or may not be associated with this great and critical battle was found in 1958. Near the village of Bredgar on the North Downs a hoard of thirty-four coins came to light, the latest of which are four of Claudius, struck between A.D. 41 and 42 (one year before the Claudian invasion). Webster and Dudley, in their book *The Roman Conquest of Britain* (1965) suggest that this "may well represent the savings of a soldier or centurion, buried for safety before the engagement and never reclaimed. The hoard was found nine miles from Aylesford, just before the descent to the Medway."

On such fragile tight-ropes of fact must the student of Roman Britain walk . . .

Richborough (Rutupiae)

Further excavations on this site have not yet confirmed definitely that it was the main landing place and assembly point for the legions which Aulus Plautius brought to Britain. It is admitted that, apart from traces of the Early Iron Age, the earliest evidences of occupation are coins, potter and military equipment of the invasion period. Two great parallel V-shaped ditches of military profile have been traced for a length of 2,000 yards, but the area enclosed—about 10 acres—would only have sufficed to protect about 2,500 men, no more than a task force sent to secure a bridgehead. "There is," writes Bush-Fox, "no evidence of a heavy occupation at this period, and only a small detachment may have been in garrison there." But beyond the area of the present Saxon Shore fort, very little excavation has yet been carried out. Possibly the defences of a much larger camp may still be found; unless, as Professor Webster and others have hinted, the three units of the Roman attacking force did *not* assemble at Richborough but landed at separate points, one of which might have been Chichester.

2. Colchester, Aldenham, Harlow

Colchester (Comuloolunum)

There have been a number of important archaeological investigations in Colchester and district, but most of these have been conducted during rebuilding operations, and while much interesting information has been obtained, and additions made to the Museum collection, there is little new for the casual visitor to see.

In several places, remains of the pre-Boudiccan city have come to light under the 'burnt layer' which speaks eloquently of the wrath of the Iceni. Perhaps the most interesting news item was the sale, for £15,500, of the sculptured head of the Emperor Claudius which was originally found in 1907 by a boy fishing in the river Alde near Saxmundham, Suffolk. The boy, Arthur Godbold, whitewashed the head and stuck it on a wall outside his cottage. Later an estate foreman bought it from him for 5/-d. The statue of which this head once formed part almost certainly came from Colchester where stood the Temple of the deified Claudius. After Boudicca sacked and destroyed the town one of her followers may have stuck it on a pole and carried it in triumph. Later, realising the danger of being found with it when Boudicca's forces were in retreat, he may have thrown it into the river.

At North Hill, Colchester, Miss B. B. K. Dunnett, excavating on behalf of the Colchester Excavation Society, discovered the foundations of eight Roman buildings, of which at least one antedates the Boudiccan revolt. Several mosaic pavements were found and are being removed before the site becomes (inevitably) a parking lot. Some coins were found, including one of Titus (40–81 A.D.).

Aldenham, near Watford

Excavations in 1965 revealed what appear to be remains of a Roman marching-camp on a hill-top. It was originally detected by aerial photography; crop-marks showed two 500 ft. lines with rounded corners. This could have been one of Caesar's marching-camps set up perhaps when he was marching along the Colne Valley to attack the fortress of the Belgic king Cassivelaunus. At the time of writing, excavation is impossible as the land is under wheat, but one hopes that the Watford and South-west Herts Archaeological Society, which has already discovered a Roman villa and bathhouse, may be able to explore the site before it is obliterated by a sewage farm. The society reports the findings of a Chape—the tip of a Roman scabbard—not far away, and this has been dated to the first century.

Harlow, Essex

On a slight rise in the Stort Valley near Harlow, on waste ground belonging to the Harlow Development Corporation, remains of a Romano-British temple have been found. Its excavation was completed in 1965 by Miss B. M. Gebel on behalf of the West Essex Archaeological Group. The temple had evidently been sacred from as far back as the Bronze Age, since burial urns of this period were found in association with a flint axe which has been dated to between 1400 and 1100 B.C.

Then came a thick Iron Age deposit and above that a large cobbled area found in association with coins of Claudius, Nero and Vespasian. There are remains of a still later building of the second century, but to date no trace of a settlement has been found, nor is it known whether the site will be reburied or opened for public inspection.

3. CHICHESTER

New Fishbourne, near Chichester

Quite the most impressive discovery for many years was made in 1960 when a civil engineer, Mr. A. N. Burgess of the Chichester Water Board, was laying a water-main between Fishbourne and Wittering. His mechanical excavator turned up a great amount of pottery and red tiles which appeared to be Roman. A phone call to Miss Margaret Rule, secretary of the Joint Archaeological Committee in her part of Hampshire and Sussex, led to the saving of one of the most spectacular Roman civilian sites in England from burial under a new housing estate.

When the archaeologists (enthusiastically aided by many volunteer helpers) began to dig they were amazed at the extent of the building uncovered. The word "villa" hardly does it justice; in dimensions and planning, it is palatial, and some scholars are already speculating whether or not this could have been the residence of Cogidubnus, the British "Client-King" of the Regnenses who is known to have been an ally of the Romans and was honoured by the title *rex et legatus Augusti in Britannia.* (This appears on an inscribed stone found in 1723 and now let into the wall of Chichester's Town Hall.)

Five seasons' excavation, mainly under the direction of the brilliant young archaeologist Barry Cunliffe of Bristol University, have revealed a structure covering over six acres and showing evidence of successive rebuilding from the first to the third century A.D. Four fine large mosaic floors have been discovered, two polychrome and two black and white; four others, in black and white, have been badly damaged. There are remains of substantial baths, an audience-chamber with a vestibule or 'waiting-room' with remains of bench seating, and many fragments of painted wall-frescoes. It is good to know that this fascinating survival from the earliest days of the Roman occupation is to be preserved *in situ* as a national monument; the whole of the north wing, measuring 270 ft. by 70 ft. is to be put under cover to protect the mosaic pavements, but at the time of writing the site is not yet open to the public.

Much less spectacular, but of great archaeological interest, was the discovery of post-holes which had supported a timber building going back to the time of Claudius. They were discovered under the foundations of a masonry house of the first century A.D. These indicate clearly that the site was occupied by the Romans during the initial period of the invasion of 43 A.D., and this has its bearing on a current theory which has aroused much controversy among scholars. Professor Graham Webster in his provocative book *The Roman Conquest of Britain* (written in collaboration with Donald R. Dudley) has suggested that Aulus Plautius, while mounting his main attack from Richborough, also made a diversionary landing near Chichester, where Cogidubnus, king of the Regnenses, was known to be a firm ally of the Romans.

4. Hampshire, Wiltshire, Dorset

Hampshire has yielded some remarkable Roman discoveries, including the ruins of a 46-roomed villa at West Park, Rockbourne, which at the time of writing is still being excavated. Its presence was first discovered in 1942 when a farmer, digging out a ferret, turned up oyster-shells which are frequently found on Roman-British settlements, but it is only in recent years that systematic excavations have been carried out. Like Chedworth in Gloucestershire and other Roman villas, it was both residence and substantial farmhouse. The south-west wing alone had a frontage of 136 ft. and baths were found at the north-east end of the main north-west wing, belonging to the second century. Later, however, they were converted to other purposes. Tesselated pavements of geometric design have been uncovered.

Winchester also continues to reveal more traces of its predecessor, *Venta Belgarum*, during building or rebuilding operations. In 1964, remains of a defensive ditch 30 ft. wide and 15 ft. deep were traced for 1,000 ft. in an east-west direction at Ashley Terrace, immediately outside the walled area. The western defences of the city have also been examined in recent years, notably at Tower Street where the primary rampart was carefully coursed in flint and chalk, and under the parish hall of St. Thomas's Church in St. Swithun Street, where it was observed that the south town wall, made of stone, had been inserted in a pre-existing gravel bank. Evidences of the Belgic settlement which the Romans took over have come to light in several places, e.g. seven cremation burials at Bottom Pond Farm, Owlesbury, of which three were pre-Roman.

In 1960, while digging the foundations of a new hotel near the Cathedral, a further section of the north-south Roman road (already detected under Middle Brook Street) came to light, and showed traces of frequent re-metalling which had built up to a total thickness of *7 ft.* The lowest and therefore earliest surface could be dated to the first century, a fact which speaks eloquently of the longevity of the Roman occupation.

Sparsholt, near Winchester

Mr. David Johnston, a classics master at Raynes Park Grammar School, aided by four skilled workers and about 20 volunteers, has uncovered part of a fine roman villa on this site. It was of the courtyard type with finely-decorated walls in panels of red, saffron, green and turquoise and was found in a woodland thicket. It is believed to have been one of the largest villa estates in the whole of Britain, dating from the third or fourth century A.D. It is hoped that excavations will continue in future years if funds and facilities are available.

Hinton St. Mary, Dorset

Roman villas seem to be sprouting like mushrooms nowadays, their long sleep being usually disturbed by the roar of the mechanical excavator. Sometimes, however, their discovery is the result of prolonged and patient research by archaeologists working on the slenderest of clues. At other times they are found in remote rural areas which are neither threatened by housing development or being probed by archaeologists. Such an event occurred in 1963 in the village of Hinton

St. Mary, when the village blacksmith, Mr. White, was preparing to build a shed on a plot of land he had purchased from Captain G. H. L. F. Pitt-Rivers, descendent of the famous General Pitt-Rivers and proprietor of the Pitt-Rivers Museum in Farnham.

His spade struck stone walls and soon, under a thin blanket of soil, Mr. White found himself gazing at one of the most remarkable Roman mosaic pavements ever discovered in Britain. British Museum archaeologists were called to the spot, and found that the pavement belonged to a group of buildings, most of which had been destroyed by stone-robbers, presumably in Saxon times. But the pavement remained, almost intact, and on close examination revealed a feature which sets it apart from all Roman pavements discovered in these islands.

It has two panels, one containing a roundel representing the Greek hero Bellerophon spearing the Chimera, but the other, larger, panel has as its centrepiece the face of a young man, and near it the monogram CHI-RHO, which in the early years of Christianity was one of the symbols of Christ. At each corner of the same panel is a male figure which may present the Four Winds, or possibly the Four Evangelists. There has been hot debate over this now famous mosaic. Some, such as Captain Pitt-Rivers, an anthropologist and ethnographer, argue that as the mongram was used in pre-Christian times, the central figures does not necessarily represent Christ; others, notably Professor J. M. C. Toynbee marshalled some powerful arguments to support the theory that it is. He dates the pavement firmly to the fourth century, when Christianity had been recognised by Rome, and it is now generally accepted that the Hinton Mary Mosaic is the earliest known picture of Christ found in Britain.

Excavations conducted in 1964 revealed three wings of a villa ranged round a courtyard. The now-famous mosaic was found in the north-east range; the south-east and north-west ranges had been severely damaged by stone-robbers. It has been carefully lifted by the experts and is to be put on display at the British Museum.

Old Sarum

The Antonine Itinerary, the Roman "road-guide," gives the name *Sorviodunum* to a settlement which may have been near Old Sarum but which, until recently, has been unlocated. However, in 1965, members of the Salisbury Museum Research Committee, directed by John Stratton, were making excavations to define the Roman road known as the Portway when they struck the foundations of buildings which appeared to be Roman. As the land was under cultivation the main structure, a substantial building of flint and worked stone, could not be completely uncovered. Work will continue in 1966 and ensuing seasons.

Vespasian's campaign in the North-West

Professor Graham Webster has drawn my attention to other evidences of Vespasian's attack on south-western Britain beside that at Maiden Castle. According to Vespasian's biographer, Suetonius Tranquillus, the future Emperor, who in 43 A.D. commanded the Second Augustan Legion, "fought thirty battles, subjugated two warlike tribes and captured more than twenty *oppida*, beside the Isle of Wight." These *oppida* or Belgic "strong-points" must have included the hill-forts of Wessex, including of course Maiden Castle.

The first question is: from which point did Vespasian start? I have suggested that he followed a landward route via Silchester, Winchester and Southampton, but his main supply-base could have been at Chichester which, in the friendly hands of Cogidubnus, would have enabled him to bring troops and heavy equipment (e.g. *ballistae*) by sea.

Besides the Legionary helmet dredged from Bosham Harbour, and which has been known for many years, other items of military equipment, of Claudian date, have turned up in the neighbourhood of Chichester and are now in the Museum; they include military bronzes and a fine horse-pendant found on Lancing Down. Again, at the recently-discovered villa at Fishbourne, near Chichester, post-holes have been found which had supported timber buildings of Claudian date. Mr. Barry Cunliffe suggests that these might have been store houses or granaries, part of a military base.

Now we come to the *oppida* themselves. If only facilities and funds were available, what interesting discoveries might be made at such hill-forts as Badbury Rings, Woodbury Hill, Cadbury Castle, Hambledon, Abbotsbury and others which have scarcely been scratched yet! Meanwhile, at one or two sites, one can obtain a preview of what some lucky excavator of the future may discover.

At Hod Hill, near Stourpaine, about 18 miles from Maiden Castle, the late Sir Ian Richmond excavated a Roman fort built in one of the corners of the Iron Age camp. During the course of his work Richmond had to examine some Iron Age hut-circles to establish whether or not the British tribesmen remained there during the military occupation. Around one of the larger huts, he came upon a number of Roman ballista—bolts which had clearly been aimed at this target. Was it perhaps the hut of the Chief, and was this where the last stand was made?

Much more gruesome evidence came to light over one hundred years ago at a place called Spettisbury Rings, three miles from Blandford. When, in 1857, the Central Dorset Railway was being built between Wimborne and Blandford, the engineers had to dig a deep cutting and in so doing cut off part of the defences of the hill-fort. They found what was described as 'a large pit' but which was probably part of the defensive ditch, and in it, eighty or ninety skeletons. Some of these showed battle wounds; one man had had part of his skull sliced away; in another a spearhead was embedded. Among the objects discovered with the dead, and now in the British Museum, were Roman lance and spearheads of military type, fragments of bronze scabbard bindings, and a length of shield binding.

Here also, as at Maiden Castle, we probably see the Second Augusta at work. Probably the dead were flung into the ditch and the earth from the demolished rampart was tipped over them when the Romans partially dismantled the fortress.

Again, at Ham Hill in Somerset, St. George Grey discovered Roman military equipment in considerable quantity, among it a large piece of a jerkin with scales of bronze. You may see this in the Taunton Museum. The remains were found on a small plateau near the hill-fort, which covers 200 acres. Among the inland forts, that at Hod Hill has been completely excavated, and proves to have been occupied at the same time both by legionaries and auxiliaries, which is unusual. Their barracks, unearthed by Richmond, provided for four centuries of legionaries (380 men) and ten troops of auxiliary cavalry (320 men). Professor Webster, from whose fascinating new book, *The Roman Conquest of Britain*, some of this information has been gathered, adds this amusing comment:

"There are two houses for the Commanding Officers, the larger and more elaborate clearly belonging to the cavalry *praefectus*. This arrangement of putting together two different kinds of unit together in the same fort had serious dangers. At a later period when the fort of Newstead in Scotland was so provided, it was necessary to build a wall between the two units and give each a separate bath-house."

Veterans of World Wars I and II will no doubt agree with Webster (and the Roman Commanders) about these serious dangers!

At Waddon Hill near Beaminster, a similar situation apparently existed; six seasons' excavations have shown that three large Roman buildings had been erected in what had been a Belgic hill-fort. Besides bits of military equipment there were pottery dishes, bowls, etc. used by the garrison. Some had been made locally by the Durotriges, the conquered tribe, and others, such as mixing-bowls and flagons were either imported or imitated locally to meet the troops' demands. We also know something about the food which Vespasian's men ate; 101 bones of hare were found, of which 81 were from the foot; there were also fish-bones, including those of a very bony creature called the Giant Wrasse. Most modern anglers throw them back into the sea, but no doubt the legionaries accepted it as a change from hare.

5. Roman Somerset

Bath

The most interesting discovery in Roman Bath for many years was made by Mr. Barry Cunliffe in 1965, when he located part of the altar of the great Temple of Sul, the deity of the waters. The existence of this structure, which lay near the Roman baths, has been known for a long time and parts of it have been uncovered at various times during the past two hundred years, when rebuilding operations have revealed them. The famous "Gorgon's Head" from Minerva's shield, for example, came from the Temple's pediment as did a corner stone depicting a naked Hercules and a clothed Jupiter, discovered in 1790. Again, in 1867, when the Pump Room was being rebuilt, a Mr. James Irving, who was helping Gilbert Scott to restore the Abbey, glanced down a hole made by the excavators and glimpsed another part of the buried Temple. Fortunately he made a detailed plan of what he could see; a section of the platform and the north-west colonnade. More evidence was found by archaeologists in 1890 and then, in 1960, a "rescue dig" confirmed the accuracy of Irving's observations of nearly a century before.

This "subterranean archaeology" has a fascination of its own. Here, lying deep beneath the foundations of relatively recent buildings lay one of the most important Roman temples in Britain, adjoining—indeed forming part of—the elaborate complex of baths which were the *raison d'être* for the Roman city. There was no hope of uncovering it, but could perhaps its plan be ascertained? Fragments of the jigsaw had been found. Could the others be fitted into place, if only on paper?

Mr. Barry Cunliffe, fresh from his triumph at Fishbourne, near Chichester, thought they could. Mr. Cunliffe, one of the new school of British archaeologists, had shown such outstanding brilliance that whilst still an undergraduate at Cambridge he had been put in charge of the Fishbourne excavations. Arriving at Bath in 1965, after carefully studying all the available evidence on the Temple of Sul, he selected a spot and drove straight down till he hit the entrance of the Temple.

His problem now was to locate the altar, the position of which he estimated from his extensive knowledge of other Roman buildings. Plotting eastward from the temple entrance, he selected another point from which to sink his second trench, which he dug in the floor of a cellar. Some fifty feet from the start of the trench he and his team struck a huge block of sculptured stone weighing a ton, lying in a bed of peat. Lifting tackle was brought in, and under the supervision of a civil engineer the block was swung clear and removed. It proved to be sculptured on two sides; one side bore a figure of Sylvanus, the god of hunting, the other that of Ceres, goddess of fertility.

Soon it became clear that this was the opposite corner-stone to the one discovered in 1790, and which showed a naked Hercules and a clothed Jupiter. In this case Cere was draped and Sylvanus naked. Although two more corner-stones remain to be discovered, it is now certain that this one formed part of the altar, or at least the altar-screen, of the Temple of Sul.

So another piece of the jigsaw falls into place, and a most important one, because now that the position of the altar is known (it stood in the forecourt of the temple) we have a much clearer picture of how the great building stood in relation to the adjoining baths. Sul was a local god of the waters and, as the Archaeological Correspondent of *The Sunday Times* observes, the altar "forms, in fact, the focal point of two views; for a Roman, entering the adjacent baths from the south, would have also seen the altar across a pool and the spring that feeds it. And it establishes the religious and social centre of all Roman Bath."

The 'Curse-tablet'

Until recently only two other "curse-tablets" had been found in Britain, apart from that addressed to the lover (or lovers) of the wayward Miss Vilbia. In 1960 a fourth example was found after ploughing had taken place on the slopes of Red Hill in the parish of Raticliffe-on-Soar, Nottinghamshire. Like the Bath tablet it is of lead, but this one lays a curse on a stealer, not of hearts but of cash. It has been translated as follows:

"To the god Jupiter, best and greatest, there is given (this offering?) that he may hound . . . through his mind, through his memory, his inner parts, his intestines, his heart, his marrow, his veins . . . whoever he was, man or woman, who stole away the *denarii* of Canius Dignus, that in his own person in a short time he may balance the account. There is also given to the god above-named a tenth part of the money when he has (repaid it)."

The translation is by Mr. Eric G. Turner, to whose article in the *Journal of Roman Studies* (Vol. LIII) I am indebted for this information.

6. Monmouthshire

Caerwent (Venta Silurum), Monmouthshire.

Between the north gate and the north-east corner of the city the foundations of three more projecting bastions were discovered in 1962.

Abergavenny (Gobannium) Monmouthshire

Many objects dating from the first and second centuries have been dug up recently, but these could not be associated with any known buildings. Two miles away, at Ty Aur Farm, Llanellen, an almost unworn *aureus* of Claudius I was found; it may have been loot from a Silurian raid in the early years of the Occupation.

Caerleon (Isca Silurum) Monmouthshire

Further excavations within this great Legionary fortress have continued since Dr. Nash-William's death; by Mr. G. C. Boon on behalf of the National Museum of Wales and the Ministry of Public Buildings and Works, and also by Mrs. L. Murray Threipland on behalf of the latter. These, though not spectacular, have added to our knowledge of Isca Silurum, the extent of its buildings and the length of time during which it was occupied. For instance in the Priory Grounds adjoining the Broadway, a street was found running off the *via principalis* at right-angles, and another road at right-angles to the first, cutting off a block about 85 ft. wide. Four distinct periods of building were identified along the first street, beginning in about 75–100 A.D. when a long timber structure existed, and continuing with successive stone buildings down to the fourth century.

In 1964, Mr. Boon found a massive bath-building in the angle between Blackhall Street and Museum Street and a courtyard, 150 ft. long and 78 ft. wide, leading from the *via principalis* to a suite of rooms (mostly under Blackhall Street) which included a frigidarium 50 ft. wide, ending in a rectangular plunge-bath and an apsed tepidarium 48 ft. wide. Here again there was evidence of successive rebuilding throughout the centuries, e.g. the second century structure was refurbished in the following century when new floors were laid and two tanks dug in the courtyard. Still later these tanks were filled in and the courtyard made up with hard core.

To date the sought-for Temple of Diana and the shrines dedicated to Mithras and Dolichenus have not been found, and a note in the Journal of Roman Studies for 1962 comments that "contractors' work removed all traces of the *vicus* in the area partially examined in 1954–55" (by Dr. Nash-Williams).

7. Wales

The fascination of Roman Wales, like the Roman North, lies less in villas and cities than in the evidences of military campaigns revealed in forts, marching-camps and strategic roads. The new discoveries made during the past decade confirm this. There is nothing of a spectacular nature to add to what is written in the foregoing chapters, but a great deal of new information and some hitherto-unknown sites have come to light, mainly associated with the Legions and Auxiliaries.

The only way to appreciate these fully is to study the articles in the learned journals bearing on the problem, e.g. those of Dr. J. K. St. Joseph on aerial photography in *The Journal of Roman Studies* (Vols. LI (1961) and LV (1965) and that of Professor Graham Webster, "The Roman Advance under Ostorius Scapula" (*The Archaeological Journal*, Vol. CXV, 1958). Another fascinating article, also in *The Archaeological Journal*, Vol. CXXI, is "Early Roman Campaigns in Wales" by Dr. Michael G. Jarrett.

Here I can only summarise a few discoveries made in recent years in the areas described in Chapter 11.

Site of the battle against Caratacus and the Ordovices

The most recent comment I can find on this much-debated subject is the following in Dr. Jarrett's above-mentioned article. "Dr. Webster suggests that the site should be sought in the Severn Valley above Newtown; Dr. St. Joseph favours a site further upriver, above Caerws. The general area of the Upper Severn is probably correct."

Marching-camp at Y Pigwyn on the borders of Brecnock and Camarthenshire. It has been suggested by Mr. Jarrett that this was one of the camps built by Ostorius Scapula in about A.D. 52 when campaigning against the Ordovices, since, he says, "it is precisely the route up the Usk valley and over Trecastle Mountain which appears likely for one of his campaigns" and adds,

"The two marching-camps at Y Pigwyn and the early fort suggest that the Usk valley was an important campaigning route in the first century." But some scholars believe that neither of the Y Pigwyn camps was built before 75 A.D.

In 1964 Dr. G. D. B. Jones examined marching-camps at Arosfa Gareg, Carmarthenshire, and at Ystradfellte, Brecknockshire.

North Wales

A new fort has been discovered at Rhyd Sarn, 2¾ miles south west of the fort at Caergai, from which it can be seen on the skyline. It is 148 ft. square and lies close to the Roman road leading to Cardigan Bay. Originally recognised in air photographs it has now been identified on the ground.

The auxiliary fort at Llystyn, Caernarvonshire, has now been almost completely destroyed by gravel-quarrying. Rescue-excavations revealed four further barracks on each side of the *via decumana*, and that the north-west and north-east gates had double carriage-ways between flanking towers.

Other forts excavated in recent years are Tomen-y-Mur, Merionethshire, where Dr. Jarrett cut sections through the defences and showed that these had been altered several times, at Trawscoed, in Cardiganshire, where pottery of the Flavian-Trajanic period was found; at Llandovery, where the earliest fort seems to have been pre-Flavian, and at Clyro, Radnorshire, which shows two periods, both apparently pre-Flavian.

Air photography has revealed a hitherto unsuspected Roman camp at Twyn y Briddallt, in Glamorganshire, covering 16 acres and lying on a spur of moorland at a height of 1,500 ft. It was a temporary camp, like two others known in this district. Air reconnaisance has added much to our knowledge of Roman Wales during recent years. For instance, near the already-known fort at Tomen-y-Mur, in Merionethshire, mentioned above, ploughing in fields adjoining the fort enable the camera lens to reveal the outlines of two 'practice-camps'; two-thirds of a mile away a small square platform was detected near the Braich-Ddu slate quarry. This also was probably another practice-camp, erected by the auxiliaries in the course of their arduous training or to keep them occupied between campaigns.

Perhaps most striking of all is a concentration of no less than seven marching-camps along a short stretch of the Watling Street as it approaches the Welsh Marches. There is one near Leintwardine, another at Walford, a third, only a mile away, near Brampton Bryan, a fourth eight miles to the north-east near Stretford Bridge, two more near Craven Arms and another at Upper Affcot. These strong evidences of troop-movements were probably built at the time when Roman units, advancing on the Severn, first began to penetrate the hills of the Welsh Marches. And all were first seen, in modern times, from the air.

8. Gloucestershire and Berkshire

Cirencester (Corinium) Gloucestershire

A considerable amount of excavation has been carried on in and near Cirencester, with interesting results. In 1960, the eastern defences of the city were examined in St. Mary's Abbey Estate, and it was found that the earliest defences, dating from the first half of the second century, consisted of a turf and clay rampart, about 15 ft. wide, with a ditch into which the waters of the river Churn had been diverted. The massive "Verulium Gate," over 100 ft. wide with twin D-shaped towers, was apparently contemporary with this earth rampart, though the gateway was of stone. About A.D. 200, part of the rampart was cut away to receive a stone wall. Still later, in the fourth century, when the flooding Church had damaged the masonry, a timber groyne was erected to protect the angle between the wall and the gate; a flood-gate carried away excess waters and bastions were added to wall at 200 ft. intervals.

An interesting discovery was a hoard of 480 coins found in the silty deposit left after the river had been diverted to an outer ditch. The latest coin was of A.D. 346.

In 1962, further work was carried out by Mr. J. S. Wacher on behalf of the Cirencester Excavation Committee. Five sites were examined with the purpose of discovering more about the layout of ancient Corinium, most of which lies buried under the modern town. Like Mr. Barry Cunliffe's work at Bath, this work was intended to fit together more pieces of the "jigsaw" so that eventually a complete town-plan, with streets, *insulae* (blocks enclosed by streets), public and private buildings, etc., might be drawn up. Little of any of these discoveries will ever be seen by the general public, but that does not make these any less important to archaeologists.

To the lay observer, perhaps the most interesting aspect of these patient diggings has been their revelation of the changes and developments which took place in Corinium over a period of four centuries. For instance, it appears that one of the problems which the citizens of Corinium had to face was flooding. For instance in *Insula XXIII*, "continuous raising of the floor-levels was thought to be caused by silt from Ermin Street washing in to an inferred portico, and led to a complete rebuilding about the middle of the second century." Again, the archaeologists report: "In Period III, probably in the fourth century, this last structure was rebuilt, but in spite of raised floor-levels it was submerged in further accumulations of silt from Ermin Street."

The Amphitheatre, which stood south-west of the West gate of Corinium, also showed traces of repeated rebuilding, testifying to continuous use over some three centuries.

An auxiliary fort was found on Ermin Street south of the later basilica. The fort had a rampart 20 ft. high, of turf reinforced with timber and was defended by two flat-bottomed ditches with steep sides. Evidences of timber structures dating from a few years after A.D. 43 were found. The basilica was built later, in the middle of the Flavian period, presumably after the troops had been evacuated, but being built on top of the filled-in ditches of the fort it soon collapsed and had to be rebuilt.

The fort and basilica now lie under Leaholme Gardens south of The Avenue.

In 1964 further excavations were carried out when, in the garden of Ashcroft House, the archaeologists revealed the house of a wealthy citizen of Corinium, dating from the fourth century, with fine mosaic pavements of the "Corinium School" similar to those found in Dyer Street many years ago.

Gloucester (Glevum) has also yielded new information. In 1960 a further length of the Roman south-east town wall was unearthed in Kings Square; as at Corinium and other cities several phases of building were noted, beginning with an earth bank and timber foundation and developing through (a) interval turrets (b) stone-faced walls with rubble core and (c) solid stone wall of large dressed stones. In the same year, while rebuilding operations were going on within the corner of Eastgate and Northgate, workmen came on a large jar containing no less than 10,000 coins which had been hidden in a pit within a Roman building. The coins ranged from late issues of Aurelian to those of Diocletian and Maximinian, and a few of Carausius and Allectus.

Excavations in 1961 threw light on the military occupation of the area before the *colonia* (settlement for veterans of the Roman Army) was founded under the Emperor Nerva. Digging in the grounds of the Technical College at a point 270 ft. from the Roman South Gate, the walls of the colonia were found embedded in the front of an earlier rampart; within this were found pottery of Claudian to Flavian times.

Three years later further excavations, this time in the headmaster's garden in the King's School, revealed military defences beneath the north-east colonia rampart at a point diagonally opposite the similar discovery on the south-west side, proving beyond doubt that these belonged to a legionary fortress, the one built to guard the Severn crossing and keep watch on the turbulent Silures.

Among other Gloucestershire sites which have yielded fresh discoveries or information are Chedworth, where, in the north range of the villa, the four eastern rooms were found to be fourth-century addition to the original third-century wing, and constituted "a uniquely appointed self-contained dining suite;" Great Witcombe—another famous villa site, where a hypocaust was cleared in Room 9, Barnsley Park, potentially a very rich site where Professor Webster and his team are excavating the remains of an extensive villa under land which has never been under the plough; Frocester Court, where another large villa has been found, with a corridor 85 ft. long paved with good geometric mosaics; and at Ebrington, in the Cotswolds where, in the bath-suite of an elegant villa, the cold plunge-bath was found to have been lined with white marble.

The richness of these well-appointed Gloucestershire villas testifies to the high standard of civilisation enjoyed by the Romanised *Dobunni* after the Legions had safeguarded their peace and Corinium had become the focal point of their wealth and culture. Today the Cotswold manor-houses offer a modern parallel, though the source of their wealth sometimes comes from cities much further afield than Cirencester!

9. Calleva Atrebatum

Most of *Calleva Atrebatum* still lies under its thick blanket of earth, as mysterious as ever. However, there have been some interesting and important excavations on the site during the intervening years, of which probably the most fascinating was one carried out in 1961 by the late Sir Ian Richmond on behalf of the

Silchester Excavation Committee. As I mentioned previously, in 1892 a building was unearthed which was then identified as a Christian church. Details can be found in *Arch.* LIII (1893) and in *Vict. Co. Hist. Hants I* (1900).

The building was reburied and for more than nearly seventy years has lain hidden under the fields. In the meantime, archaeology has become more scientific, and the findings of an earlier generation of excavators were being re-assessed. Was this building really a Christian church? Was the evidence sufficient, in the light of modern knowledge, to confirm it as a fact? Professor Richmond and his colleagues decided to disinter it to find out.

A summarised account of his excavation published in the 1962 issue of *The Journal of Roman Studies* contains these words:

"Among the churned mud and flooring-material filling the hollows was a group of Constantinian coins, to three of which still adhered the white mortar of the pavement, in which they have evidently once been embedded. The three coins in question are a *follis* of A.D. 309–313, an *Urbis Roma* (A.D. 330–335) and a *Fel. Temp. Reparatio* copy (A.D. 348–353), the last somewhat worn. This gives a *terminus post quem* of at least A.D. 360 for the laying of the pavement and the construction of the building".

Later in the article the writer adds:

". . . the combination of date and type of buildings strongly favours the notion of a Christian church, with a table of offerings at the north end of the vestibule and a baptistery in an axial position in front of the church. The plan of the transeptal rooms echoes that of the famous large Constantinian churches, such as St. Peter's and the Lateran in Rome, and the Church of the Nativity in Bethlehem".

It now seems almost certain that some 250 years before St. Augustine landed in Kent to convert the pagan Saxons, Christ was being worshipped in a small building, the foundations of which now lie buried beneath a Hampshire meadow, and that that humble structure bore distinct resemblances, in planning, to three of the holiest shrines in Christendom.

This is not the only excavation undertaken at Silchester, of course, but the others, though important to archaeologists, are more of specialised than general interest. But all students of Roman Britain, professional or amateur will rejoice in the news, recently published, that the Ministry of Works is to clear the great city walls from overgrowth and even construct "viewing-platforms" from which visitors can approach and view the walls without encroaching on neighbouring farmland. One hopes that this is only the first stage in a process which may, in the end, lead to the complete uncovering and exhibition of this great city of the Atrebates. Protection of walls and pavements would of course be necessary, but this has been successfully done at other places, e.g. Bignor and Chedworth villas. How much more exciting it would be to see an entire Romano-British city!

10. Suffolk, North Midlands, Lincoln

Caistor-by-Yarmouth

In 1961 excavations disclosed the palisade trench and the stone wall, with an interval-tower, at the south-east angle of the defences. The inner of two defensive ditches of the second century was re-cut at the beginning of the fourth century, when the outer ditch was almost obliterated by a larger ditch, 30 ft. wide and 9 ft. deep. This indicated clearly the need for stronger defences at a time when Saxon invaders were threatening this eastern coast of Britain.

In the following year, 1962, full excavation of the north-east angle of the town wall defined the wall area as a square of between 9 and 10 acres.

Burgh Castle, Suffolk

In 1960, work on this coastal fortress revealed a lean-to structure which had existed near the turret-like building on the south-east wall, which was also dug out and its collapsed roof found lying on the floor. The footings of the wall were of rammed chalk on a bed of stiff clay over natural sand, reinforced with horizontal timbers.

Later excavations in 1961 "revealed the technical limitations of the rounded form of the north-east and south-east angles; the ballista-mountings (for artillery defence) on the bastions lie within the lines of the walls when these are produced to meet in an angle, making complete enfilade fire-cover an impossibility." (J.R.S. Vol. III).

Very early post-Roman occupation of the fort is indicated by a wattle-and-daub building and a group of Saxon huts. Yet Romano-British glass vessels of the fourth and fifth centuries were also found. At *Feltwell*, Norfolk, remains were found off a small Fen settlement which included a stable and remains of a timber-framed building with a chalk floor.

Other Fenland settlements of early Roman times have been identified at *Hockwold*, where remains of narrow drainage ditches were uncovered, together with timber-framed buildings of Romano-Celtic type, including a temple. South-west of this temple, in 1962, archaeologists found a hoard of fine silver wine-cups of Italo-Greek manufacture; that these had been deliberately concealed is indicated by the fact that the bases of the pedestals and the handles had been removed and packed in two of the cups; the three others were crushed. Curiously the date of this concealment, according to the J.R.S. Vol. LIII is the first century A.D. and not, as one would have expected, during the last troubled century of the Occupation. The cups may have been the treasured property of some Belgic chieftan *before* the Roman invasion.

The North Midlands

Great Casterton (Rutland)

A Roman fort was identified from the air in 1959, with two widely-spaced ditches showing as an extra-green growth in a crop of winter oats. There is a gate at the centre of the south-east front, and the internal area was about 590 ft. by 395 ft. Ground excavation by Richmond showed that there had been two separate occupations of this fort, in the second of which its size was reduced. Pottery dates it firmly to the Governorship of Ostorius Scapula. Another fort has been found at *Water Newton*, guarding the point where the river Nene was crossed by the Ermine Street. This may be of Claudian date, i.e. from the early years of the invasion. Again, at *Holme*, 3½ miles north of Newark, Notts, aerial reconnaisance has identified a large marching-camp on level ground east of the Trent. Large enough to have contained a Legion, it may possibly date from the Conquest, suggests Dr. St. Joseph.

Among civil sites investigated is one at *Thistleton Dyer;* a winged corridor house of the "tripartite" type with a central entrance, mosaic pavements, and hypocausts testify to a substantial residence with attached farm-buildings. There are others at *Wakefield Lodge*, in Whittlewood Forest, Pottersbury; at *Briary Wood* where a settlement 500 ft. long and 240 ft. broad was found; and at the east end of *Redmoor Copse*, near Wakefield Lodge.

The site of *Ancaster* was known in Roman times as Causennae where an east-west road crossed the Ermine Street. In 1965, while digging out a cemetery, excavators came on a V-shaped ditch of military profile, partly filled with turf. It seems that a former turf rampart had been deliberately dismantled, probably at a time when former military sites were being systematically destroyed when the 9th Hispana Legion moved from its old base at Lincoln to its new headquarters at York.

Lincoln (Lindum)

Excavations have been concentrated mainly on tracing the development of the legionary fortress and *colonia;* their foundation and subsequent rebuilding, alteration and enlargement through four centuries. Very little of what has been uncovered could remain so, nor would piecemeal sections of wall have meant much to the lay visitor anyway. But from photographs, plans and drawings in the museum, and in the publications of Lincoln Archaeological Research Committee, the interested reader can learn much that is new.

Probing deep beneath one of the masonry towers of the east gate of the upper colonia, Mr. D. F. Petch and his team found large post-holes which had supported the massive timber gateway of the first legionary fortress, with evidence of rebuilding. In part of the lower colonia excavated under 291 High Street, remains of a third-century fountain were discovered. These, it is hoped, will eventually be re-erected in the garden of the Usher Art Gallery where visitors can see them.

A Roman industrial site of the first and second centuries was identified at *Holbeach*, in the Lincoln Fens, with extensive remains of baked-clay, peat ash, soot and charcoal; to date, however, the precise nature of the industry is uncertain. A hoard of over 9,000 silver or silver-washed coins was found in a pot during ploughing at Kirmington, seven miles from the well-known Roman site at Caistor, and an extensive villa with mosaic pavements was excavated at *Winterton*.

One of the most interesting discoveries in the north-east Midlands was made at *Longthorpe*, near Peterborough, Notts. It was an aerial sighting, made, as usual, by the keen, experienced eyes of Dr. J. K. S. St. Joseph, Director of Aerial Photography in the Department of Geography, Cambridge. In the Nene Valley, he identified a large Roman fort, 1,200 ft. by 1,000 ft. and enclosing nearly 28 acres. The camp had never been seen on the ground, and the only clue to its existence was the fact that when a light sprinkling of snow had fallen on it, the snow melted more quickly along the lines of buried ditches than elsewhere. Aerial photographs, taken during the few hours when this phenomenon was observable, enabled Dr. St. Joseph to identify the fort, with its three gateways, ramparts and surrounding ditches. Another line of ditches and embankments is also discernable within the larger enclosure and this may represent either a temporary camp or a second phase in the permanent fortifications. The main camp is large enough to have contained a legion and may possibly date from the conquest.

"Of internal structures," writes Dr. St. Joseph, "nothing is now visible, but Roman levels cannot lie deep and buildings, in timber, should not be difficult to trace." So an interesting dig awaits some fortunate archaeologists in Nottinghamshire.

11. From York to the Wall

York (Eboracum)

As at Lincoln, which preceded York as a legionary base, archaeological research is hindered by the fact that ancient *Eboracum* lies buried deep beneath the medieval and modern city. Excavations, when they take place, are confined to small areas, perhaps temporarily revealed by rebuilding operations. Nevertheless, discoveries continue to be made which help archaeologists to delineate more clearly the great northern capital in which two Emperors died. Another section of the Roman wall was discovered near the Praetorian Gate during extensions to a bank in St. Helen's Square. In the garden of St. William's College, in what had been part of the legionary fortress "more than 200 sherds of Flavian pottery were found and also some of Claudio-Neronian date," i.e. from the early years of the Occupation. These lay below a Roman layer of rubble.

In the vicarage garden beside the church of St. Mary, Bishophill Junior archaeologists found an apsed building with elaborate drainage; pottery was mainly of the fourth century, but coins were found dating from the first to the fourth. When builders were excavating at the junction of Tanner Row and Tanner Street they uncovered three feet of the metalling of the Roman road to Chester. During the excavations of the foundations of flats in Long Close Lane, south of Walmgate, three stone coffins were unearthed, lying north-south (*J.R.S.* Vol. LII).

Aldborough (Isurium Brigantium)

Elements of the Brigantian capital, superseded by Roman Eboracum, have come to light in recent years. The defences, including a rock-cut ditch 20 ft. wide and 8 ft. deep, have been partially identified, and also evidence of reorganisation and improvement of these fortifications in later years. In 1964 the Ministry of Public Buildings and Works made excavations, under the direction of Mr. and Mrs. W. T. Jones. They discovered the east corner of the presumed south gate, and, 165 ft. to the east of it, a bastion 27¾ ft. wide. In front of the bastion was "a 25 ft. berm" (level space), "a ditch 40 ft. in width, a counterscarp bank 50 ft. wide and an outer rock-cut ditch of unknown width."

At another West Riding site, *Ilkley*, the fort was excavated, revealing a north-south dimension of nearly 400 ft. over the ramparts; the principia lies beneath the churchyard. No less than five main periods of construction were noted. First came timber buildings of Agricola's time; later the fort was abandoned, but timber barracks were built again in the Mid-Antonone period; these were destroyed by fire in about 196–7 A.D. Under Septimium Severus new barracks were rebuilt with stone foundations, and still later, in the time of Constantius (fourth century) more enlargements and improvements were made. There was a double range of rooms on either side of a central courtyard, granaries, and a timber workshop containing bronze-workers' crucibles and many fragments of scale-armour.

Details such as these, which can only be discovered by patient excavation, reveal that the fort at Ilkley, like many other Roman military sites in the north, was occupied and reoccupied, altered and adapted, clear evidence of the stubborn, never-ending struggle between the Roman army and the turbulent tribes of Northern Britain.

Civil settlements are much scarcer than they are in the south. An exception is the villa at *Cockle Pits*, Brantingham, East Yorkshire, excavated by the Ministry of Public Buildings and Works under the direction of Mr. Stead. A fine mosaic pavement with a central panel showing a crowned goddess surrounded by water-nymphs is to be exhibited in the Hull Museum.

Hadrian's Wall

This much-examined, much-admired monument to Roman genius receives more archaeological attention than lesser-known sites. It has fascinated antiquaries for more than two centuries. Only occasionally does something unexpected turn up, e.g. the remains of the Mithraic temple at Carrowburgh. But legionary inscriptions, milestones and tombstones turn up from time to time and usually find their way to the museums at Carlisle and Newcastle-on-Tyne, if not to the British Museum. Not all of them, however; patient enquiry by visitors with time to explore may reveal private collections in farmhouses within the area.

Some recent research has been directed to investigating the flanking defences of the Wall which existed along the coasts of the North Sea and the Atlantic. For instance, a sequence of four watch-towers and two mile fortlets has been identified in the *Crosscanonbury* area. The famous forts along the Wall, e.g. Housesteads, Chesterholm, Haltonchesters continue to yield information mainly of interest to archaeologists at this stage; later, when fully digested and correlated it will enable historians to tell us much more about the stormy history of the frontier troop-movements, the disposition of garrisons, the successive constructions and reconstructions, occupations, abandonments and reoccupations from the time of Hadrian down to the final abandonment of the Wall.

At *Hardknot* (*Mediobogdum*) high on the windswept Hardknot Pass in Cumberland, clearance and restoration has been done to this most impressively-sited of all auxiliary fortresses, a miniature "Mycenae" set down in the English Lake District, and like Mycenae, looking towards the sea.

12. Scotland, North England

Discoveries in Scotland and in northern England have been so numerous and important that even an extensive summary could hardly do justice to them all. The reader is advised, therefore, to consult the section on Roman Britain published each year in *The Journal of Roman Studies*, and especially Dr. St. Joseph's article "Air Reconnaissance in Britain 1961–64" published in Volume LV, 1965 of the *J.R.S.*

Here I have space to mention only a few.

At *Learmouth*, in Northumberland, 1½ miles south of the Tweed at Cornhill a large temporary camp has been discovered, lying on undulating ground now divided between four fields and 925 ft. long along its west side. In Roxburghshire, south of Cappuck, another marching-camp has been identified on sloping ground south-west of Dere Street. A third camp of 165 acres, was revealed by aerial photographs in 1960 at *St. Leonards* in Lauderdale; a fourth was identified at *Channelkirk*, one side of which appears to have been 3,500 ft. long, and a fifth at *Pathhead* in Midlothian where air photography revealed a fortified enclosure with an axis of some 1,725 ft.

All these evidences of military activity—temporary camps, signal stations, military roads, and permanent or semi-permanent forts—provide material for extensive study, and it will be some time before they can be firmly linked with known campaigns, but some undoubtedly were made during Agricola's initial advance into Scotland. In this study, reliable guides may be found in the works of Dr. St. Joseph and the late Sir Ian Richmond. For example, Dr. St. Joseph writes: "The wild hilly country of the Segolvae contained between the trunk roads to the Forth-Clyde frontier and bounded to north by the Tweed, was no doubt subject to Roman patrols. A fort and camp at Oakwood indicated provision for watching the upper Ettrick. Penetration up the Teviot Valley is suggested by the observation in 1960, 1½ miles west of Denholm, in Roxburghshire, of a crop mark revealing a ditch, 1,000 ft. long, interrupted at one point as at a gate. The site, some 8 miles upstream from the crossing by Dere Street at *Jedfoot*, on even ground above flood-level at a local widening of the alluvial plain, is typically Roman choice of terrain. Confirmation that this is a temporary camp may be expected from future reconnaissance." (*J.R.S.* Vol. LI).

No less than *eighteen* hitherto unrecognised temporary camps came to light in Scotland between 1961 and 1964, of which five are in the valley of the Tweed (in fact one, *Carham*, is just over the Northumberland border). Twelve miles upstream, a day's marching distance, lies another at *Maxton* in Roxburghshire and yet another a mile to the north-west within the great loop of the river. Other camps have been identified in the Teviot valley, near *Denholm*, and at *Cavers Mains* farm, less than a mile away.

In addition to these "new" camps, such as the one recently found near *Castlecraig* (4½ miles from the known fort at Lyne), air photography and ground excavations have filled in many important details concerning the already-known sites, e.g. at the fort of *Glenlochar* in the Dee Valley and along the Antonine Wall where, in 1955, a camp was identified south east of *Inveravon* and has since been revealed along its entire perimeter, about 550 ft. square, and two other camps have been observed within a distance of 5 miles.

At *Camelon*, on the Antonine Wall, 1½ acres of the

northern annex were examined in 1962, and though little datable material was found, the timber structures appeared to be older than the Antonine fortress. Excavations at *Cramond*, Edinburgh, in the same year revealed a "well-built stone structure, perhaps the Commandant's house, about 30 ft. west of the storehouse."

Over a number of years Dr. St. Joseph and the late Sir Ian Richmond have worked at Inchtuthil, Perthshire. This was the great legionary fortress above the Tay built during the occupation of Scotland and subsequently abandoned when the legion was withdrawn. Among other features examined was a large temporary compound outside the walls of the fortress itself. It had contained "a large and elaborate timber-framed house, 274 by 35 ft. in which two of the principal rooms were built in by masonry and furnished with hypocausts. This can be recognised as the quarters of the *praefectus sastorum* and *praefectus fabrum* during the construction of the fortress, protected by appropriate guard and defences. . . ." (*J.R.S.* Vol. LV).

Between this building and another to the west, identified as the officers' baths, was a large open space bordered by offices and a long shed; on the other side, near the north-east corner of the compound, were remains of barracks. The whole compound, which was fortified by an embankment, has been identified as the temporary headquarters of the senior officers during the building of the main fortress, which lies to the north of it.

There was also a huge fortified enclosure, almost as big as the fortress itself, which was evidently a labour camp. "Internal features" commented Richmond, "were limited to occasional gullies, as if occupation, attested by Flavian pottery, had been in tents."

Considerable interest was aroused some years ago by the excavation of another legionary fortress at *Carpow*, in Perthshire. It occupies 30 acres but was occupied only for a short period at the beginning of the third century. No Flavian material has been found. Marching camps and auxiliary forts are fairly common, but a legionary fort is a rare and remarkable discovery. At Carpow the Strathallan School Archaeological Society, directed by Mr. R. E. Birley, excavated a number of buried foundations, including those of a substantial building, tentatively identified as the Legate's Palace, with sixteen rooms built around a courtyard. These include a double suite of baths (later reduced to one), also the Principia, (headquarters building) with an underground strong-room (sacellum) located beneath the tribunal at the north end of the cross-hall. The legionaries' pay was kept in such strong-rooms; at Carpow two coins of A.D. 202–5 in mint condition, with pottery of the same period, testify to a brief occupation at the beginning of the third century.

One wonders if this powerful base is associated with the arrival in Britain, in 208 A.D. of the Emperor Septimium Severus with Geta and Caracolla, who campaigned in Scotland in the following year when they "received the surrender of the Caledonians."

Finally, Scottish readers interested in hunting for Roman roads may like to try this one, as described in Vol. LV, 1965, of the *Journal of Roman Studies*. "The road traced along the Ayrshire coast follows the ridge of Blackhouse Moor to its summit (NS213644) where a signal-station is indicated by a green mound measuring 39 x 31 ft. with a depression near its centre within a surrounding bank of turf. From here the presumed signal-station at Hillside Hill is just visible. The road then passes by Craighton Farm and climbs on to Girtley Hill."

13. Roman Midlands

At Watercrook, near Kendal, Westmorland, where there is a known fort on a bend of the river Kent, the Ministry of Public Buildings and Works is planning an excavation in 1966. At *Kirby Thore*, also in Westmorland, a "new" fort has been identified from the air. A section cut across the east angle revealed a turf rampart and a thick layer of burning, with stone buildings above. This excavation was carried out by Miss D. Charlesworth, on behalf of the Ministry of Public Buildings and Works. She has also excavated at *Hardknot*, mentioned in a previous chapter, and at *Papcastle* in Cumberland, where she found parts of a late stone building, probably the commandant's headquarters, and "heavily robbed barracks."

At *Chester* (Deva) new building developments have necessitated a number of "rescue digs" in recent years, throwing fresh light on the fortress of the 20th Legion. When the inner ring-road was being built archaeologists were able to locate the north-west and south-west angles; it was found that the Roman fortress wall, embedded in the medieval wall, still stood to a height of 15 feet. Excavations west of the Town Hall proved that the barracks of the First Cohort had guard-chambers at their northern ends. Beyond was an extensive area devoted to the legionary workshops. There was also an extensive range of bath-buildings between these buildings and the via praetoria. Particularly interesting was the excavation of part of the amphitheatre, which revealed that there had been an earlier timber structure before the present building was erected.

In parts of Cheshire hitherto unmapped sections of Roman roads were discovered, e.g. at *Appleton*, where the total width of the Sandbach-Wilderspool road was 34 ft. and at *Sproston Wood Farm*, ¾ miles north-east of Wrenbury, where the *agger* of a road was uncovered, 58 ft. in width, of sand and pebbles.

A great deal of new information relating to the Roman Midlands has been gathered during the past ten years. Archaeologists such as Professor Graham Webster and Mr. Adrian Oswald have been extremely active in the region, with stimulating results. The area, once described as "archaeologically a barren waste," has proved to be unusually prolific in finds, thanks to modern techniques, especially aerial photography followed by ground survey. Only a few examples can be quoted here, but fuller details can be found in the *Journal of Roman Studies* and the *Archaeological Journal.*

That, after the first thrust, the Romans drew a frontier along the line of the later Foss Way has long been suspected, and though not fully proven, this theory is gaining more adherents. Many forts and marching camps have been discovered, e.g. at *Chesterton*, where the robbed foundation of the north gate were exposed, and two periods of the town's defences. In Staffordshire, a second fort has been observed from the air at *Greensforge*, a little to the south-west of one previously noted. At *Wall* (*Letocetum*) on the Watling Street, the western ditches of a first century fort were examined and within the modern town of *Rocester*, also in Staffordshire, trenches laid bare the western defences of the Roman fort and town, with material dating from the first to the fourth centuries. Iron-smelting was evidently carried on one mile north of the modern village of *Shenstone*, not far from Wall (Letocetum).

Early settlement was observed at *Baginton*, near Coventry, where two first-century ditches were unearthed with a palisade enclosing timber buildings, and at *Princethorpe*, where the Fosse Way passes through a small settlement, its early and later courses were seen to diverge.

Warwickshire has also yielded some interesting finds. When the first edition of this book was published, several readers wrote querying my statement that Roman remains had been discovered near *Alcester*. In recent years substantial remains of the settlement have been unearthed during excavations for a new housing estate, with evidences of a leather-working industry. 100 undated burials were found in a cemetery alongside Ryknield Street and early timber buildings in the Cattle Market Field.

The same is true of Nottinghamshire, where at *Thorpe* two overlapping enclosures were found, one astride the Fosse Way, and another along its eastern flank. Ditches contained native and very early Romano-British pottery. Evidences of domestic iron-working were discovered at Normangate Field, Castor, in Northamptonshire.

In Leicestershire the story is the same, not only in Leicester itself, where further remains of Roman *Ratae* have been discovered in Great Central Street, and an east-west street parallel to the well-known "Jewry Wall," but also on the east side of the Watling Street at Tripontium, 100 yds. north-west of Caves Inn Farm, Shawell.

Wroxeter (Uriconium) continues to yield information, thanks to continued excavation, including those undertaken by Professor Webster as part of his training scheme for young amateur archaeologists. This great city on the edge of the Welsh Marches, however, continues to present unsolved problems. Although the presence of the 14th Gemina Legion is attested by tiles and tomb-inscriptions, there is still no firm evidence that Uriconium was the legionary fortress from which this, and possibly the 20th Valeria Victrix, operated when they were advancing into Wales. Yet surely it must exist somewhere? Chocks away, Dr. St. Joseph!

Coming further south, at *Gadebridge Park*, near Hemel Hempstead, Hertfordshire, one of the rare examples of a Roman swimming bath has come to light, very well preserved, and almost as large as the Great Bath at Bath. It adjoined a substantial villa, but was not in use for very long, as soot from the furnace of a large heated room was dumped into it at a later stage. Perhaps our climate had a lot to do with this. The swimming pool at Bath, which was used down to the end of the fourth century, enjoyed the advantages of warm water perpetually supplied by the sulphur-springs, and this no doubt accounts for its continued popularity among the hedonists of Aquae Sulis.

As for Verulamium (St. Albans), so many discoveries have been made in recent years, largely due to the expansion of the modern town, that several new chapters would barely do justice to them. The best source of information is of course the fine Museum, which continues to add to its treasures, and where a guide can be obtained listing some of the more recent discoveries, and maps and diagrams fill in new details of this great Roman city.

14. London

So many alterations have overtaken London that the rapid successive revelations of Roman Londinium, followed all too often by their final obliteration, are like death agonies. If that seems too morbid a comparison, consider what has been happening since 1954, compared with the rebuildings of former centuries. When Stuart, Hanoverian and even Victorian contractors rebuilt the city, they destroyed much of Roman London, but often left foundations buried beneath their own constructions. When these were in turn destroyed, as in the bombardment of the Second World War, parts of the Roman city were seen again; in a few cases, e.g. the stretch of Roman wall in Cooper's Row, the bath-buildings underneath the former Coal Exchange, the tessellated pavement under an office building in Ironmonger Lane, were permanently preserved, *in situ*.

But mid-twentieth century is remorseless. To sink the foundations of multi-storey skyscrapers, mechanical excavators disembowel the city, so that even the temple of Mithras, a unique monument which, had it been found under Cologne, would undoubtedly have been spared—whatever the cost—had to be grubbed up and re-assembled, a pathetic little relic, now floored with crazy pavement, standing outside the steel and concrete monster which occupies its former site.

The result has been a frenzy of "rescue digging;" every week teams of archaeologists, hurriedly assembled by the Guildhall Museum, the London Museum or some other authority, have had to grab what information they could extract from doomed sites, while the bulldozers waited impatiently to complete the destruction. To do them justice, most of the contractors working on newly-discovered Roman sites have co-operated gladly with the archaeologists, but when time is literally money, the excavators grubbing in the mud of Blackfriars, or beside Cannon Street Station, have had to work at high and continuous pressure.

All the more credit is due to them for what they have achieved, to Dr. Grimes for his splendid work on the buried Mithraeum and other sites, to young Peter Marsden, who discovered and removed the remains of a Roman barge near Blackfriars Bridge, to Ralph Merrifield, who has recently published a fully-documented account of Roman London with maps and plans and of course to the energetic, enthusiastic, indefatigable Keeper of the Guildhall Museum, Norman Cook, and his staff of equally-dedicated enthusiasts.

Thanks to these men and the many volunteer helpers who have assisted them, more has been learned about Roman London in the last ten years than was known in the previous half-century. For full details readers should read Mr. Merrifield's book.

And despite the inevitable destruction, some elements of Londonium have been preserved fcr posterity and are now more readily accessible than they were before. The wonderful stretch of the city wall which used to be concealed with a warehouse in Cooper's Row is now fully visible from the street, thanks to the public spirit of the warehouse's owners. It divides two office blocks north of Tower Hill, not far from the famous inscription to Julius Classicianus.

The West Gateway of the Roman Fort has been permanently exposed, and can be visited any day between 12 noon and 2 p.m. and at other times by arrangement with the Keeper of the Guildhall Museum (Royal Exchange). The other remains described in the foregoing chapter can still be seen, and though the old Coal Exchange has been demolished, the Roman bath-building beneath it can be visited.

Among the most fascinating discoveries made in recent years was that of a Roman barge found in the mud beneath the Thames near Blackfriars Bridge. In the space where the mast had stood still lay a Roman coin, on one side of which was the Goddess Fortuna with a ship's rudder in her hand. . . . A few weeks after the discovery was made, a press announcement describing the building of a new racing yacht mentioned that a coin had been placed beneath its mast "for good luck." The custom has survived 2,000 years.

The cargo found in the sunken barge was Kentish ragstone. Mr. Norman Cook, himself a Kentish man, told me that as a boy he remembers seeing barges loaded with the same stone moving down the Medway on their way to the Thames and London. Mr. Cook, who, with Mr. Harden, Keeper of the London Museum, has promoted a splendid plan to amalgamate the contents of the two Museums which are now housed in Kensington Palace and the Royal Exchange, in one modern museum which may be built in the heart of the city, within sight of the fortress. At the time of writing, some difficulties are being encountered but it is to be hoped that they may eventually be overcome, as a worthy crowning of Mr. Cook's labours and a fascinating addition to the amenities of the City.

Mr. Cook sometimes talks as if he himself had been a citizen of Londinium. "We were never a garrison town," he remarked, somewhat deprecatingly, when I commented on the comparative lack of elegance and smartness in Roman London. "If we'd had had a crack regiment here, there might have been more social life and better amenities. There was probably a body of household troops for ceremonial duties but that is all. No, we were always a commercial city—merchants, tradesmen, manufacturers, you know. I suppose a few V.I.P.s passed through en route for the West or the North, and they probably stayed in a building near Cannon Street Station which some people think may have been the Governor's Palace. That was rather fine, with terraces set above the river bank; there was no wall there. But we *were* one of the largest Roman cities north of the Alps in our prime. And that's something to be proud of."

So if you see a chubby-faced, smiling citizen in a toga stepping smartly down Ludgate Hill, and you want to know the way to the Forum, do not hesitate to ask him. He will certainly know, and probably take you there himself.

INDEX